Understanding Cryptography

Understanding Cryptography

Ethan Scott

Larsen & Keller
www.larsen-keller.com

Understanding Cryptography
Ethan Scott
ISBN: 978-1-64172-638-2 (Hardback)

 Larsen & Keller

Published by Larsen and Keller Education,
5 Penn Plaza,
19th Floor,
New York, NY 10001, USA

Cataloging-in-Publication Data

Understanding cryptography / Ethan Scott.
    p. cm.
Includes bibliographical references and index.
ISBN 978-1-64172-638-2
1. Cryptography. 2. Data encryption (Computer science). I. Scott, Ethan.
QA268 .U53 2021
003.54--dc23

For more information regarding Larsen and Keller Education and its products, please visit the publisher's website www.larsen-keller.com

TABLE OF CONTENTS

It is with great pleasure that I present this book. It has been carefully written after numerous discussions with my peers and other practitioners of the field. I would like to take this opportunity to thank my family and friends who have been extremely supporting at every step in my life.

The study of the techniques that are utilized to ensure secure communication in the presence of adversaries is known as cryptography. It includes the analysis and construction of the protocols to prevent the public or third parties from reading private messages. The aspects that are central to modern cryptography are related to confidentiality of data, authentication, data integrity, and non-repudiation. Modern cryptography is classified into various areas of study such as symmetric-key cryptography, cryptanalysis, cryptosystems, public-key cryptography and cryptographic primitives. Various disciplines that contribute to cryptography are computer science, communication science, mathematics, physics and electrical engineering. Cryptography is applied in fields such as electronic commerce, computer passwords, military communications, chip-payment cards and digital currencies. This book attempts to understand the multiple branches that fall under the discipline of cryptography and how such concepts have practical applications. Most of the topics introduced herein cover new techniques and the applications of this field. This book is a complete source of knowledge on the present status of this important field.

The chapters below are organized to facilitate a comprehensive understanding of the subject:

Chapter – Introduction

Cryptography refers to the practice and study of the techniques for secure communication in the presence of third parties. It is used for trusted timestamping and digital signatures. This is an introductory chapter which will introduce briefly all these significant applications of cryptography.

Chapter – Branches of Cryptography

Some of the various branches of cryptography are quantum cryptography, post-quantum cryptography, visual cryptography, multivariate cryptography and DNA cryptography. The topics elaborated in this chapter will help in gaining a better perspective about these branches of cryptography.

Chapter – Information Security

The practice of protecting information by reducing the information risks is referred to as information security. It falls under the domain of information risk management. The chapter closely examines the key applications of Information security such as authentication and non-repudiation to provide an extensive understanding of the subject.

Chapter – Cryptosystem

The suit of cryptographic algorithms needed to implement a specific security service in order to achieve confidentiality is known as a cryptosystem. The algorithms within this field are primarily used for encryption and decryption. This chapter discusses in detail these components of cryptosystems.

Chapter – Cryptographic Algorithms and Keys

Cryptographic algorithms are sets of well-defined mathematical instructions which are used to encrypt or decrypt data. Cryptographic keys refer to a string of data which is used to lock or unlock cryptographic functions. The chapter closely examines the key concepts of cryptographic algorithms and keys to provide an extensive understanding of the subject.

Chapter – Classical Ciphers

Classical cipher is a type of cipher that was used historically, but is no longer used. The main types of classical ciphers are substitution ciphers that include Caesar cipher and playfair cipher, and transportation ciphers such as Hill cipher and polyalphabetic cipher. All the diverse principles related to these types of classical ciphers have been carefully analyzed in this chapter.

Ethan Scott

Introduction

Cryptography refers to the practice and study of the techniques for secure communication in the presence of third parties. It is used for trusted timestamping and digital signatures. This is an introductory chapter which will introduce briefly all these significant applications of cryptography.

CRYPTOGRAPHY

Cryptography is the study of message secrecy. One of cryptography's primary purposes is hiding the meaning of messages, but not usually their existence. In modern times, cryptography is considered to be a branch of both mathematics and computer science, and is affiliated closely with information theory, computer security, and engineering.

Cryptography is used in many applications encountered in everyday life; examples include security of ATM cards, computer passwords, and electronic commerce. It is also valuable for confidential governmental communications, on both domestic and international levels, especially during times of conflict.

The German Lorenz cipher machine used in World War II for encryption of very high-level general staff messages.

Before the modern era, cryptography was concerned solely with message confidentiality (encryption) — conversion of messages from a comprehensible form into an incomprehensible one, and back again at the other end, rendering it unreadable by interceptors or eavesdroppers without secret knowledge (namely, the key needed for decryption of that message). In recent decades, the field has expanded beyond confidentiality concerns to include techniques for message integrity checking, sender/receiver identity authentication, digital signatures, interactive proofs, and secure computation, amongst others.

The earliest forms of secret writing required little more than a pen and paper, as most people could not read. An increase in literacy over time required actual cryptography. The main classical cipher types are transposition ciphers, which rearrange the order of letters in a message (e.g. 'help me' becomes 'ehpl em' in a trivially simple rearrangement scheme), and substitution ciphers, which systematically replace letters or groups of letters with other letters or groups of letters (e.g., 'fly at once' becomes 'gmz bu podf' by replacing each letter with the one following it in the alphabet). Simple versions of either offered little confidentiality from enterprising opponents, and still don't. An early substitution cipher was the Caesar cipher, in which each letter in the plaintext was replaced by a letter some fixed number of positions further down the alphabet. It was named after Julius Caesar who is reported to have used it, with a shift of 3, to communicate with his generals during his military campaigns.

Encryption attempts to ensure secrecy in communications, such as those of spies, military leaders, and diplomats, but it has also had religious applications. For instance, early Christians used cryptography to obfuscate some aspects of their religious writings to avoid the near certain persecution they would have faced had they been less cautious; famously, 666 the Number of the Beast from the Christian New Testament Book of Revelation, is sometimes thought to be a ciphertext referring to the Roman Emperor Nero, one of whose policies was persecution of Christians. There is record of several, even earlier, Hebrew ciphers as well. Steganography (hiding even the existence of a message so as to keep it confidential) was also first developed in ancient times. An early example, from Herodotus, concealed a message - a tattoo on a shaved man's head - under the regrown hair. More modern examples of steganography include the use of invisible ink, microdots, and digital watermarks to conceal information.

Ciphertexts produced by classical ciphers (and some modern ones) always reveal statistical information about the plaintext, which can often be used to break them. After the Arab discovery of frequency analysis (circa 1000 C.E.), nearly all such ciphers became more or less readily breakable by an informed attacker. Such classical ciphers still enjoy popularity today, though mostly as puzzles. Essentially all ciphers remained vulnerable to cryptanalysis using this technique until the invention of the polyalphabetic cipher, most clearly by Leon Battista Alberti around the year 1467 (there is some indication of early Arab knowledge of them). Alberti's innovation was to use different ciphers (i.e., substitution alphabets) for various parts of a message (often each successive plaintext letter). He also invented what was probably the first automatic cipher device, a wheel which implemented a partial realization of his invention. In the polyalphabetic Vigenère cipher, encryption uses a key word, which controls letter substitution depending on which letter of the key word is used. In the mid 1800s Babbage showed that polyalphabetic ciphers of this type remained partially vulnerable to frequency analysis techniques.

The Enigma machine, used in several variants by the German military between the late 1920s and the end of World War II, implemented a complex electro-mechanical polyalphabetic cipher to protect sensitive communications. Breaking the Enigma cipher at the Biuro Szyfrów, and the subsequent large-scale decryption of Enigma traffic at Bletchley Park, was an important factor contributing to the Allied victory in WWII.

Although frequency analysis is a powerful and general technique, encryption was still often effective in practice; many a would-be cryptanalyst was unaware of the technique. Breaking a message without frequency analysis essentially required knowledge of the cipher used, thus encouraging espionage, bribery, burglary, and defection to discover it. It was finally recognized in the nine-teenth century that secrecy of a cipher's algorithm is not a sensible or practical safeguard; in fact, any adequate cryptographic scheme (including ciphers) should remain secure even if the adversary knows the cipher algorithm itself. Secrecy of the key should alone be sufficient for confidentiality when under attack — for good ciphers. This fundamental principle was first explicitly stated in 1883 by Auguste Kerckhoffs and is generally called Kerckhoffs' principle; alternatively and more bluntly, it was restated by Claude Shannon as *Shannon's Maxim* — 'the enemy knows the system'.

Various physical devices and aids have been used to assist with ciphers. One of the earliest may have been the scytale of ancient Greece, a rod supposedly used by the Spartans as an aid for a transposition cipher. In medieval times, other aids were invented such as the cipher grille, also used for a kind of steganography. With the invention of polyalphabetic ciphers came more sophis-ticated aids such as Alberti's cipher disk, Johannes Trithemius' tabula recta scheme, and Thomas Jefferson's multi-cylinder (invented independently by Bazeries around 1900). Early in the twenti-eth century, several mechanical encryption/decryption devices were invented, and many patented, including rotor machines — most famously the Enigma machine used by Germany in World War II. The ciphers implemented by better quality examples of these designs brought about a substan-tial increase in cryptanalytic difficulty after WWI.

The development of digital computers and electronics after WWII made possible much more complex ciphers. Furthermore, computers allowed for the encryption of any kind of data that is represented by computers in any binary format, unlike classical ciphers which only encrypted written language texts, dissolving the utility of a linguistic approach to cryptanalysis in many cases. Many computer ciphers can be characterized by their operation on binary bit sequences (sometimes in groups or blocks), unlike classical and mechanical schemes, which generally manipulate traditional characters (letters and digits) directly. However, computers have also assisted cryptanalysis, which has compensated to some extent for increased cipher complexity. Nonetheless, good modern ciphers have stayed ahead of cryptanalysis; it is usually the case that use of a quality cipher is very efficient (i.e., fast and requiring few resources), while breaking it requires an effort many orders of magnitude larger, making cryptanalysis so inefficient and impractical as to be effectively impossible.

The 3 by 5 mm chip embedded in the card is shown enlarged in the insert. Smart cards attempt to combine portability with the power to compute modern cryptographic algorithms.

Extensive open academic research into cryptography is relatively recent — it began only in the mid-1970s with the public specification of DES (the Data Encryption Standard) by the NBS, the Diffie-Hellman paper, and the public release of the RSA algorithm. Since then, cryptography has become a widely used tool in communications, computer networks, and computer security generally. The present security level of many modern cryptographic techniques is based on the difficulty of certain computational problems, such as the integer factorization problem or the discrete logarithm problem. In many cases, there are proofs that cryptographic techniques are secure if a certain computational problem cannot be solved efficiently. With one notable exception— the one-time pad—these proofs are contingent, and thus not definitive, but are currently the best available for cryptographic algorithms and protocols.

As well as being aware of cryptographic history, cryptographic algorithm and system designers must also sensibly consider probable future developments in their designs. For instance, the continued improvements in computer processing power have increased the scope of brute-force attacks when specifying key lengths. The potential effects of quantum computing are already being considered by some cryptographic system designers; the announced imminence of small implementations of these machines is making the need for this preemptive caution fully explicit.

Essentially, prior to the early twentieth century, cryptography was chiefly concerned with linguistic patterns. Since then the emphasis has shifted, and cryptography now makes extensive use of mathematics, including aspects of information theory, computational complexity, statistics, combinatorics, abstract algebra, and number theory. Cryptography is also a branch of engineering, but an unusual one as it deals with active, and intelligent opposition; most other kinds of engineering deal only with natural forces. There is also active research examining the relationship between cryptographic problems and quantum physics.

Cryptographic Primitives

Much of the theoretical work in cryptography concerns cryptographic primitives — algorithms with basic cryptographic properties — and their relationship to other cryptographic problems. For example, a one-way function is a function intended to be easy to compute but hard to invert. In a very general sense, for any cryptographic application to be secure (if based on such computational feasibility assumptions), one-way functions must exist.

Currently known cryptographic primitives provide only basic functionality. These are usually noted as confidentiality, message integrity, authentication, and non-repudiation. Any other functionality in a cryptosystem must be built in using combinations of these algorithms and assorted protocols. Such combinations are called cryptosystems and it is they which users will encounter. Examples include PGP and its variants, SSH, SSL/TLS, all PKIs, and digital signatures. Other cryptographic primitives include the encryption algorithms themselves, one-way permutations, trapdoor permutations, etc.

Cryptographic Protocols

In many cases, cryptographic techniques involve back and forth communication among two or more parties in space (for example between a home office and a branch office). The term cryptographic protocol captures this general idea.

Cryptographic protocols have been developed for a wide range of problems, including relatively simple ones like interactive proofs, secret sharing, and zero-knowledge.

When the security of a good cryptographic system fails, it is rare that the vulnerability leading to the breach will have been in a quality cryptographic primitive. Instead, weaknesses are often mistakes in the protocol design (often due to inadequate design procedures, or less than thoroughly informed designers), in the implementation (for example a software bug), in a failure of the assumptions on which the design was based (for example the proper training of those who will be using the system), or some other human error. Many cryptographic protocols have been designed and analyzed using *ad hoc* methods, but they rarely have any proof of security. Methods for formally analyzing the security of protocols, based on techniques from mathematical logic, and more recently from concrete security principles, have been the subject of research for the past few decades. Unfortunately, to date these tools have been cumbersome and are not widely used for complex designs.

CRYPTOGRAPHY TECHNIQUES FOR SECURE COMMUNICATIONS

Electronic communication is the lifeblood of many organizations. Much of the information communicated on a daily basis must be kept confidential. Information such as financial reports, employee data and medical records needs to be communicated in a way that ensures confidentiality and integrity. This makes good business sense and may even be regulated by legislation like the Health Insurance Portability and Accountability Act (HIPAA). The problem of unsecure communication is compounded by the fact that much of this information is sent over the public Internet and may be processed by third parties, as in e-mail or instant messaging (IM).

Cryptography can be used to provide message confidentiality and integrity and sender verification. The basic functions of cryptography are encryption, decryption and cryptographic hashing. In order to encrypt and decrypt messages, the sender and recipient need to share a secret. Typically this is a key, like a password, that is used by the cryptographic algorithm. The key is used by the sender to encrypt the message (transform it into cipher text) and by the recipient to decrypt the message (reverse the cipher text back to clear text). This process can be done on a fixed message, such as an e-mail, or a communications stream, such as a TCP/IP connection.

Cryptographic hashing is the process of generating a fixed-length string from a message of arbitrary length. If the sender provides a cryptographic hash with the message, the recipient can verify its integrity. Modern cryptographic systems are based on complex mathematical relationships and processes.

The three basic types of cryptography in common use are symmetric key, asymmetric (public) key systems and cryptographic hash functions. Typically, the strength of a crypto system is directly related to the length of the key. This assumes that there is no inherent weakness in the algorithm and that the keys are chosen in a way that fully utilizes the key space (the number of possible keys). There are many kinds of attacks that can be used against crypto systems, if you use public algorithms with no known vulnerabilities, use reasonable key lengths (most defaults are fine) and choose good keys (which are normally chosen for you), your communications will be very secure.

Symmetric key cryptography uses the same key to encrypt and decrypt data. Some common symmetric key algorithms are the Data Encryption Standard (DES), Triple DES, Blowfish and the Advanced Encryption Standard (AES). DES is ineffective because it uses a 64-bit key and has been broken. Be careful, because some crypto security, like Microsoft's Windows XP Encrypted File System (EFS), defaults to DES and must be changed to provide good security.

The main advantage of symmetric key cryptography is speed. The principle problems with this system are key distribution and scalability. Keys need to be distributed securely, and each secure channel needs a separate key. Symmetric key systems provide confidentiality but do not provide authenticity of the message, and the sender can deny having sent the message.

Asymmetric (public) key cryptography uses a pair of mathematically related keys. Each key can be used to encrypt or decrypt. However, a key can only decrypt a message that has been encrypted by the related key. The key pair is called the public/private key pair. Some common public key systems are Rivest-Shamir-Adelman (RSA), Diffe-Hellman and Digital Signature Standard (DSS).

Asymmetric key systems solve the key distribution and scalability problems associated with symmetric systems, although it's not trivial to manage and implement a public key infrastructure (PKI). However, you can take advantage of companies like Thawte, Verisign and PGP Corp. that provide key distribution and trust services. Asymmetric key systems provide a greater range of security services than symmetric systems. They provide for confidentiality, authenticity and nonrepudiation. The principle problem with these systems is speed. It takes significantly more computer resources to encrypt and decrypt with asymmetric systems than symmetric ones.

Cryptographic hash functions take a message of arbitrary length and compute a fixed signature, often called a message digest, for the message. This can be done for a file, e-mail message or your entire hard-drive image. The main properties of these functions are that it is difficult to find different files that produce the same digest and that the function is one-way. Therefore, it is not computationally feasible to recover a message given its digest.

Two common examples of hash functions are the Secure Hash Algorithm (SHA), commonly SHA-1, and Message-Digest algorithm 5 (MD5). SHA-1 is used in many common security applications including SSL, TLS, S/MIME and IPSec. MD5 is generally used to create a digital fingerprint for verifying file integrity.

So symmetric is fast, but exchanging keys is a problem; and asymmetric has more security services, but it's slow. The solution: Combine them in a hybrid system. This is what is done in the digital-certificate-based crypto systems that are in common use for e-mail, IM and SSL Web traffic. The basic idea is to use an asymmetric system, as is done with Diffie-Hellman key exchange, to exchange a symmetric key to do the bulk of the data encryption.

CAs and Webs of Trust

Trust is one of the services provided by certificate vendors. There are two common trust models: certificate authorities (CA) and webs of trust (WOT).

The CA model is based on the notion that you trust the CA to vouch for the validity and integrity of the certificate that is being presented to you. For example, you might visit a Web site to purchase something, and the site will use SSL to secure the site. As part of that process, your browser asks the server to authenticate its identity. The server does this by providing its digital certificate, typically signed by the CA. By signing the certificate, the CA is assuring you that it has verified the identity of the entity that it gave the certificate to. This might involve verifying business records, domain registration information, company contacts, etc. Your Web browser has many CA certificates in its Trusted Root Library. It uses the appropriate root certificate to verify that the certificate presented by the Web server is in fact signed by the CA. Other parameters, such as expiration date, also are checked. Without using the CA model, you would be told who signed the certificate (it might be self-signed), and then you would have to independently decide if you trusted the site.

WOTs use a process of elevating trust in a certificate by having others in the web vouch for the owner of the certificate. This usually starts as simply verifying an e-mail address by requiring you to respond to an e-mail before you can obtain a certificate that uses that e-mail address for identity. In Thawte's WOT, you must physically meet a certificate notary and present various forms of identification to elevate your level of trust. The notary will then add trust points to your certificate, allowing people to have a greater certainty that you are who you claim to be. Self-signing certificates is fine if you only communicate with people you know, and they know how to verify that the certificate is yours.

When you communicate with someone who doesn't know you, then a CA or WOT enables them to have confidence that it is really you. A certificate also can be revoked, by the CA or the owner, so that people will know that the certificate is no longer valid. Certificate revocation can be a more complicated problem because it assumes that everyone will check for revocation each time a certificate is used.

CRYPTANALYSIS

Cryptanalysis is the investigation of systems, ciphertext, and ciphers in order to reveal the hidden meaning or details of the system itself. It takes a successful blend of persistence, mathematics, intuition, inquisitiveness, and a working computer to make a good cryptanalyst. This type of code breaking is extremely important especially in today's technologically dependent world. Cryptology is constantly being pushed and pulled forward by both cryptographers trying to secure valuable information and by those who are trying to break the code to reveal the secrets. Careers in this field are typically on the federal level.

Types of Ciphers and Methods of Cryptanalysis

There are several different methods that can be utilized in order to break ciphers. The easiest codes to crack are those which have existed the longest time. Modern cryptography is becoming increasingly difficult to solve with the wide use of computers to create previously inconceivable algorithms.

Text Characterization

When trying to find the key to solving a certain text there are a number of methods a cryptanalyst can use to come closer to their goal. The main techniques that are used to characterize the text are counting frequency, identifying patterns, and using CRANK, the cryptanalysis tool kit. There are much more complex methods such as the Index of Coincidence which roughly estimates the frequency in which certain letters are distributed in certain languages. By comparing this to the code certain patterns may help reveal the key. Another and more complicated method is called Quadgram Statistics. It can be used in a similar manner by adding up all the likelihoods of ciphertext appearing in a length of four blocks which will tell the cryptanalyst how close the code is to true English.

Modern Cryptanalysis

One example of a modern technique is timing or differential power analysis. Basically the analyst will measure differences in the consumption of electricity when a microchip is securing information. Over time information can be gained about the encryption algorithm and can be helpful in getting information about other security functions of the chip. There are several more modern and unorthodox methods of cryptanalysis. With technology it is possible to fool individuals into giving up their passwords and keys or trick them into utilizing a weak and breakable cryptosystem. Another modern technique of cryptanalysis is using Trojan horse viruses to steal the secret key from the individual's computer.

Security Careers in Cryptanalysis

Currently the FBI has a cryptanalysis and Racketeering Records Unit which is responsible for studying encrypted records and documents to assist in identifying criminal or terrorist activities. The cryptanalysis agent will be responsible for examining all kinds of ciphers and codes in written communications, e-mails, and records. The goal is to identify illegal activities. Codes are commonly used by those in prison, international terrorist, violent criminals, and foreign intelligence agents. The members in these security fields are expected to provide information as well as expert testimony in legal proceedings in order to stop criminal behavior.

The National Security Agency values cryptanalysis highly and regards this type of discipline as necessary regardless of the passing of time. The NSA believes that this decryption of codes is absolutely necessary in order to provide intelligence to nations around the world and protect the nation's security. They hire a wide variety of people from different backgrounds and do not seek out any type of specific major for these security careers. Once accepted into their program the NSA will provide formal training for these security fields. The intelligence these agents are able to collect from their work can be used in various ways from combating crime and terrorism to discovering ground-breaking technology.

This extremely challenging line of work is usually performed at the federal level and has proven throughout history to be extremely important to the security of individuals, companies, and even nations. During WWII, for example, the United States employed Navajo Native Americans in order to encode messages based on their language. This type of coded language was so unique and challenging that it was never broken by the enemy and played an integral role in the United State's victory. With technology always increasing and the modern day reliance on the internet it seems that the field of cryptanalysis will grow even more and become increasingly important for our nation's security.

USES OF CRYPTOGRAPHY

Cryptography was used only to ensure secrecy of information. Encryption was used to ensure confidentiality in communications by spies, military leaders and diplomats. The Egyptian hieroglyphs, the scytale transposition cipher used by the Spartans of Greece, waxed seals and different physical devices to assist with ciphers were used throughout history right up to modern times. These devices underwent further changes when computers and electronics came into the picture, immensely helping in cryptanalysis. Cryptography has become more mathematical now and also finds applications in day-to-day security. It helps you safely transfer or withdraw money electronically and you'd be hard-pressed to come across an individual without a credit or debit card. The public-key encryption system introduced the concept of digital signatures and electronic credentials. Cryptography has a definitive existence in our lives today and the whole system will crumble in its absence.

Secrecy in Transmission

The major goal of cryptography is to prevent data from being read by any third party. Most transmission systems use a private-key cryptosystem. This system uses a secret key to encrypt and decrypt data which is shared between the sender and receiver. The private keys are distributed and destroyed periodically. One must secure the key from unauthorized access, because any party that has the key can decrypt the encrypted information.

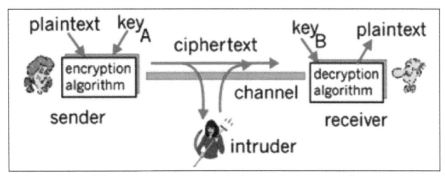

How an encrypted transmission can be intercepted.

Alternately a key-generating-key, called a master key, can be used to electronically generate a one-time session-key for every transaction. The secrecy of the master-key should be maintained by all parties privy to the information. The disadvantage of this method is there's too much hope riding on the master-key, which if cracked, collapses the entire system.

A better method is to use a public-key cryptosystem. In this system, data can be encrypted by anyone with the public-key, but it can be decrypted only by using the private-key, and data that is signed with the private key can be verified only with the public key. With the development of publickey systems, secrecy can be maintained without having to keep track of a large number of keys or sharing a common master-key. If, say, Alex wants to communicate with Neil, she first generates her public/private key pair and sends the public key to Neil over a non-secure channel. Neil to encrypt information and sends it back to Alex. Only Alex has the private key with which she can decrypt the information. Anyone who intercepts the public key or the encrypted data can't decrypt the message due to the protocols followed during information transfer.

Secrecy in Storage

Storage encryption refers to the application of cryptographic techniques on data, both during transit and while on storage media. Storage encryption is gaining popularity among enterprises that use storage area networks (SANs). Secrecy in storage is maintained by storing data in encrypted form. The user has to provide the key to the computer only at the beginning of a session to access the data and it then takes care of encryption and decryption throughout the course of normal use. Hardware devices can also be used for PCs to automatically encrypt all information stored on disk. When the computer is turned on, the user must supply a key to the encryption hardware. The information is plain gibberish without its key thus preventing misuse if the disk is stolen.

Multiple ciphers can be used for individual files and folders. The ciphers and keys should be changed frequently to ensure security of data. However, if the user forgets a key, all of the information encrypted with it makes no sense and is rendered useless. This is why backups of encrypted information are advised to be stored in plaintext. The data is only encrypted while in storage, not when in use. This leaves a loophole for the attackers. The system is vulnerable to a security breach if the encryption and decryption are done in software, or if the key is stored somewhere in the system.

Integrity in Transmission

We can use cryptography to provide a means to ensure that data is not altered during transmission, i.e. its integrity is preserved. In electronic funds transfer, it is very important that integrity be maintained. A bank can lose millions if a transaction is illicitly intercepted. Cryptographic techniques are employed to prevent accidental or intentional modification of data during transmission, leading to erroneous actions. One of the ways to ensure integrity is to perform a checksum on the information being transmitted and to transmit the checksum in an encrypted form as well.

The information is received on the other end and again checksummed. The transmitted checksum is decrypted and compared with the previous checksum. If the checksums agree, the information is most likely unaltered. The problem with this scheme is that the checksum of the original message can be known and another message with the same checksum can be generated and sent instead of the original one. This problem can be overcome by using a public-key cryptosystem. After generating the public-key/private-key pair, if we throw away the private-key and use only the public-key to encrypt the checksum, the checksum becomes impossible to decrypt. In order to verify the checksum, we generate a new checksum for the received information, encrypt it using the public-key and match it with the encrypted checksum. This is also known as a one-way function as it is hard to invert.

Integrity in Storage

Integrity in storage had been ensured by access control systems with lock and keys and other guards to prevent unauthorized access to stored data. The existence of computer viruses has changed the scenario and the need of integrity against intentional attack has become a problem of epic proportions. Cryptographic checksums to ascertain validity of stored data are of help here. As in the case of transmission, a cryptographic checksum is produced and compared to the expected value. However, storage media are more vulnerable to attacks than transmission channels due to longer exposure and larger volumes of information.

Authentication of Identity

Authentication is the process of verifying if the user has enough authority for data access. Simple passwords are used to identify someone. You must also have seen in classic gangster movies, the exchange of keywords to prove identity. Cryptography is similar to the practice of providing passwords for identity authentication. Modern systems use cryptographic transforms in conjunction with other characteristics of individuals to provide more reliable and efficient authentication of identity. Many systems allow passwords to be stored in an encrypted form, with read access available to all programs which may use them. Since passwords are not stored as plaintext, an accidental of data doesn't compromise the system's security. Passwords are analogous to the key in a cryptosystem that allows encryption and decryption of anything the password has access to. The principal element of this system is the password selection process. the longer the password, the more random it will be and the harder it is to guess. So if you think it's easy for you to remember, you should know that it will be all the easier to crack.

Credentialing Systems

A credential is a proof of qualification or competence that is attached to a person to indicate suitability for something. Suppose you go to a bank for a loan, they check your credentials before approving the loan. Your credenctials are checked not only from the paperwork, but also from your past record and your references. Your driver's license and passport are forms of credentials. Progress in the field of implementing electronic credentials has been rather slow. Electronic credentials allow electronic verification of the credence of a claim. It's not a standalone system, but is being used in conjunction with other devices such as smart cards which perform cryptographic functions and store secret information.

Electronic Money

Electronic information has replaced cash for financial transactions between individuals for quite a long time now. Such a system uses cryptography to keep the assets of individuals in electronic form. Electronic funds transfer (EFT), digital gold currency, virtual currency and direct deposit are all examples of electronic money. Electronic funds transfer (EFT) is the electronic exchange of money between two accounts through computer-based systems. This includes online payments, debit card payments, ATM withdrawals, direct deposits, wire transfers and the like. Another application of electronic money is in e-commerce, and businesses such as PayPal mediate the transfer. Clearly any attack on such a system would allow wipe out national economies in the blink of an eye. The significance of integrity in such a system is staggering.

The merchant doesn't know who you are or ask for your credentials when you pay in cash. On the other hand, when you buy something with a credit card, you have to tell the merchant who you are, and you have to tell the credit card company who you're purchasing from. Anonymity is not maintained thus failing to protect your privacy. Concerns that anonymity in e-money could encourage tax evasion and money laundering led to demands by various institutions for digital cash to be traceable. This called for an elaborate method of encryption so that the information wouldn't get into the wrong hands.

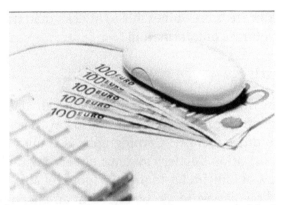

The key property of cash is anonymity: when you take money out of the bank, the bank gives you the cash without knowing what you do with that money.

The man behind it all is Dr. David Chaum. He formulated the blinded signature, a special form of a cryptographic signature that allowed a virtual coin to be signed without the signer seeing the actual coin, and permitted a form of digital money that offered anonymity and untraceability. This form of currency is known as Digital Cash.

Threshold Cryptosystem

Threshold systems are designed to allow use only if a minimum number of parties, exceeding a threshold, agree to the said use. Technically, it means that in order to decrypt a ciphertext a minimum number of parties are required to collaborate in the process. Any less than that won't have sufficient information. For example, if in a bank at least 5 out of 10 people authorize the transaction, only then will it occur. Such systems obviate a single individual acting alone, while at the same time allowing many of the parties to be absent without the transaction being halted. Most threshold cryptosystems have keys which are distributed into parts. The most common technique for partitioning a key is to form the key as the solution to equations in N variables. Only if all the N equations are known, the key can be determined by solving them. If any less than N equations are known, the key can't be determined since there's at least one independent variable in each equation. The minimum required threshold number can be chosen for N and the equations can be held by separate individuals. The same general concept can be used to form arbitrary combinations of key requirements by forming ORs and ANDs of encryptions using different sets of keys for different combinations of key holders. The major difficulties with such a system lie in the key distribution problem and the large number of keys necessary to achieve arbitrary key holder combinations.

Such systems are mostly employed in organizations with very valuable secrets, such as militaries and the governments. One of the applications is to store the secret information in multiple locations to prevent access to the ciphertext itself and thus prevent cryptanalysis on it.

Secure Multi-party Computation

Secure multi-party computation involves a set of parties with private inputs who wish to jointly compute a function of their inputs so that certain security properties (such as privacy and correctness) are preserved. It provides solutions to various real-life problems such as private auctions, distributed voting, sharing of signature or decryption functions, and situations that require private information retrieval. One popular application of secure MPC (multi-party computation) is solving the Yao's millionaire problem, i.e. two millionaires want to know which one of them is richer but without revealing their net worth to the other. The millionaires' problem is a secure two-party computation problem.

It has been generalized for multi-party computations. In a secure MPC, if no party can learn more from the public function and its result then what can it learn from its own input.

It has been proved that the multi-party computation problem can be solved if there exist unconditionally secure authenticated channels between pairs of participants. Consider four individuals Alice, Bob, Carol and Dave who want to calculate their average salary without revealing their salary to others.

One way to calculate the salary is as follows:

1. Alice adds a secret random number to her salary, encrypts the result with Bob's public key and sends it to Bob.

2. Bob decrypts Alice's result with his private key. He adds his salary to Alice's message, encrypts the result with Carol's public key and sends it to Carol.

3. Carol decrypts Bob's result with her private key. She adds her salary to Bob's message, encrypts the result with Dave's public key and sends it to Dave.

4. Dave decrypts Carol's result with his private key. He adds his salary to Carol's message, encrypts the result with Alice's public key and sends it to Alice.

5. Alice decrypts Dave's result with her private key. She subtracts the random number from Step 1 to recover the sum of everyone's salaries.

6. Alice divides the result by the number of people (four, in this case) and announces the result.

This way no one knew anybody else's salary and the function to calculate average salary was successfully computed.

Applications of cryptography help us understand that its use transcends almost all aspects of human dealings. Cryptography ensures security and integrity of information and prevents misuse of data by unauthorized persons. It also makes our lives convenient by providing such instruments as electronic cash and digital signatures. It was used by early man to pass on secret messages to one another, and has evolved continuously to serve our ever increasing demands.

APPLICATIONS OF CRYPTOGRAPHY

Trusted Timestamping

Trusted timestamping is the process of securely keeping track of the creation and modification time of a document. Security here means that no one—not even the owner of the document—should be able to change it once it has been recorded provided that the timestamper's integrity is never compromised.

The administrative aspect involves setting up a publicly available, trusted timestamp management infrastructure to collect, process and renew timestamps.

The idea of timestamping information is centuries old. For example, when Robert Hooke discovered Hooke's law in 1660, he did not want to publish it yet, but wanted to be able to claim priority. So he published the anagram *ceiiinosssttuv* and later published the translation *ut tensio sic vis* ("as is the extension, so is the force"). Similarly, Galileo first published his discovery of the phases of Venus in the anagram form.

Sir Isaac Newton, in responding to questions from Leibniz in a letter in 1677, concealed the details of his "fluxional technique" with an anagram:

> "The foundations of these operations is evident enough, in fact; but because I cannot proceed with the explanation of it now, I have preferred to conceal it thus: 6accdae13eff7i3l-9n4o4qrr4s8t12ux. On this foundation I have also tried to simplify the theories which concern the squaring of curves, and I have arrived at certain general Theorems".

Classification

There are many timestamping schemes with different security goals:

- PKI-based - timestamp token is protected using PKI digital signature.

- Linking-based schemes - timestamp is generated such a way that it is related to other timestamps.

- Distributed schemes - timestamp is generated in cooperation of multiple parties.

- Transient key scheme - variant of PKI with short-living signing keys.

- MAC - simple secret key based scheme, found in ANSI ASC X9.95 Standard.

- Database - document hashes are stored in trusted archive; there is online lookup service for verification.

- Hybrid schemes - the linked and signed method is prevailing.

Coverage in standards:

Scheme	RFC 3161	X9.95	ISO/IEC 18014
PKI	Yes	Yes	Yes
Linked		Yes	Yes
MAC		Yes	
Database			Yes
Transient key		Yes	
Linked and signed		Yes	

Trusted (Digital) Timestamping

Getting a timestamp from a trusted third party.

According to the RFC 3161 standard, a trusted timestamp is a timestamp issued by a Trusted Third Party (TTP) acting as a Time Stamping Authority (TSA). It is used to prove the existence of certain data before a certain point (e.g. contracts, research data, medical records,) without the possibility that the owner can backdate the timestamps. Multiple TSAs can be used to increase reliability and reduce vulnerability.

The newer ANSI ASC X9.95 Standard for trusted timestamps augments the RFC 3161 standard with data-level security requirements to ensure data integrity against a reliable time source that is provable to any third party. This standard has been applied to authenticating digitally signed data for regulatory compliance, financial transactions, and legal evidence.

Creating a Timestamp

The technique is based on digital signatures and hash functions. First a hash is calculated from the data. A hash is a sort of digital fingerprint of the original data: a string of bits that is practically impossible to duplicate with any other set of data. If the original data is changed then this will result in a completely different hash. This hash is sent to the TSA. The TSA concatenates a timestamp to the hash and calculates the hash of this concatenation. This hash is in turn digitally signed with the private key of the TSA. This signed hash + the timestamp is sent back to the requester of the timestamp who stores these with the original data.

Since the original data cannot be calculated from the hash (because the hash function is a one way function), the TSA never gets to see the original data, which allows the use of this method for confidential data.

Checking the Timestamp

Anyone trusting the timestamper can then verify that the document was not created after the date that the timestamper vouches. It can also no longer be repudiated that the requester of the timestamp was in possession of the original data at the time given by the timestamp. To prove this the hash of the original data is calculated, the timestamp given by the TSA is appended to it and the hash of the result of this concatenation is calculated, call this hash A.

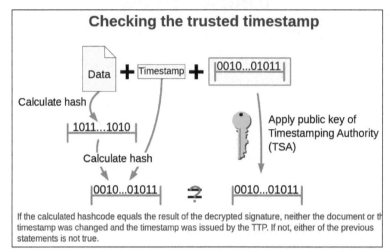

Checking correctness of a timestamp generated by a time stamping authority (TSA).

Then the digital signature of the TSA needs to be validated. This can be done by checking that the signed hash provided by the TSA was indeed signed with their private key by digital signature verification. The hash A is compared with the hash B inside the signed TSA message to confirm they are equal, proving that the timestamp and message is unaltered and was issued by the TSA. If not, then either the timestamp was altered or the timestamp was not issued by the TSA.

Decentralized Timestamping on the Blockchain

With the advent of cryptocurrencies like bitcoin, it has become possible to securely timestamp information in a decentralized and tamper-proof manner. Digital data can be hashed and the hash can be incorporated into a transaction stored in the blockchain, which serves as a secure proof of the exact time at which that data existed. The proof is due to a tremendous amount of computational effort performed after the hash was submitted to the blockchain. Tampering with the timestamp would require more computational resources than the rest of the network combined, and cannot be done unnoticed.

The decentralized timestamping approach using the blockchain has also found applications in other areas, such as in dashboard cameras, to secure the integrity of video files at the time of their recording, or to prove priority for creative content and ideas shared on social media platforms.

Digital Signatures

Digital signatures are the public-key primitives of message authentication. In the physical world, it is common to use handwritten signatures on handwritten or typed messages. They are used to bind signatory to the message.

Similarly, a digital signature is a technique that binds a person/entity to the digital data. This binding can be independently verified by receiver as well as any third party.

Digital signature is a cryptographic value that is calculated from the data and a secret key known only by the signer.

In real world, the receiver of message needs assurance that the message belongs to the sender and he should not be able to repudiate the origination of that message. This requirement is very crucial in business applications, since likelihood of a dispute over exchanged data is very high.

Model of Digital Signature

The digital signature scheme is based on public key cryptography. The model of digital signature scheme is depicted in the following illustration –

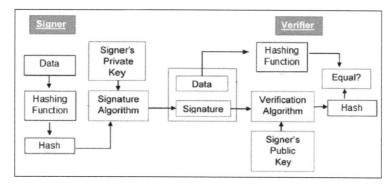

The following points explain the entire process in detail –

- Each person adopting this scheme has a public-private key pair.

- Generally, the key pairs used for encryption/decryption and signing/verifying are different. The private key used for signing is referred to as the signature key and the public key as the verification key.

- Signer feeds data to the hash function and generates hash of data.

- Hash value and signature key are then fed to the signature algorithm which produces the digital signature on given hash. Signature is appended to the data and then both are sent to the verifier.

- Verifier feeds the digital signature and the verification key into the verification algorithm. The verification algorithm gives some value as output.

- Verifier also runs same hash function on received data to generate hash value.

- For verification, this hash value and output of verification algorithm are compared. Based on the comparison result, verifier decides whether the digital signature is valid.

- Since digital signature is created by 'private' key of signer and no one else can have this key; the signer cannot repudiate signing the data in future.

It should be noticed that instead of signing data directly by signing algorithm, usually a hash of data is created. Since the hash of data is a unique representation of data, it is sufficient to sign the hash in place of data. The most important reason of using hash instead of data directly for signing is efficiency of the scheme.

Let us assume RSA is used as the signing algorithm. The encryption/signing process using RSA involves modular exponentiation.

Signing large data through modular exponentiation is computationally expensive and time consuming. The hash of the data is a relatively small digest of the data, hence signing a hash is more efficient than signing the entire data.

Importance of Digital Signature

Out of all cryptographic primitives, the digital signature using public key cryptography is considered as very important and useful tool to achieve information security.

Apart from ability to provide non-repudiation of message, the digital signature also provides message authentication and data integrity.

- Message authentication – When the verifier validates the digital signature using public key of a sender, he is assured that signature has been created only by sender who possess the corresponding secret private key and no one else.

- Data Integrity – In case an attacker has access to the data and modifies it, the digital signature verification at receiver end fails. The hash of modified data and the output provided by the verification algorithm will not match. Hence, receiver can safely deny the message assuming that data integrity has been breached.

- Non-repudiation – Since it is assumed that only the signer has the knowledge of the signature key, he can only create unique signature on a given data. Thus the receiver can present data and the digital signature to a third party as evidence if any dispute arises in the future.

By adding public-key encryption to digital signature scheme, we can create a cryptosystem that can provide the four essential elements of security namely – Privacy, Authentication, Integrity, and Non-repudiation.

Encryption with Digital Signature

In many digital communications, it is desirable to exchange an encrypted messages than plaintext to achieve confidentiality. In public key encryption scheme, a public (encryption) key of sender is available in open domain, and hence anyone can spoof his identity and send any encrypted message to the receiver.

This makes it essential for users employing PKC for encryption to seek digital signatures along with encrypted data to be assured of message authentication and non-repudiation.

This can archived by combining digital signatures with encryption scheme. There are two possibilities, sign-then-encrypt and encrypt-then-sign.

However, the crypto system based on sign-then-encrypt can be exploited by receiver to spoof identity of sender and sent that data to third party. Hence, this method is not preferred. The process of encrypt-then-sign is more reliable and widely adopted. This is depicted in the following illustration.

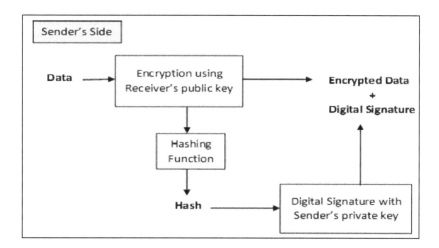

The receiver after receiving the encrypted data and signature on it, first verifies the signature using sender's public key. After ensuring the validity of the signature, he then retrieves the data through decryption using his private key.

CRYPTOGRAPHY BENEFITS AND DRAWBACKS

Nowadays, the networks have gone global and information has taken the digital form of bits and bytes. Critical information now gets stored, processed and transmitted in digital form on computer systems and open communication channels.

Since information plays such a vital role, adversaries are targeting the computer systems and open communication channels to either steal the sensitive information or to disrupt the critical information system.

Modern cryptography provides a robust set of techniques to ensure that the malevolent intentions of the adversary are thwarted while ensuring the legitimate users get access to information.

Benefits

Cryptography is an essential information security tool. It provides the four most basic services of information security:

- Confidentiality – Encryption technique can guard the information and communication from unauthorized revelation and access of information.

- Authentication – The cryptographic techniques such as MAC and digital signatures can protect information against spoofing and forgeries.

- Data Integrity – The cryptographic hash functions are playing vital role in assuring the users about the data integrity.

- Non-repudiation – The digital signature provides the non-repudiation service to guard against the dispute that may arise due to denial of passing message by the sender.

All these fundamental services offered by cryptography has enabled the conduct of business over the networks using the computer systems in extremely efficient and effective manner.

Drawbacks

Apart from the four fundamental elements of information security, there are other issues that affect the effective use of information:

- A strongly encrypted, authentic, and digitally signed information can be difficult to access even for a legitimate user at a crucial time of decision-making. The network or the computer system can be attacked and rendered non-functional by an intruder.

- High availability, one of the fundamental aspects of information security, cannot be ensured through the use of cryptography. Other methods are needed to guard against the threats such as denial of service or complete breakdown of information system.

- Another fundamental need of information security of selective access control also cannot be realized through the use of cryptography. Administrative controls and procedures are required to be exercised for the same.

- Cryptography does not guard against the vulnerabilities and threats that emerge from the poor design of systems, protocols, and procedures. These need to be fixed through proper design and setting up of a defensive infrastructure.

- Cryptography comes at cost. The cost is in terms of time and money:

  o Addition of cryptographic techniques in the information processing leads to delay.

  o The use of public key cryptography requires setting up and maintenance of public key infrastructure requiring the handsome financial budget.

- The security of cryptographic technique is based on the computational difficulty of mathematical problems. Any breakthrough in solving such mathematical problems or increasing the computing power can render a cryptographic technique vulnerable.

Future of Cryptography

Elliptic Curve Cryptography (ECC) has already been invented but its advantages and disadvantages are not yet fully understood. ECC allows to perform encryption and decryption in a drastically lesser time, thus allowing a higher amount of data to be passed with equal security. However, as other methods of encryption, ECC must also be tested and proven secure before it is accepted for governmental, commercial, and private use.

Quantum computation is the new phenomenon. While modern computers store data using a binary format called a "bit" in which a "1" or a "0" can be stored; a quantum computer stores data using a quantum superposition of multiple states. These multiple valued states are stored in "quantum bits" or "qubits". This allows the computation of numbers to be several orders of magnitude faster than traditional transistor processors.

To comprehend the power of quantum computer, consider RSA-640, a number with 193 digits, which can be factored by eighty 2.2 GHz computers over the span of 5 months, one quantum computer would factor in less than 17 seconds. Numbers that would typically take billions of years to compute could only take a matter of hours or even minutes with a fully developed quantum computer.

In view of these facts, modern cryptography will have to look for computationally harder problems or devise completely new techniques of archiving the goals presently served by modern cryptography.

References

- Cryptography, entry: newworldencyclopedia.org, Retrieved 26 July, 2019

- Cryptography-techniques-for-secure-communications: certmag.com, Retrieved 21 May, 2019

- What-is-cryptanalysis: securitydegreehub.com, Retrieved 8 January, 2019

- Uses-of-cryptography, fasttrack-to-cryptography, technology-guides: digit.in, 1 February, 2019

- Jones, Shawn M. (2017-04-20). "2017-04-20: Trusted Timestamping of Mementos". Ws-dl.blogspot.de. Retrieved 2017-10-30

- Cryptography-digital-signatures, cryptography: tutorialspoint.com, Retrieved 13 May, 2019

- Benefits-and-drawbacks, cryptography: tutorialspoint.com, Retrieved 6 July, 2019

Branches of Cryptography

Some of the various branches of cryptography are quantum cryptography, post-quantum cryptography, visual cryptography, multivariate cryptography and DNA cryptography. The topics elaborated in this chapter will help in gaining a better perspective about these branches of cryptography.

QUANTUM CRYPTOGRAPHY

The uncertainty principle of quantum physics builds the earliest foundations for quantum cryptography. With quantum computers of future being expected to solve discrete logarithmic problem and the popularly know cryptography methods such as AES, RSA, DES, quantum cryptography becomes the foreseen solution. In practice it is used to establish a shared, secret and random sequence of bits to communicate between two system let's say Alice and Bob. This is known as Quantum Key Distribution. After this key is shared between Alice and Bob, further exchange of information can take place through known cryptographic strategies.

Based on Heisenberg's Uncertainty Principle: BB84 and Variants

A single photon pulse is passed through a polarizer .Alice can use a particular polarizer to polarize a single photon pulse and encode binary value bits to outcome of a particular type (vertical, horizontal, circular etc) of polarizer. On receiving the photon beam, Bob would guess the polarizer and Bob can thus match the cases with Alice and know the correctness of his guesses. If Eve would have been trying to decode then due to poarization by Eve's polarizer would have caused discrepencies in match cases of Bob and Alice and thus they would know about eavesdropping. Thus in such a system if Eve tries to eavesdrop it will get into notice of Alice and Bob.

- The B92 protocol has only two polarization states unlike four in original BB84.

- BB84 has similar protocol SSP that uses 6 states to encode the bits.

- SARG04 is another protocol that uses attenuated lasers and provides better result than BB84 in more than one photon syetems.

Based on Quantum Entanglement: E91 and Variants

There is a single source that emits a pair of entangled photons with Alice and Bob receiving each particle. Similar to BB84 scheme Alice and Bob would exchange encoded bits and match cases for each photon transferred. But in this scenario the outcome of results of match cases of Alice and Bob will be opposite as a consequence of Entanglement principle. Either of them will have complement bits in bit strings interpreted. One of them can then invert bits to agree upon a key. Since Bell's Inequality should not hold for entagled particles thus this test can confirm absence of eavesdropper. Since practically it is not possible to have a third photon in entanglement with energy levels sufficient for non detect ability, thus this system is fully secure.

- SARG04 and SSP protocol models can be extended to Entangled particles theory.

Possible Attacks in Quantum Cryptography

- Photon Number Splitting (PNS) Attack –Since it is not possible to send a single photon thus a pulse is sent. Some of the photons from a pulse can be captured by Eve and after matching of bits by Alice and Bob, Eve can use the same polarizer as done by Bob and thus get the key without being detected.

- Faked-State Attack –Eve uses a replica of Bob's photon detector and thus captures the photons intended for Bob and further passed it to Bob. Though Eve knows about the encoded bit, Bob thinks that he received it from Alice.

POST-QUANTUM CRYPTOGRAPHY

Post-quantum cryptography (sometimes referred to as quantum-proof, quantum-safe or quantum-resistant) refers to cryptographic algorithms (usually public-key algorithms) that are thought to be secure against an attack by a quantum computer. As of 2018, this is not true for the most popular public-key algorithms, which can be efficiently broken by a sufficiently strong hypothetical quantum computer. The problem with currently popular algorithms is that their security relies on one of three hard mathematical problems: the integer factorization problem, the discrete logarithm problem or the elliptic-curve discrete logarithm problem. All of these problems can be easily solved on a sufficiently powerful quantum computer running Shor's algorithm. Even though current, publicly known, experimental quantum computers lack processing power to break any real cryptographic algorithm, many cryptographers are designing new algorithms to prepare for a time when quantum computing becomes a threat. This work has gained greater attention from academics and industry through the PQCrypto conference series since 2006 and more recently by several workshops on Quantum Safe Cryptography hosted by the European Telecommunications Standards Institute (ETSI) and the Institute for Quantum Computing.

In contrast to the threat quantum computing poses to current public-key algorithms, most current symmetric cryptographic algorithms and hash functions are considered to be relatively secure against attacks by quantum computers. While the quantum Grover's algorithm does speed up attacks against symmetric ciphers, doubling the key size can effectively block these attacks. Thus post-quantum symmetric cryptography does not need to differ significantly from current symmetric cryptography.

Algorithms

Currently post-quantum cryptography research is mostly focused on six different approaches:

Lattice-based Cryptography

This approach includes cryptographic systems such as learning with errors, ring learning with errors (ring-LWE), the ring learning with errors key exchange and the ring learning with errors signature, the older NTRU or GGH encryption schemes, and the newer NTRU signature and BLISS signatures. Some of these schemes like NTRU encryption have been studied for many years without anyone finding a feasible attack. Others like the ring-LWE algorithms have proofs that their security reduces to a worst-case problem. The Post Quantum Cryptography Study Group sponsored by the European Commission suggested that the Stehle–Steinfeld variant of NTRU be studied for standardization rather than the NTRU algorithm. At that time, NTRU was still patented. Studies have indicated that NTRU may have more secure properties than other lattice based algorithms.

Multivariate Cryptography

This includes cryptographic systems such as the Rainbow (Unbalanced Oil and Vinegar) scheme which is based on the difficulty of solving systems of multivariate equations. Various attempts to build secure multivariate equation encryption schemes have failed. However, multivariate signature schemes like Rainbow could provide the basis for a quantum secure digital signature. There is a patent on the Rainbow Signature Scheme.

Hash-based Cryptography

This includes cryptographic systems such as Lamport signatures and the Merkle signature scheme and the newer XMSS and SPHINCS schemes. Hash based digital signatures were invented in the late 1970s by Ralph Merkle and have been studied ever since as an interesting alternative to number-theoretic digital signatures like RSA and DSA. Their primary drawback is that for any hash-based public key, there is a limit on the number of signatures that can be signed using the corresponding set of private keys. This fact had reduced interest in these signatures until interest was revived due to the desire for cryptography that was resistant to attack by quantum computers. There appear to be no patents on the Merkle signature scheme and there exist many non-patented hash functions that could be used with these schemes. The stateful hash-based signature scheme XMSS is described in RFC 8391. Note that all the above schemes are one-time or bounded-time signatures, Moni Naor and Moti Yung invented UOWHF hashing in 1989 and designed a signature based on hashing (the Naor-Yung scheme) which can be unlimited-time in use (the first such signature that does not require trapdoor properties).

Code-based Cryptography

This includes cryptographic systems which rely on error-correcting codes, such as the McEliece and Niederreiter encryption algorithms and the related Courtois, Finiasz and Sendrier Signature scheme. The original McEliece signature using random Goppa codes has withstood scrutiny for over 30 years. However, many variants of the McEliece scheme, which seek to introduce more structure into the code used in order to reduce the size of the keys, have been shown to be insecure. The post quantum cryptography study group sponsored by the european commission has recommended the McEliece public key encryption system as a candidate for long term protection against attacks by quantum computers.

Supersingular Elliptic Curve Isogeny Cryptography

This cryptographic system relies on the properties of supersingular elliptic curves and supersingular isogeny graphs to create a Diffie-Hellman replacement with forward secrecy. This cryptographic system uses the well studied mathematics of supersingular elliptic curves to create a Diffie-Hellman like key exchange that can serve as a straightforward quantum computing resistant replacement for the Diffie-Hellman and elliptic curve Diffie–Hellman key exchange methods that are in widespread use today. Because it works much like existing Diffie–Hellman implementations, it offers forward secrecy which is viewed as important both to prevent mass surveillance by governments but also to protect against the compromise of long term keys through failures. In 2012, researchers Sun, Tian and Wang of the Chinese State Key Lab for Integrated Service Networks and Xidian University, extended the work of De Feo, Jao, and Plut to create quantum secure digital signatures based on supersingular elliptic curve isogenies. There are no patents covering this cryptographic system.

Symmetric Key Quantum Resistance

Provided one uses sufficiently large key sizes, the symmetric key cryptographic systems like AES and SNOW 3G are already resistant to attack by a quantum computer. Further, key management systems and protocols that use symmetric key cryptography instead of public key cryptography like Kerberos and the 3GPP Mobile Network Authentication Structure are also inherently secure against attack by a quantum computer. Given its widespread deployment in the world already, some researchers recommend expanded use of Kerberos-like symmetric key management as an efficient and effective way to get post quantum cryptography today.

Security Reductions

In cryptography research, it is desirable to prove the equivalence of a cryptographic algorithm and a known hard mathematical problem. These proofs are often called "security reductions", and are used to demonstrate the difficulty of cracking the encryption algorithm. In other words, the security of a given cryptographic algorithm is reduced to the security of a known hard problem. Researchers are actively looking for security reductions in the prospects for post quantum cryptography. Current results are given here.

Lattice-based Cryptography – Ring-LWE Signature

In some versions of Ring-LWE there is a security reduction to the shortest-vector problem (SVP) in a lattice as a lower bound on the security. The SVP is known to be NP-hard. Specific ring-LWE systems that have provable security reductions include a variant of Lyubashevsky's ring-LWE signatures defined in a paper by Güneysu, Lyubashevsky, and Pöppelmann. The GLYPH signature scheme is a variant of the Güneysu, Lyubashevsky, and Pöppelmann (GLP) signature which takes into account research results that have come after the publication of the GLP signature in 2012. Another Ring-LWE signature is Ring-TESLA.

Lattice-based Cryptography – NTRU, BLISS

The security of the NTRU encryption scheme and the BLISS signature is believed to be related to, but not provably reducible to, the Closest Vector Problem (CVP) in a Lattice. The CVP is known to be NP-hard. The Post Quantum Cryptography Study Group sponsored by the European Commission suggested that the Stehle–Steinfeld variant of NTRU which does have a security reduction be studied for long term use instead of the original NTRU algorithm.

Multivariate Cryptography – Rainbow

The Rainbow Multivariate Equation Signature Scheme is a member of a class of multivariate quadratic equation cryptosystems called "Unbalanced Oil and Vinegar Cryptosystems" (UOV Cryptosystems) Bulygin, Petzoldt and Buchmann have shown a reduction of generic multivariate quadratic UOV systems to the NP-Hard Multivariate Quadratic Equation Solving problem.

Hash-based Cryptography – Merkle Signature Scheme

In 2005, Luis Garcia proved that there was a security reduction of Merkle Hash Tree signatures to the security of the underlying hash function. Garcia showed in his paper that if computationally one-way hash functions exist then the Merkle Hash Tree signature is provably secure.

Therefore, if one used a hash function with a provable reduction of security to a known hard problem one would have a provable security reduction of the Merkle tree signature to that known hard problem.

Code-based Cryptography – McEliece

The McEliece Encryption System has a security reduction to the Syndrome Decoding Problem (SDP). The SDP is known to be NP-hard. The Post Quantum Cryptography Study Group sponsored by the European Commission has recommended the use of this cryptography for long term protection against attack by a quantum computer.

Code-based Cryptography – RLCE

In 2016, Wang proposed a random linear code encryption scheme RLCE which is based on McEliece schemes. RLCE scheme can be constructed using any linear code such as Reed-Solomon code by inserting random columns in the underlying linear code generator matrix.

Supersingular Elliptic Curve Isogeny Cryptography

Security is related to the problem of constructing an isogeny between two supersingular curves with the same number of points. The most recent investigation of the difficulty of this problem is by Delfs and Galbraith indicates that this problem is as hard as the inventors of the key exchange suggest that it is. There is no security reduction to a known NP-hard problem.

Comparison

One common characteristic of many post-quantum cryptography algorithms is that they require larger key sizes than commonly used "pre-quantum" public key algorithms. There are often tradeoffs to be made in key size, computational efficiency and ciphertext or signature size. The table lists some values for different schemes at a 128 bit post-quantum security level.

Algorithm	Type	Public Key	Private Key	Signature
NTRU Encrypt	Lattice	6130 B	6743 B	
Streamlined NTRU Prime	Lattice	1232 B		
Rainbow	Multivariate	124 KB	95 KB	
SPHINCS	Hash Signature	1 KB	1 KB	41 KB
SPHINCS+	Hash Signature	32 B	64 B	8 KB
BLISS-II	Lattice	7 KB	2 KB	5 KB
GLP-Variant GLYPH Signature	Ring-LWE	2 KB	0.4 KB	1.8 KB
New Hope	Ring-LWE	2 KB	2 KB	
Goppa-based McEliece	Code-based	1 MB	11.5 KB	
Random Linear Code based encryption	RLCE	115 KB	3 KB	
Quasi-cyclic MDPC-based McEliece	Code-based	1232 B	2464 B	
SIDH	Isogeny	751 B	48 B	
SIDH (compressed keys)	Isogeny	564 B	48 B	
3072-bit Discrete Log	not PQC	384 B	32 B	96 B
256-bit Elliptic Curve	not PQC	32 B	32 B	65 B

A practical consideration on a choice among post-quantum cryptographic algorithms is the effort required to send public keys over the internet. From this point of view, the Ring-LWE, NTRU, and SIDH algorithms provide key sizes conveniently under 1KB, hash-signature public keys come in under 5KB, and MDPC-based McEliece takes about 1KB. On the other hand, Rainbow schemes require about 125KB and Goppa-based McEliece requires a nearly 1MB key.

Lattice-based Cryptography – LWE Key Exchange and Ring-LWE Key Exchange

The fundamental idea of using LWE and Ring LWE for key exchange was proposed and filed at the University of Cincinnati in 2011 by Jintai Ding. The basic idea comes from the associativity of matrix multiplications, and the errors are used to provide the security.

In 2014, Peikert presented a key transport scheme following the same basic idea of Ding's, where the new idea of sending additional 1 bit signal for rounding in Ding's construction is also utilized. For somewhat greater than 128 bits of security, Singh presents a set of parameters which have 6956-bit public keys for the Peikert's scheme. The corresponding private key would be roughly 14,000 bits.

In 2015, an authenticated key exchange with provable forward security following the same basic idea of Ding's was presented at Eurocrypt 2015, which is an extension of the HMQV construction in Crypto 2005.

Lattice-based Cryptography – NTRU Encryption

For 128 bits of security in NTRU, Hirschhorn, Hoffstein, Howgrave-Graham and Whyte, recommend using a public key represented as a degree 613 polynomial with coefficients $\mod\left(2^{10}\right)$. This results in a public key of 6130 bits. The corresponding private key would be 6743 bits.

Multivariate Cryptography – Rainbow Signature

For 128 bits of security and the smallest signature size in a Rainbow multivariate quadratic equation signature scheme, Petzoldt, Bulygin and Buchmann, recommend using equations in $\mathbb{F}_{31}$ with a public key size of just over 991,000 bits, a private key of just over 740,000 bits and digital signatures which are 424 bits in length.

Hash-based Cryptography – Merkle Signature Scheme

In order to get 128 bits of security for hash based signatures to sign 1 million messages using the fractal Merkle tree method of Naor Shenhav and Wool the public and private key sizes are roughly 36,000 bits in length.

Code-based Cryptography – McEliece

For 128 bits of security in a McEliece scheme, The European Commissions Post Quantum Cryptography Study group recommends using a binary Goppa code of length at least $n = 6960$ and dimension at least $k = 5413$, and capable of correcting $t = 119$ errors. With these parameters the public key for the McEliece system will be a systematic generator matrix whose non-identity part takes $k \times (n-k) = 8373911$ bits. The corresponding private key, which consists of the code support with $n = 6960$ elements from $GF(2^{13})$ and a generator polynomial of with $t = 119$ coefficients from $GF(2^{13})$, will be 92,027 bits in length

The group is also investigating the use of Quasi-cyclic MDPC codes of length at least $n = 2^{16} + 6 = 65542$ and dimension at least $= 2^{15} + 3 = 32771$, and capable of correcting $t = 264$ errors. With these parameters the public key for the McEliece system will be the first row of a systematic generator matrix whose non-identity part takes $k = 32771$ bits. The private key, a quasi-cyclic parity-check matrix with $d = 274$ nonzero entries on a column (or twice as much on a row), takes no more than $d \times 16 = 4384$ bits when represented as the coordinates of the nonzero entries on the first row.

Barreto et al. recommend using a binary Goppa code of length at least $n = 3307$ and dimension at least $k = 2515$, and capable of correcting $t = 66$ errors. With these parameters the public key for the McEliece system will be a systematic generator matrix whose non-identity part takes $k \times (n-k) = 1991880$ bits. The corresponding private key, which consists of the code support with $n = 3307$ elements from $GF(2^{12})$ and a generator polynomial of with $t = 66$ coefficients from $GF(2^{12})$, will be 40,476 bits in length.

Supersingular Elliptic Curve Isogeny Cryptography

For 128 bits of security in the supersingular isogeny Diffie-Hellman (SIDH) method, De Feo, Jao and Plut recommend using a supersingular curve modulo a 768-bit prime. If one uses elliptic curve point compression the public key will need to be no more than 8×768 or 6144 bits in length. A March 2016 paper by authors Azarderakhsh, Jao, Kalach, Koziel, and Leonardi showed how to cut the number of bits transmitted in half, which was further improved by authors Costello, Jao, Longa, Naehrig, Renes and Urbanik resulting in a compressed-key version of the SIDH protocol with public keys only 2640 bits in size. This makes the number of bits transmitted roughly equivalent to the non-quantum secure RSA and Diffie-Hellman at the same classical security level.

Symmetric–key-based Cryptography

As a general rule, for 128 bits of security in a symmetric-key-based system, one can safely use key sizes of 256 bits. The best quantum attack against generic symmetric-key systems is an application of Grover's algorithm, which requires work proportional to the square root of the size of the key space. To transmit an encrypted key to a device that possesses the symmetric key necessary to decrypt that key requires roughly 256 bits as well. It is clear that symmetric-key systems offer the smallest key sizes for post-quantum cryptography.

Forward Secrecy

A public-key system demonstrates a property referred to as perfect forward secrecy when it generates random public keys per session for the purposes of key agreement. This means that the compromise of one message cannot lead to the compromise of others, and also that there is not a single secret value which can lead to the compromise of multiple messages. Security experts recommend using cryptographic algorithms that support forward secrecy over those that do not. The reason for this is that forward secrecy can protect against the compromise of long term private keys associated with public/private key pairs. This is viewed as a means of preventing mass surveillance by intelligence agencies.

Both the Ring-LWE key exchange and supersingular isogeny Diffie-Hellman (SIDH) key exchange can support forward secrecy in one exchange with the other party. Both the Ring-LWE and SIDH can also be used without forward secrecy by creating a variant of the classic ElGamal encryption variant of Diffie-Hellman.

The other algorithms such as NTRU, do not support forward secrecy as is. Any authenticated public key encryption system can be used to build a key exchange with forward secrecy.

Open Quantum Safe Project

Open Quantum Safe (OQS) project was started in late 2016 and has the goal of developing and prototyping quantum-resistant cryptography. It aims to integrate current post-quantum schemes in one library: liboqs. Liboqs is an open source C library for quantum-resistant cryptographic algorithms. liboqs initially focuses on key exchange algorithms. liboqs provides a common API suitable for post-quantum key exchange algorithms, and will collect together various implementations. liboqs will also include a test harness and benchmarking routines to compare performance of post-quantum implementations. Furthermore, OQS also provides integration of liboqs into OpenSSL.

Table: As of April 2017, the following key exchange algorithms are supported.

Algorithm	Type
BCNS15	Ring learning with errors key exchange
NewHope	Ring learning with errors key exchange
Frodo	Learning with errors
NTRU	Lattice-based cryptography
SIDH	Supersingular isogeny key exchange
McBits	Error-correcting codes

Implementation

One of the main challenges in post-quantum cryptography is considered to be the implementation of potentially quantum safe algorithms into existing systems. There are tests done, for example by Microsoft Research implementing PICNIC in a PKI using Hardware security modules. Test implementations for Google's NewHope algorithm have also been done by HSM vendors.

VISUAL CRYPTOGRAPHY

Visual cryptography is a cryptographic technique which allows visual information (pictures, text, etc.) to be encrypted in such a way that the decrypted information appears as a visual image.

One of the best-known techniques has been credited to Moni Naor and Adi Shamir, who developed it in 1994. They demonstrated a visual secret sharing scheme, where an image was broken up into n shares so that only someone with all n shares could decrypt the image, while any $n - 1$ shares revealed no information about the original image. Each share was printed on a separate transparency, and decryption was performed by overlaying the shares. When all n shares were overlaid, the original image would appear. There are several generalizations of the basic scheme including k-out-of-n visual cryptography.

Using a similar idea, transparencies can be used to implement a one-time pad encryption, where one transparency is a shared random pad, and another transparency acts as the ciphertext. Normally, there is an expansion of space requirement in visual cryptography. But if one of the two shares is structured recursively, the efficiency of visual cryptography can be increased to 100%.

Some antecedents of visual cryptography are in patents from the 1960s. Other antecedents are in the work on perception and secure communication.

Visual cryptography can be used to protect biometric templates in which decryption does not require any complex computations.

(2, N) Visual Cryptography Sharing Case

Sharing a secret with an arbitrary number of people N such that at least 2 of them are required to decode the secret is one form of the visual secret sharing scheme presented by Moni Naor and Adi Shamir in 1994. In this scheme we have a secret image which is encoded into N shares printed on transparencies. The shares appear random and contain no decipherable information about the underlying secret image, however if any 2 of the shares are stacked on top of one another the secret image becomes decipherable by the human eye.

Every pixel from the secret image is encoded into multiple subpixels in each share image using a matrix to determine the color of the pixels. In the (2,N) case a white pixel in the secret image is encoded using a matrix from the following set, where each row gives the subpixel pattern for one of the components:

$$\{\text{all permutations of the columns of}\} : C_0 = \begin{bmatrix} 1 & 0 & ... & 0 \\ 1 & 0 & ... & 0 \\ ... & & & \\ 1 & 0 & ... & 0 \end{bmatrix}.$$

While a black pixel in the secret image is encoded using a matrix from the following set:

$$\{\text{all permutations of the columns of}\} : C_1 = \begin{bmatrix} 1 & 0 & ... & 0 \\ 0 & 1 & ... & 0 \\ ... & & & \\ 0 & 0 & ... & 1 \end{bmatrix}.$$

For instance in the (2,2) sharing case (the secret is split into 2 shares and both shares are required to decode the secret) we use complementary matrices to share a black pixel and identical matrices to share a white pixel. Stacking the shares we have all the subpixels associated with the black pixel now black while 50% of the subpixels associated with the white pixel remain white.

Cheating the (2,N) Visual Secret Sharing Scheme

Horng et al. proposed a method that allows $N - 1$ colluding parties to cheat an honest party in visual cryptography. They take advantage of knowing the underlying distribution of the pixels in the shares to create new shares that combine with existing shares to form a new secret message of the cheaters choosing.

We know that 2 shares are enough to decode the secret image using the human visual system. But examining two shares also gives some information about the 3rd share. For instance, colluding participants may examine their shares to determine when they both have black pixels and use that information to determine that another participant will also have a black pixel in that location. Knowing where black pixels exist in another party's share allows them to create a new share that will combine with the predicted share to form a new secret message. In this way a set of colluding parties that have enough shares to access the secret code can cheat other honest parties.

MULTIVARIATE CRYPTOGRAPHY

Multivariate cryptography is the generic term for asymmetric cryptographic primitives based on multivariate polynomials over a finite field F. In certain cases those polynomials could be defined over both a ground and an extension field. If the polynomials have the degree two, we talk about multivariate quadratics. Solving systems of multivariate polynomial equations is proven to be NP-hard or NP-complete. That's why those schemes are often considered to be good candidates for post-quantum cryptography. Multivariate cryptography has been very productive in terms of design and cryptanalysis. Overall, the situation is now more stable and the strongest schemes have withstood the test of time. It is commonly admitted that Multivariate cryptography turned out to be more successful as an approach to build signature schemes primarily because multivariate schemes provide the shortest signature among post-quantum algorithms.

In 1988, T. Matsumoto and H. Imai [MI88] presented their so-called C* scheme at the Eurocrypt conference. Although C* has been broken [P95], the general principle of Matsumoto and Imai has inspired a generation of improved proposals. In later work, the "Hidden Monomial Cryptosystems" was developed by (in French) Jacques Patarin. It is based on a ground and an extension field. "Hidden Field Equations" (HFE), developed by (in French) Jacques Patarin in 1996, remains a popular multivariate scheme today [P96]. The security of HFE has been thoroughly investigated, beginning with a direct Gröbner basis attack [FJ03, GJS06], key-recovery attacks [KS99b, BFP13], and more. The plain version of HFE is considered to be practically broken, in the sense that secure parameters lead to an impractical scheme. However, some simple variants of HFE, such as the *minus variant* and the *vinegar variant* allow one to strengthen the basic HFE against all known attacks.

In addition to HFE, J. Patarin developed other schemes. In 1997 he presented "Balanced Oil & Vinegar" and 1999 "Unbalanced Oil and Vinegar" in cooperation with Aviad Kipnis and Louis Goubin.

Construction

Multivariate Quadratics involves a public and a private key. The private key consists of two affine transformations, S and T, and an easy to invert quadratic map $P' : F^m \rightarrow F^n$. We denote the n by n matrix of the affine endomorphisms $S : F^n \rightarrow F^n$ by M_S and the shift vector by $v_S \in F^n$ and similarly for $T : F^m \rightarrow F^m$. In other words,

- $S(x) = M_S x + v_S$ and

- $T(y) = M_T y' + v_T$.

The triple $(S^{-1}, P'^{-1}, T^{-1})$ is the private key, also known as the trapdoor. The public key is the composition $P = S \circ P' \circ T$ which is by assumption hard to invert without the knowledge of the trapdoor.

Signature

Signatures are generated using the private key and are verified using the public key as follows. The message is hashed to a vector in $y \in F^n$ via a known hash function. The signature is

$$x = P^{-1}(y) = T^{-1}\left(P'^{-1}\left(S^{-1}(y)\right)\right).$$

The receiver of the signed document must have the public key P in possession. He computes the hash y and checks that the signature x fulfils $P(x) = y$.

Applications

- Unbalanced Oil and Vinegar

- Hidden Field Equations

- SFLASH by NESSIE

- Rainbow

- TTS

- QUARTZ

- QUAD (cipher)

DNA CRYPTOGRAPHY

DNA Cryptology combines cryptology and modern biotechnology.

Why DNA Cryptography

- DNA Cryptography is one of the rapidly evolving technologies in the world.

- Adelman showed the world how it can be used to solve complex problems like directed Hamilton path problem and NP-complete problem (for example Travelling Salesman problem). Hence user can design and implement more complex Crypto algorithms.

- It brings forward new hope to break unbreakable algorithms. This is because DNA computing offers more speed, minimal storage and power requirements.

- DNA stores memory at a density of about 1 bit/nm3 where conventional storage media requires 1012 nm3/bit.

- No power is required for DNA computing while the computation is taking place.

- Surprisingly, one gram of DNA contains 1021 DNA bases which is equivalent to 108 TB of data. Hence can store all the data in the world in a few milligrams.

DNA Cryptography can be defined as a hiding data in terms of DNA Sequence. Just like the RSA and DES algorithms, in DNA Cryptology user have DNA algorithms like "Public-key system using DNA as a one-way function for key distribution," "DNASC cryptography system", DNA Steganography Systems, Triple stage DNA Cryptography, Encryption algorithm inspired by DNA and Chaotic computing.

So, how do encode data in a DNA strand which is mainly made, up of 4 nitrogenous bases namely:

- Adenine (A)

- Thymine (T)

- Cytosine (C)

- Guanine (G)

The easiest way to encode is to represent these four units as four figures:

```
A(0) -00

T(1) -01

C(2)-10

G(3)-11
```

- By these encoding rules, there are 4!=24 possible encoding methods. Based on some principles as A and G make pairs while T and C make pairs.

- Of those 24 methods, only 8 match the DNA pairing rule but the best encoding scheme is 0123/CTAG.

So now converted our initial number into a sequence of A, T, G and C theoretically. This is then physically implemented using various DNA synthesizing techniques like Chemical Oligonucleotide Synthesis and Oligo Synthesis Platforms (this includes Column-Based Oligo Synthesis, Array-based Oligo Synthesis, Complex Strand and Gene Synthesis and Error Correction).

Let's take an example of the classic XOR One Time Pad and see how its implemented using DNA Cryptography:

Example — Let M be the message and K be the key. The Ciphertext is obtained by finding M xor K = C. User can again obtain the Encoded message by doing: C xor K = M xor K xor K= M. Hence, get our original message. The steps involved in implementing it is:

- The message and the OTP key are converted to ASCII bits.

- Zero Padding is added to the message and the key in order to make the size of their binary codes even.

- The message and the key are XORed together.

- The XOR output is represented in DNA bases format. This is our enciphered text.

The decryption process involves the following processes and hence it is also prone to eavesdropping:

- All the DNA bases are transformed into bits.

- These bits are then XORed with the OTP key bits to reproduce the original plain text.

- This text so obtained in binary format is then converted into a sequence of ASCII characters.

Similarly, user can implement other crypto algorithms like AES and even DES. Instead of storing data as a sequence of 0s and 1s, storing them as a sequence of nitrogenous bases. Storing information in the form a DNA enables us to store a lot of data in a small area.

STEGANOGRAPHY

Steganography is a method of hiding secret data, by embedding it into an audio, video, image or text file. It is one of the methods employed to protect secret or sensitive data from malicious attacks.

Cryptography and steganography are both methods used to hide or protect secret data. However, they differ in the respect that cryptography makes the data unreadable, or hides the *meaning* of the data, while steganography hides the *existence* of the data.

In layman's terms, cryptography is similar to writing a letter in a secret language: people can read it, but won't understand what it means. However, the existence of a (probably secret) message would be obvious to anyone who sees the letter, and if someone either knows or figures out your secret language, then your message can easily be read.

If you were to use *steganography* in the same situation, you would hide the letter inside a pair of socks that you would be gifting the intended recipient of the letter. To those who don't know about the message, it would look like there was nothing more to your gift than the socks. But the intended recipient knows what to look for, and finds the message hidden in them.

Similarly, if two users exchanged media files over the internet, it would be more difficult to determine whether these files contain hidden messages, than if they were communicating using cryptography. Crpytography is often used to supplement the security offered by steganography. Crypography algorithms are used to encrypt secret data before embedding it into cover files.

Image Steganography

As the name suggests, Image Steganography refers to the process of hiding data within an image file. The image selected for this purpose is called the cover-image and the image obtained after steganography is called the stego-image.

How is it Done

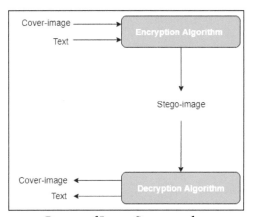

Process of Image Stegaography.

An image is represented as an N*M (in case of greyscale images) or N*M*3 (in case of colour images) matrix in memory, with each entry representing the intensity value of a pixel. In image steganography, a message is embedded into an image by altering the values of some pixels, which are chosen by an encryption algorithm. The recipient of the image must be aware of the same algorithm in order to known which pixels he or she must select to extract the message.

Detection of the message within the cover-image is done by the process of steganalysis. This can be done through comparison with the cover image, histogram plotting, or by noise detection. While efforts are being invested in developing new algorithms with a greater degree of immunity against such attacks, efforts are also being devoted towards improving existing algorithms for steganalysis, to detect exchange of secret information between terrorists or criminal elements.

References

- Quantum-cryptography: geeksforgeeks.org, Retrieved 6 January, 2019

- Alkim, Erdem; Ducas, Léo; Pöppelmann, Thomas; Schwabe, Peter (2015). "Post-quantum key exchange - a new hope" (PDF). Cryptology eprint Archive, Report 2015/1092. Retrieved 1 September 2017

- Dna-cryptography: geeksforgeeks.org, Retrieved 5 August, 2019

- Overbeck, Raphael; Sendrier (2009). Bernstein, Daniel (ed.). Code-based cryptography. Post-Quantum Cryptography. Pp. 95–145. Doi:10.1007/978-3-540-88702-7-4. ISBN 978-3-540-88701-0

- Image-steganography-in-cryptography: geeksforgeeks.org, Retrieved 30 March, 2019

Information Security

The practice of protecting information by reducing the information risks is referred to as information security. It falls under the domain of information risk management. The chapter closely examines the key applications of Information security such as authentication and non-repudiation to provide an extensive understanding of the subject.

Information security (infosec) is a set of strategies for managing the processes, tools and policies necessary to prevent, detect, document and counter threats to digital and non-digital information. Infosec responsibilities include establishing a set of business processes that will protect information assets regardless of how the information is formatted or whether it is in transit, is being processed or is at rest in storage.

Many large enterprises employ a dedicated security group to implement and maintain the organization's infosec program. Typically, this group is led by a chief information security officer. The security group is generally responsible for conducting risk management, a process through which vulnerabilities and threats to information assets are continuously assessed, and the appropriate protective controls are decided on and applied. The value of an organization lies within its information -- its security is critical for business operations, as well as retaining credibility and earning the trust of clients.

Principles of Information Security

Infosec programs are built around the core objectives of the CIA triad: maintaining the confidentiality, integrity and availability of IT systems and business data. These objectives ensure that sensitive information is only disclosed to authorized parties (confidentiality), prevent unauthorized modification of data (integrity) and guarantee the data can be accessed by authorized parties when requested (availability).

The first security consideration, confidentiality, usually requires the use of encryption and encryption keys. The second consideration, integrity, implies that when data is read back, it will be exactly the same as when it was written. (In some cases, it may be necessary to send the same data to two different locations in order to protect against data corruption at one place.) The third part of the CIA is availability. This part of the triad seeks to ensure that new data can be used in a timely manner and backup data can be restored in an acceptable recovery time.

Threats and Threat Responses

Threats to sensitive and private information come in many different forms, such as malware and phishing attacks, identity theft and ransomware. To deter attackers and mitigate vulnerabilities at various points, multiple security controls are implemented and coordinated as part of a layered defense in depth strategy. This should minimize the impact of an attack. To be prepared for a security breach, security groups should have an incident response plan (IRP) in place. This should allow them to contain and limit the damage, remove the cause and apply updated defense controls.

Information security processes and policies typically involve physical and digital security measures to protect data from unauthorized access, use, replication or destruction. These measures can include mantraps, encryption key management, network intrusion detection systems, password policies and regulatory compliance. A security audit may be conducted to evaluate the organization's ability to maintain secure systems against a set of established criteria.

Information Security vs. Network Security

In modern enterprise computing infrastructure, data is as likely to be in motion as it is to be at rest. This is where network security comes in. While technically a subset of cybersecurity, network security is primarily concerned with the networking infrastructure of the enterprise. It deals with issues such as securing the edge of the network; the data transport mechanisms, such as switches and routers; and those pieces of technology that provide protection for data as it moves between computing nodes. Where cybersecurity and network security differ is mostly in the application of security planning. A cybersecurity plan without a plan for network security is incomplete; however, a network security plan can typically stand alone.

CIA Triad

Confidentiality, integrity and availability, also known as the CIA triad, is a model designed to guide policies for information security within an organization. The model is also sometimes referred to as the AIC triad (availability, integrity and confidentiality) to avoid confusion with the Central Intelligence Agency. The elements of the triad are considered the three most crucial components of security.

In this context, confidentiality is a set of rules that limits access to information, integrity is the assurance that the information is trustworthy and accurate, and availability is a guarantee of reliable access to the information by authorized people.

Confidentiality

Confidentiality is roughly equivalent to privacy. Measures undertaken to ensure confidentiality are designed to prevent sensitive information from reaching the wrong people, while making sure that the right people can in fact get it: Access must be restricted to those authorized to view the data in question. It is common, as well, for data to be categorized according to the amount and type of damage that could be done should it fall into unintended hands. More or less stringent measures can then be implemented according to those categories.

Sometimes safeguarding data confidentiality may involve special training for those privy to such documents. Such training would typically include security risks that could threaten this information. Training can help familiarize authorized people with risk factors and how to guard against them. Further aspects of training can include strong passwords and password-related best practices and information about social engineering methods, to prevent them from bending data-handling rules with good intentions and potentially disastrous results.

A good example of methods used to ensure confidentiality is an account number or routing number when banking online. Data encryption is a common method of ensuring confidentiality. User IDs and passwords constitute a standard procedure; two-factor authentication is becoming the norm. Other options include biometric verification and security tokens, key fobs or soft tokens. In addition, users can take precautions to minimize the number of places where the information appears and the number of times it is actually transmitted to complete a required transaction. Extra measures might be taken in the case of extremely sensitive documents, precautions such as storing only on air gapped computers, disconnected storage devices or, for highly sensitive information, in hard copy form only.

Integrity

Integrity involves maintaining the consistency, accuracy, and trustworthiness of data over its entire life cycle. Data must not be changed in transit, and steps must be taken to ensure that data cannot be altered by unauthorized people (for example, in a breach of confidentiality). These measures include file permissions and user access controls. Version control maybe used to prevent erroneous changes or accidental deletion by authorized users becoming a problem. In addition, some means must be in place to detect any changes in data that might occur as a result of non-human-caused events such as an electromagnetic pulse (EMP) or server crash. Some data might include checksums, even cryptographic checksums, for verification of integrity. Backups or redundancies must be available to restore the affected data to its correct state.

Availability

Availability is best ensured by rigorously maintaining all hardware, performing hardware repairs immediately when needed and maintaining a correctly functioning operating system environment that is free of software conflicts. It's also important to keep current with all necessary system upgrades. Providing adequate communication bandwidth and preventing the occurrence of bottlenecks are equally important. Redundancy, failover, RAID even high-availability clusters can mitigate serious consequences when hardware issues do occur. Fast and adaptive disaster recovery is essential for the worst case scenarios; that capacity is reliant on the existence of a comprehensive disaster recovery plan (DRP). Safeguards against data loss or interruptions in connections must include unpredictable events such as natural disasters and fire. To prevent data loss from such occurrences, a backup copy may be stored in a geographically-isolated location, perhaps even in a fireproof, waterproof safe. Extra security equipment or software such as firewalls and proxy servers can guard against downtime and unreachable data due to malicious actions such as denial-of-service (DoS) attacks and network intrusions.

AUTHENTICATION

Authentication is the process of determining whether someone or something is, in fact, who or what it declares itself to be. Authentication technology provides access control for systems by checking to see if a user's credentials match the credentials in a database of authorized users or in a data authentication server.

Users are usually identified with a user ID, and authentication is accomplished when the user provides a credential, for example a password, that matches with that user ID. Most users are most familiar with using a password, which, as a piece of information that should be known only to the user, is called a knowledge authentication factor. Other authentication factors, and how they are used for two-factor or multifactor authentication (MFA), are described below.

Authentication in Cybersecurity

Authentication is important because it enables organizations to keep their networks secure by permitting only authenticated users (or processes) to access its protected resources, which may include computer systems, networks, databases, websites and other network-based applications or services.

Once authenticated, a user or process is usually subjected to an authorization process as well, to determine whether the authenticated entity should be permitted access to a protected resource or system. A user can be authenticated but fail to be given access to a resource if that user was not granted permission to access it.

The terms authentication and authorization are often used interchangeably; while they may often be implemented together the two functions are distinct. While authentication is the process of validating the identity of a registered user before allowing access to the protected resource, authorization is the process of validating that the authenticated user has been granted permission to access the requested resources. The process by which access to those resources is restricted to a certain number of users is called access control. The authentication process always comes before the authorization process.

How Authentication is Used

User authentication occurs within most human-to-computer interactions outside of guest accounts, automatically logged-in accounts and kiosk computer systems. Generally, a user has to choose a username or user ID and provide a valid password to begin using a system. User authentication authorizes human-to-machine interactions in operating systems and applications, as well as both wired and wireless networks to enable access to networked and internet-connected systems, applications and resources.

Many companies use authentication to validate users who log into their websites. Without the right security measures, user data, such as credit and debit card numbers, as well as Social Security numbers, could get into the hands of cybercriminals.

Organizations also use authentication to control which users have access to corporate networks and resources, as well as to identify and control which machines and servers have access. Companies also use authentication to enable remote employees to securely access their applications and networks.

For enterprises and other large organizations, authentication may be accomplished using a single sign-on (SSO) system, which grants access to multiple systems with a single set of login credentials.

How Authentication Works

During authentication, credentials provided by the user are compared to those on file in a database of authorized users' information either on the local operating system or through an authentication server. If the credentials match, and the authenticated entity is authorized to use the resource, the process is completed and the user is granted access. The permissions and folders returned define both the environment the user sees and the way he can interact with it, including hours of access and other rights such as the amount of resource storage space.

Traditionally, authentication was accomplished by the systems or resources being accessed; for example, a server would authenticate users using its own password system, implemented locally, using loginIDs (user names) and passwords. Knowledge of the login credentials is assumed to guarantee that the user is authentic. Each user registers initially (or is registered by someone else, such as a systems administrator), using an assigned or self-declared password. On each subsequent use, the user must know and use the previously declared password.

However, the web's application protocols, HTTP and HTTPS, are stateless, meaning that strict authentication would require end users reauthenticate each time they access a resource using HTTPS. Rather than burden end users with that process for each interaction over the web, protected systems often rely on token-based authentication, in which authentication is performed once at the start of a session. The authenticating system issues a signed authentication token to the end-user application, and that token is appended to every request from the client.

Entity authentication for systems and processes can be carried out using machine credentials that work like a user's ID and password, except the credentials are submitted automatically by the device in question. They may also use digital certificates that were issued and verified by a certificate authority as part of a public key infrastructure to authenticate an identity while exchanging information over the internet.

Authentication Factors

Authenticating a user with a user ID and a password is usually considered the most basic type of authentication, and it depends on the user knowing two pieces of information: the user ID or username, and the password. Since this type of authentication relies on just one authentication factor, it is a type of single-factor authentication.

Strong authentication is a term that has not been formally defined, but usually is used to mean that the type of authentication being used is more reliable and resistant to attack; achieving that is generally acknowledged to require using at least two different types of authentication factors.

An authentication factor represents some piece of data or attribute that can be used to authenticate a user requesting access to a system. An old security adage has it that authentication factors can be "something you know, something you have or something you are." These three factors correspond to the knowledge factor, the possession factor and the inherence factor. Additional factors have been proposed and put into use in recent years, with location serving in many cases as the fourth factor, and time serving as the fifth factor.

Currently used authentication factors include:

- Knowledge factor: "Something you know." The knowledge factor may be any authentication credentials that consist of information that the user possesses, including a personal identification number (PIN), a user name, a password or the answer to a secret question.

- Possession factor: "Something you have." The possession factor may be any credential based on items that the user can own and carry with them, including hardware devices like a security token or a mobile phone used to accept a text message or to run an authentication app that can generate a one-time password or PIN.

- Inherence factor: "Something you are." The inherence factor is typically based on some form of biometric identification, including finger or thumb prints, facial recognition, retina scan or any other form of biometric data.

- Location factor: "Where you are." While it may be less specific, the location factor is sometimes used as an adjunct to the other factors. Location can be determined to reasonable accuracy by devices equipped with GPS, or with less accuracy by checking network routes. The location factor cannot usually stand on its own for authentication, but it can supplement the other factors by providing a means of ruling out some requests. For example, it can prevent an attacker located in a remote geographical area from posing as a user who normally logs in only from home or office in the organization's home country.

- Time factor: "When you are authenticating." Like the location factor, the time factor is not sufficient on its own, but it can be a supplemental mechanism for weeding out attackers who attempt to access a resource at a time when that resource is not available to the authorized user. It may also be used together with location as well. For example, if the user was last authenticated at noon in the U.S., an attempt to authenticate from Asia one hour later would be rejected based on the combination of time and location.

Despite being used as supplemental authentication factors, user location and current time by themselves are not sufficient, without at least one of the first three factors, to authenticate a user. However, the ubiquity of smartphones is helping to ease the burdens of multifactor authentication for many users. Most smartphones are equipped with GPS, enabling reasonable confidence in confirmation of the login location; smartphone MAC addresses may also be used to help authenticate a remote user, despite the fact that MAC addresses are relatively easy to spoof.

Two-factor and Multifactor Authentication

Adding authentication factors to the authentication process typically improves security. Strong authentication usually refers to authentication that uses at least two factors, where those factors are of different types. The distinction is important; since both username and password can be considered types of knowledge factor, basic username and password authentication could be said to use two knowledge factors to authenticate - however, that would not be considered a form of two-factor authentication (2FA). Likewise for authentication systems that rely on "security questions," which are also "something you know," to supplement user ID and passwords.

Two-factor authentication usually depends on the knowledge factor combined with either a biometric factor or a possession factor like a security token. Multifactor authentication can include any type of authentication that depends on two or more factors, but an authentication process that uses a password plus two different types of biometric would not be considered three-factor authentication, although if the process required a knowledge factor, a possession factor and an inherence factor, it would be. Systems that call for those three factors plus a geographic or time factor are considered examples of four-factor authentication.

Authentication and Authorization

Authorization includes the process through which an administrator grants rights to authenticated users, as well as the process of checking user account permissions to verify that the user has been granted access to those resources. The privileges and preferences granted for the authorized account depend on the user's permissions, which are either stored locally or on the authentication server. The settings defined for all these environment variables are set by an administrator.

Systems and processes may also need to authorize their automated actions within a network. Online backup services, patching and updating systems and remote monitoring systems, such as those used in telemedicine and smart grid technologies, all need to securely authenticate before they can verify that it is the authorized system involved in any interaction and not a hacker.

Types of Authentication Methods

Traditional authentication depends on the use of a password file, in which user IDs are stored together with hashes of the passwords associated with each user. When logging in, the password submitted by the user is hashed and compared to the value in the password file. If the two hashes match, the user is authenticated.

This approach to authentication has several drawbacks, particularly for resources deployed across different systems. For one thing, attackers who are able to access to the password file for a system can use brute force attacks against the hashed passwords to extract the passwords. For another, this approach would require multiple authentications for modern applications that access resources across multiple systems.

Password-based authentication weaknesses can be addressed to some extent with smarter user names and password rules like minimum length and stipulations for complexity, such as including capitals and symbols. However, password-based authentication and knowledge-based authentication are more vulnerable than systems that require multiple independent methods.

Other authentication methods include:

- Two-factor authentication - Two-factor authentication adds an extra layer of protection to the process of authentication. 2FA requires that a user provide a second authentication factor in addition to the password. 2FA systems often require the user to enter a verification code received via text message on a preregistered mobile phone, or a code generated by an authentication application.

- Multifactor authentication - Multifactor authentication requires users to authenticate with more than one authentication factor, including a biometric factor like fingerprint or facial recognition, a possession factor like a security key fob or a token generated by an authenticator app.

- One-time password - A one-time password is an automatically generated numeric or alphanumeric string of characters that authenticates a user. This password is only valid for one login session or transaction, and is usually used for new users, or for users who lost their passwords and are given a one-time password to log in and change to a new password.

- Three-factor authentication - Three-factor authentication (3FA) is a type of MFA that uses three authentication factors, usually a knowledge factor (password) combined with a possession factor (security token) and inherence factor (biometric).

- Biometrics - While some authentication systems can depend solely on biometric identification, biometrics are usually used as a second or third authentication factor. The more common types of biometric authentication available include fingerprint scans, facial or retina scans and voice recognition.

- Mobile authentication - Mobile authentication is the process of verifying user via their devices or verifying the devices themselves. This lets users log into secure locations and resources from anywhere. The mobile authentication process involves multifactor authentication that can include one-time passwords, biometric authentication or QR code validation.

- Continuous authentication - With continuous authentication, instead of a user being either logged in or out, a company's application continually computes an "authentication score" that measures how sure it is that the account owner is the individual who's using the device.

- API authentication - The standard methods of managing API authentication are: HTTP basic authentication; API keys and OAuth.

- In HTTP basic authentication, the server requests authentication information, i.e., a username and password, from a client. The client then passes the authentication information to the server in an authorization header.

- In the API key authentication method, a first-time user is assigned a unique generated value that indicates that the user is known. Then each time the user tries to enter the system again, his unique key is used to verify that he is the same user who entered the system previously.

- Open Authorization (OAuth) is an open standard for token-based authentication and authorization on the internet. OAuth allows a user's account information to be used by third-party services, such as Facebook, without exposing the user's password. OAuth acts as an intermediary on behalf of the user, providing the service with an access token that authorizes specific account information to be shared.

User Authentication vs. Machine Authentication

Machines also need to authorize their automated actions within a network. Online backup services, patching and updating systems and remote monitoring systems, such as those used in telemedicine and smart grid technologies, all need to securely authenticate to verify that it is the authorized system involved in any interaction and not a hacker.

Machine authentication can be carried out with machine credentials much like a user's ID and password only submitted by the device in question. They can also use digital certificates issued and verified by a certificate authority as part of a public key infrastructure to prove identification while exchanging information over the internet, like a type of digital password.

With the increasing number of internet-enabled devices, reliable machine authentication is crucial to enable secure communication for home automation and other internet of things applications, where almost any entity or object may be made addressable and able to exchange data over a network. It is important to realize that each access point is a potential intrusion point. Each networked device needs strong machine authentication and also, despite their normally limited activity, these devices must be configured for limited permissions access as well, to limit what can be done even if they are breached.

Message Authentication

In information security, message authentication or data origin authentication is a property that a message has not been modified while in transit (data integrity) and that the receiving party can verify the source of the message. Message authentication does not necessarily include the property of non-repudiation.

Message authentication is typically achieved by using message authentication codes (MACs), authenticated encryption (AE) or digital signatures. The message authentication code, also known as digital authenticator, is used as an integrity check based on a secret key shared by two parties to authenticate information transmitted between them. It is based on using a cryptographic hash or symmetric encryption algorithm. The authentication key is only shared by at least two parties or two communicating devices but it will fail in the existence of a third party since the algorithm will no longer be effective in detecting forgeries. In addition, the key must also be randomly generated to avoid its recovery through brute force searches and related key attacks designed to identify it from the messages transiting the medium.

Some cryptographers distinguish between "message authentication without secrecy" systems - which allow the intended receiver to verify the source of the message, but don't bother hiding the plaintext contents of the message -- from authenticated encryption systems. Some cryptographers have researched subliminal channel systems that send messages that appear to use a "message authentication without secrecy" system, but in fact also transmit a secret message.

Message Authentication Code

In cryptography, a message authentication code (MAC), sometimes known as a *tag*, is a short piece of information used to authenticate a message—in other words, to confirm that the message came from the stated sender (its authenticity) and has not been changed. The MAC value protects both a message's data integrity as well as its authenticity, by allowing verifiers (who also possess the secret key) to detect any changes to the message content.

Informally, a message authentication code consists of three algorithms:

- A key generation algorithm selects a key from the key space uniformly at random.

- A signing algorithm efficiently returns a tag given the key and the message.

- A verifying algorithm efficiently verifies the authenticity of the message given the key and the tag. That is, return *accepted* when the message and tag are not tampered with or forged, and otherwise return *rejected*.

For a secure unforgeable message authentication code, it should be computationally infeasible to compute a valid tag of the given message without knowledge of the key, even if for the worst case, we assume the adversary can forge the tag of any message except the given one.

Formally, a message authentication code (MAC) is a triple of efficient algorithms (G, S, V) satisfying:

- G (key-generator) gives the key k on input 1^n, where n is the security parameter.

- S (signing) outputs a tag t on the key k and the input string x.

- V (verifying) outputs *accepted* or *rejected* on inputs: the key k, the string x and the tag t. S and V must satisfy the following:

  $\Pr[\, k \leftarrow G(1^n),\, V(\, k, x, S(k, x)\,) = accepted\,] = 1.$

A MAC is unforgeable if for every efficient adversary A

  $\Pr[\, k \leftarrow G(1^n),\, (x, t) \leftarrow A^{S(k, \cdot)}(1^n),\, x \notin \text{Query}(A^{S(k, \cdot)}, 1^n),\, V(k, x, t) = accepted] < \text{negl}(n),$

where $A^{S(k, \cdot)}$ denotes that A has access to the oracle $S(k, \cdot)$, and $\text{Query}(A^{S(k, \cdot)}, 1^n)$ denotes the set of the queries on S made by A, which knows n. Clearly we require that any adversary cannot directly query the string x on S, since otherwise a valid tag can be easily obtained by that adversary.

Security

While MAC functions are similar to cryptographic hash functions, they possess different security requirements. To be considered secure, a MAC function must resist existential forgery under chosen-plaintext attacks. This means that even if an attacker has access to an oracle which possesses the secret key and generates MACs for messages of the attacker's choosing, the attacker cannot guess the MAC for other messages (which were not used to query the oracle) without performing infeasible amounts of computation.

MACs differ from digital signatures as MAC values are both generated and verified using the same secret key. This implies that the sender and receiver of a message must agree on the same key before initiating communications, as is the case with symmetric encryption. For the same reason, MACs do not provide the property of non-repudiation offered by signatures specifically in the case of a network-wide shared secret key: any user who can verify a MAC is also capable of generating MACs for other messages. In contrast, a digital signature is generated using the private key of a key pair, which is public-key cryptography. Since this private key is only accessible to its holder, a digital signature proves that a document was signed by none other than that holder. Thus, digital signatures do offer non-repudiation. However, non-repudiation can be provided by systems that securely bind key usage information to the MAC key; the same key is in the possession of two people, but one has a copy of the key that can be used for MAC generation while the other has a copy of the key in a hardware security module that only permits MAC verification. This is commonly done in the finance industry.

Message Integrity Codes

The term message integrity code (MIC) is frequently substituted for the term MAC, especially in communications, to distinguish it from the use of *MAC* meaning MAC address (for *media access control address*). However, some authors use MIC to refer to a message digest, which is different from a MAC – a message digest does not use secret keys. This lack of security means that any message digest intended for use gauging message integrity should be encrypted or otherwise be protected against tampering. Message digest algorithms are created such that a given message will always produce the same message digest assuming the same algorithm is used to generate both. Conversely, MAC algorithms are designed to produce matching MACs only if the same message, secret key and initialization vector are input to the same algorithm. Message digests do not use secret keys and, when taken on their own, are therefore a much less reliable gauge of message integrity than MACs. Because MACs use secret keys, they do not necessarily need to be encrypted to provide the same level of assurance.

RFC 4949 recommends avoiding the term "message integrity code" (MIC), and instead using "checksum", "error detection code", "hash", "keyed hash", "message authentication code", or "protected checksum".

Implementation

MAC algorithms can be constructed from other cryptographic primitives, like cryptographic hash functions (as in the case of HMAC) or from block cipher algorithms (OMAC, CBC-MAC and PMAC). However many of the fastest MAC algorithms like UMAC and VMAC are constructed based on universal hashing.

Additionally, the MAC algorithm can deliberately combine two or more cryptographic primitives, so as to maintain protection even if one of them is later found to be vulnerable. For instance, in Transport Layer Security (TLS), the input data is split in halves that are each processed with a different hashing primitive (MD5 and SHA-1) then XORed together to output the MAC.

Standards

Various standards exist that define MAC algorithms. These include:

- FIPS PUB 113 *Computer Data Authentication*, withdrawn in 2002, defines an algorithm based on DES.

- FIPS PUB 198-1 *The Keyed-Hash Message Authentication Code (HMAC)*.

- ISO/IEC 9797-1 *Mechanisms using a block cipher*.

- ISO/IEC 9797-2 *Mechanisms using a dedicated hash-function*.

ISO/IEC 9797-1 and -2 define generic models and algorithms that can be used with any block cipher or hash function, and a variety of different parameters. These models and parameters allow more specific algorithms to be defined by nominating the parameters. For example, the FIPS PUB 113 algorithm is functionally equivalent to ISO/IEC 9797-1 MAC algorithm 1 with padding method 1 and a block cipher algorithm of DES.

An Example of MAC Use

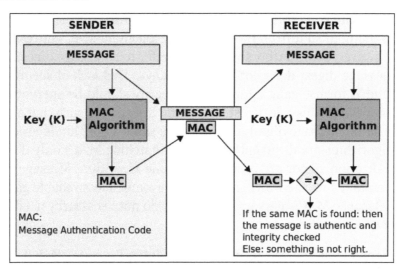

In this example, the sender of a message runs it through a MAC algorithm to produce a MAC data tag. The message and the MAC tag are then sent to the receiver. The receiver in turn runs the message portion of the transmission through the same MAC algorithm using the same key, producing a second MAC data tag. The receiver then compares the first MAC tag received in the transmission to the second generated MAC tag. If they are identical, the receiver can safely assume that the message was not altered or tampered with during transmission (data integrity).

However, to allow the receiver to be able to detect replay attacks, the message itself must contain data that assures that this same message can only be sent once (e.g. time stamp, sequence number or use of a one-time MAC). Otherwise an attacker could – without even understanding its content – record this message and play it back at a later time, producing the same result as the original sender.

One-time MAC

Universal hashing and in particular pairwise independent hash functions provide a secure message authentication code as long as the key is used at most once. This can be seen as the one-time pad for authentication.

The simplest such pairwise independent hash function is defined by the random key $key = (a,b)$, and the MAC tag for a message m is computed as $tag = (am + b) \bmod p$, where p is prime.

More generally, k-independent hashing functions provide a secure message authentication code as long as the key is used less than k times for k-ways independent hashing functions.

NON-REPUDIATION

A repudiation is a rejection or denial of something as valid or true – including the refusal to pay a debt or honor a formal contract. Flip that on its head, and non-repudiation translates into a method of assuring that something that's actually valid cannot be disowned or denied.

From the point of view of information security, non-repudiation usually applies to cases of a formal contract, a communication, or the transfer of data. Its aim is to ensure that an individual or organization bound by the terms of a contract, or the parties involved in a particular communication or document transfer are unable to deny the authenticity of their signatures on the contract documents, or that they were the originator of a particular message or transfer.

Classic analog examples of non-repudiation methods would include the signatures and documentation associated with a registered mail delivery (where by signing, the recipient is unable to deny having received that court summons from the utilities company), or the recorded presence of witnesses to the signing of a legal document or treaty.

Beyond Authenticity

Clearly, non-deniability in a communications or data transfer context cannot be achieved if the true identities of both parties to the dialog cannot be confirmed. So some reliable means of authenticating these parties has to be put in place. These methods might range from the Kerberos authentication protocol used to validate procedures on most operating systems to a simple Message Authentication Code.

But authenticity by itself isn't enough to guarantee non-deniability. For example, the SSL or TLS authentication protocols used for internet communications can provide an assurance that a given client system is "talking" to its intended server, but there's no fool-proof method of recording a session which the client could present in the case of a legal dispute with the service provider – which would introduce the element of non-repudiation into the data transfer.

So you can have authenticity/authentication without non-repudiation. But the reverse is not the case. Non-repudiation cannot be achieved without the identities of the concerned parties first having been established beyond reasonable doubt – in other words, authenticity has to be a part of the mix. But it's not all of it.

Non-Repudiation Principles

Non-repudiation requires the creation of artifacts which may be used to dispute the claims of an entity or organization that denies being the originator of an action or communication. These artifacts consist of:

- An identity.

- The authentication of that identity.

- Tangible evidence connecting the identified party to a particular communication or action.

Non-Repudiation Techniques

For email transmission, non-repudiation typically involves using methods designed to ensure that a sender can't deny having sent a particular message, or that a message recipient can't deny having received it. Techniques would include email tracking.

Cryptographic hash functions may be used to establish the integrity of transmitted documents. No encryption keys are involved, and strong hash functions are designed to be irreversible. Moreover, they're designed to avoid collision, which occurs in the rare cases where two separate documents give rise to the same hash value.

Taking this a stage further is HMAC, a technique used to provide data authentication and integrity through the hashing of a document and its transmission with a shared encryption key. However, the very fact that the key is a shared one means that this method lacks non-repudiation.

Repudiation Attacks

When a system or application doesn't include protocols or controls for tracking and logging the actions of its users, the system may be manipulated by malicious intruders, who can forge the identifying credentials of new actions, which can't be denied with certainty.

In a repudiation attack of this type, erroneous data may be fed into log files, the authoring information of actions on the system may be altered, and general data manipulation or spoofing may occur.

Some Best Practices

Since the strength of digital signature transactions lies in their private keys, care should be taken to store these keys in a secure location (such as on smart cards) to reduce the risk of them falling into the wrong hands.

With some analysts maintaining that digital signatures alone are insufficient to fully guarantee non-repudiation, a mix of measures is advised. Options include supplementing digital signatures with biometric information and other data captured from the sender of a message at the point of transmission.

References

- Information-security-infosec, definition: techtarget.com, Retrieved 2 July, 2019

- Patel, Dhiren (2008). Information Security: Theory and Practice. New Delhi: Prentice Hall India Private Lt. P. 124. ISBN 9788120333512

- Confidentiality-integrity-and-availability-CIA, definition: techtarget.com, Retrieved 1 April, 2019

- Jacobs, Stuart (2011). Engineering Information Security: The Application of Systems Engineering Concepts to Achieve Information Assurance. Hoboken, NJ: John Wiley & sons. P. 108. ISBN 9780470565124

- Authentication, definition: techtarget.com, Retrieved 4 June, 2019

- Goldreich, Oded (2004), Foundations of cryptography II: Basic Applications (1. Publ. Ed.), Cambridge [u.a.]: Cambridge Univ. Press, ISBN 978-0-521-83084-3

- What-is-non-repudiation: finjan.com, Retrieved 5 April, 2019

Cryptosystem

The suit of cryptographic algorithms needed to implement a specific security service in order to achieve confidentiality is known as a cryptosystem. The algorithms within this field are primarily used for encryption and decryption. This chapter discusses in detail these components of cryptosystems.

A cryptosystem is an implementation of cryptographic techniques and their accompanying infrastructure to provide information security services. A cryptosystem is also referred to as a cipher system.

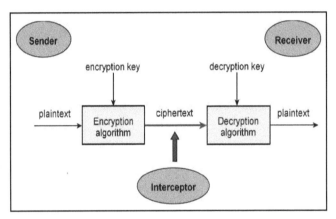

The illustration shows a sender who wants to transfer some sensitive data to a receiver in such a way that any party intercepting or eavesdropping on the communication channel cannot extract the data.

The objective of this simple cryptosystem is that at the end of the process, only the sender and the receiver will know the plaintext.

Relation between Encryption Schemes

A summary of basic key properties of two types of cryptosystems is given below –

	Symmetric Cryptosystems	Public Key Cryptosystems
Relation between Keys	Same	Different, but mathematically related
Encryption Key	Symmetric	Public
Decryption Key	Symmetric	Private

Due to the advantages and disadvantage of both the systems, symmetric key and public-key cryptosystems are often used together in the practical information security systems.

Number Theory Terms

The following are some important concepts required for cryptography from the field of number theory:

- Modulo: The remainder operator (e.g. 17 modulo 5 is 2, i.e. 17 when divided by 5 leaves a remainder of 2). This is often shortened to mod, we write $17 \equiv 2 \pmod 5$, read as "17 is congruent to 2, modulo 5".

- Coprime: In number theory two values are said to be coprime or relatively prime if they do not share any common prime factors. That's to say that their greatest common divisor (GCD) or highest common factor is 1.

Characters

It is general practice in cryptography to follow the standards of Rivest, Shamir and Adleman, the inventors of the RSA encryption algorithm, by using Alice and Bob as the main protagonists in any example of cryptosystem protocols. In examples of attacks, Eve is usually cast as the attacker. That is, Alice wants to send messages privately to Bob, and Eve is trying to spy on the messages.

Design Objectives and Goals

The design objectives of a cryptosystem can be summarized by Kerckhoff's Priniciple:

> "The system must be secure even if everything except the private key is public information. In particular, the design of the system must not be required to be kept secret."

This is the approach taken by modern cryptography (as compared to earlier cryptographic systems, which often relied on obscurity, i.e. aiming for security by keeping the system or parts of it secret or unclear).

Beyond security computational efficiency and the practicality of implementation are sub-objectives in cryptosystem design. This is shown in the development of AES whereby the US Government accepted suggestions for algorithms and 15 made it to the final. Some of the finalists were more secure than the ultimate winner but were dismissed for requiring too much processing power.

The trade-off between complexity and therefore security and ease of implementation can be further seen in the guidance for the use of AES encryption. Top secret information is encrypted using a 192 or 256 bit key whereas less highly classified information may be encrypted using a 128-bit key for efficiency. AES involves 10 rounds of encryption processes for 128-bit keys, 12 rounds for 192-bit keys and 14 rounds for 256-bit keys.

What Makes Cryptosystems Secure: One-way Functions

The security of cryptosystems comes from the one-way nature of the encryption function. These are mathematical functions such that it is efficient to calculate the value of the function given an input, but calculating the inverse (i.e. retrieving the input given the output) is computational infeasible or practically impossible. Note that:

1. We don't say completely impossible. The inverse can be calculated given infinite computational resources. The objective is to make it expensive enough (say you'd have to wait 1000 years to decrypt a message, or you need computational power of 1 million computers) so that no one would do it.

2. We also don't know with mathematical certainty that there is no way to calculate the inverse function quickly, i.e. there is no proof saying that calculating the inverse is computationally infeasible. We rely on the fact that over decades of attempts and efforts from mathematicians, no one has been able to find a method to calculate the inverse quickly.

Taking the example of the ElGamal cryptosystem where encryption is performed by exponentiation modulo a large prime, the encryption is a one-way function because calculating exponents is easy whereas working out the exponent required for a base raised to that power to yield a given value (the discrete log problem) has no known practical solution. The exponent in this case is therefore the encryption key with its inverse being the decryption key.

Novel Applications

Today encryption affects more and more of day-to-day life as the digitization of assets and systems accelerates. Some novel applications of cryptography have included the development of TOR or The Onion Router which famously allows untraceable internet use for political dissidents, whistle blowers and journalists. The system works by placing layer upon layer of encryption on each packet of information as it bounces around a network of nodes each of which either adds a layer of encryption or removes one depending on the direction of travel and thereby masks the origin and destination of the requests.

Another novel application of cryptography is blockchain technology. This is the technology behind bitcoin and other cryptocurrencies, enabling what is known as decentralized trust, i.e. the ability of a large group of people to agree on a single truth without requiring a central authoritative entity such as a government or a bank. Bitcoin was invented by a cryptography expert in 2008 due to his distrust of the American financial system which had recently caused the 2008 global financial crisis.

COMPONENTS OF A CRYPTOSYSTEM

Encryption

In cryptography, encryption is the process of encoding a message or information in such a way that only authorized parties can access it and those who are not authorized cannot. Encryption does not itself prevent interference, but denies the intelligible content to a would-be interceptor. In an encryption scheme, the intended information or message, referred to as plaintext, is encrypted using an encryption algorithm – a cipher – generating ciphertext that can be read only if decrypted. For technical reasons, an encryption scheme usually uses a pseudo-random encryption key generated by an algorithm. It is in principle possible to decrypt the message without possessing the key, but, for a well-designed encryption scheme, considerable computational resources and skills are required. An authorized recipient can easily decrypt the message with the key provided by the originator to recipients but not to unauthorized users.

Types

Symmetric Key

In symmetric-key schemes, the encryption and decryption keys are the same. Communicating parties must have the same key in order to achieve secure communication. An example of a symmetric key is the German military's Enigma Machine. There were key settings for each day. When the Allies figured out how the machine worked, they were able to decipher the information encoded within the messages as soon as they could discover the encryption key for a given day's transmissions.

Public Key

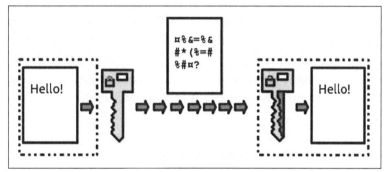

Illustration of how encryption is used within servers Public key encryption.

In public-key encryption schemes, the encryption key is published for anyone to use and encrypt messages. However, only the receiving party has access to the decryption key that enables messages to be read. Public-key encryption was first described in a secret document in 1973; before then all encryption schemes were symmetric-key (also called private-key). Although published subsequently, the work of Diffie and Hellman, was published in a journal with a large readership, and the value of the methodology was explicitly described and the method became known as the Diffie Hellman key exchange.

A publicly available public key encryption application called Pretty Good Privacy (PGP) was written in 1991 by Phil Zimmermann, and distributed free of charge with source code; it was purchased by Symantec in 2010 and is regularly updated.

Uses

Encryption has long been used by militaries and governments to facilitate secret communication. It is now commonly used in protecting information within many kinds of civilian systems. For example, the Computer Security Institute reported that in 2007, 71% of companies surveyed utilized encryption for some of their data in transit, and 53% utilized encryption for some of their data in storage. Encryption can be used to protect data "at rest", such as information stored on computers and storage devices (e.g. USB flash drives). In recent years, there have been numerous reports of confidential data, such as customers' personal records, being exposed through loss or theft of laptops or backup drives; encrypting such files at rest helps protect them if physical security measures fail. Digital rights management systems, which prevent unauthorized use or reproduction of copyrighted material and protect software against reverse engineering, is another somewhat different example of using encryption on data at rest.

Encryption is also used to protect data in transit, for example data being transferred via networks (e.g. the Internet, e-commerce), mobile telephones, wireless microphones, wireless intercom systems, Bluetooth devices and bank automatic teller machines. There have been numerous reports of data in transit being intercepted in recent years. Data should also be encrypted when transmitted across networks in order to protect against eavesdropping of network traffic by unauthorized users.

Data Erasure

Conventional methods for deleting data permanently from a storage device involve overwriting its whole content with zeros, ones or other patterns – a process which can take a significant amount of time, depending on the capacity and the type of the medium. Cryptography offers a way of making the erasure almost instantaneous. This method is called crypto-shredding. An example implementation of this method can be found on iOS devices, where the cryptographic key is kept in a dedicated 'Effaceable Storage'. Because the key is stored on the same device, this setup on its own does not offer full confidentiality protection in case an unauthorized person gains physical access to the device.

Limitations, Attacks and Countermeasures

Encryption is an important tool but is not sufficient alone to ensure the security or privacy of sensitive information throughout its lifetime. Most applications of encryption protect information only at rest or in transit, leaving sensitive data in cleartext and potentially vulnerable to improper disclosure during processing, such as by a cloud service for example. Homomorphic encryption and secure multi-party computation are emerging techniques to compute on encrypted data; these techniques are general and Turing complete but incur high computational and/or communication costs.

In response to encryption of data at rest, cyber-adversaries have developed new types of attacks. These more recent threats to encryption of data at rest include cryptographic attacks, stolen ciphertext attacks, attacks on encryption keys, insider attacks, data corruption or integrity attacks, data destruction attacks, and ransomware attacks. Data fragmentation and active defense data protection technologies attempt to counter some of these attacks, by distributing, moving, or mutating ciphertext so it is more difficult to identify, steal, corrupt, or destroy.

Integrity Protection of Ciphertexts

Encryption, by itself, can protect the confidentiality of messages, but other techniques are still needed to protect the integrity and authenticity of a message; for example, verification of a message authentication code (MAC) or a digital signature. Authenticated encryption algorithms are designed to provide both encryption and integrity protection together. Standards for cryptographic software and hardware to perform encryption are widely available, but successfully using encryption to ensure security may be a challenging problem. A single error in system design or execution can allow successful attacks. Sometimes an adversary can obtain unencrypted information without directly undoing the encryption.

Integrity protection mechanisms such as MACs and digital signatures must be applied to the ciphertext when it is first created, typically on the same device used to compose the message, to protect a message end-to-end along its full transmission path; otherwise, any node between the sender and the encryption agent could potentially tamper with it. Encrypting at the time of creation is only secure if the encryption device itself has correct keys and has not been tampered with. If an endpoint device has been configured to trust a root certificate that an attacker controls, for example, then the attacker can both inspect and tamper with encrypted data by performing a man-in-the-middle attack anywhere along the message's path. The common practice of TLS interception by network operators represents a controlled and institutionally sanctioned form of such an attack, but countries have also attempted to employ such attacks as a form of control and censorship.

Ciphertext Length and Padding

Even when encryption correctly hides a message's content and it cannot be tampered with at rest or in transit, a message's length is a form of metadata that can still leak sensitive information about the message. The well-known CRIME and BREACH attacks against HTTPS were side-channel attacks that relied on information leakage via the length of encrypted content, for example. Traffic analysis is a broad class of techniques that often employs message lengths to infer sensitive implementation about traffic flows from many messages in aggregate.

Padding a message's payload before encrypting it can help obscure the cleartext's true length, at a cost of increasing the ciphertext's size and introducing bandwidth overhead. Messages may be padded randomly or deterministically, each approach having different tradeoffs. Encrypting and padding messages to form padded uniform random blobs or PURBs is a practice guaranteeing that the cipher text leaks no metadata about its cleartext's content, and leaks asymptotically minimal $O(\log \log M)$ information via its length.

Decryption

Decryption is generally the reverse process of encryption. It is the process of decoding the data which has been encrypted into a secret format. An authorized user can only decrypt data because decryption requires a secret key or password. Decryption is the process of decoding encrypted information so that is can be accessed again by authorized users.

Encryption – Decryption Cycle

To make the data confidential, data (plain text) is encrypted using a particular algorithm and a secret key. After encryption process, plain text gets converted into cipher text. To decrypt the cipher text, similar algorithm is used and at the end the original data is obtained again.

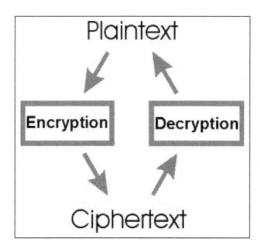

Key Management

Key management refers to management of cryptographic keys in a cryptosystem. This includes dealing with the generation, exchange, storage, use, crypto-shredding (destruction) and replacement of keys. It includes cryptographic protocol design, key servers, user procedures, and other relevant protocols.

Key management concerns keys at the user level, either between users or systems. This is in contrast to key scheduling, which typically refers to the internal handling of keys within the operation of a cipher. Successful key management is critical to the security of a cryptosystem. It is the more challenging side of cryptography in a sense that it involves aspects of social engineering such as system policy, user training, organizational and departmental interactions, and coordination between all of these elements, in contrast to pure mathematical practices that can be automated.

Types of Keys

Cryptographic systems may use different types of keys, with some systems using more than one. These may include symmetric keys or asymmetric keys. In a symmetric key algorithm the keys involved are identical for both encrypting and decrypting a message. Keys must be chosen carefully, and distributed and stored securely. Asymmetric keys, also known as public keys, in contrast are two distinct keys that are mathematically linked. They are typically used together to communicate. Public key infrastructure (PKI), the implementation of public key cryptography, requires an organization to establish an infrastructure to create and manage public and private key pairs along with digital certificates.

Inventory

The starting point in any certificate and private key management strategy is to create a comprehensive inventory of all certificates, their locations and responsible parties. This is not a trivial matter because certificates from a variety of sources are deployed in a variety of locations by different individuals and teams - it's simply not possible to rely on a list from a single certificate authority. Certificates that are not renewed and replaced before they expire can cause serious downtime and outages. Some other considerations:

- Regulations and requirements, like PCI-DSS, demand stringent security and management of cryptographic keys and auditors are increasingly reviewing the management controls and processes in use.

- Private keys used with certificates must be kept secure or unauthorised individuals can intercept confidential communications or gain unauthorised access to critical systems. Failure to ensure proper segregation of duties means that admins who generate the encryption keys can use them to access sensitive, regulated data.

- If a certificate authority is compromised or an encryption algorithm is broken, organizations must be prepared to replace all of their certificates and keys in a matter of hours.

Management Steps

Once keys are inventoried, key management typically consists of three steps: exchange, storage and use.

Key Exchange

Prior to any secured communication, users must set up the details of the cryptography. In some instances this may require exchanging identical keys (in the case of a symmetric key system). In others it may require possessing the other party's public key. While public keys can be openly exchanged (their corresponding private key is kept secret), symmetric keys must be exchanged over a secure communication channel. Formerly, exchange of such a key was extremely troublesome, and was greatly eased by access to secure channels such as a diplomatic bag. Clear text exchange of symmetric keys would enable any interceptor to immediately learn the key, and any encrypted data.

The advance of public key cryptography in the 1970s has made the exchange of keys less troublesome. Since the Diffie-Hellman key exchange protocol was published in 1975, it has become possible to exchange a key over an insecure communications channel, which has substantially reduced the risk of key disclosure during distribution. It is possible, using something akin to a book code, to include key indicators as clear text attached to an encrypted message. The encryption technique used by Richard Sorge's code clerk was of this type, referring to a page in a statistical manual, though it was in fact a code. The German Army Enigma symmetric encryption key was a mixed type early in its use; the key was a combination of secretly distributed key schedules and a user chosen session key component for each message.

In more modern systems, such as OpenPGP compatible systems, a session key for a symmetric key algorithm is distributed encrypted by an asymmetric key algorithm. This approach avoids even the necessity for using a key exchange protocol like Diffie-Hellman key exchange.

Another method of key exchange involves encapsulating one key within another. Typically a master key is generated and exchanged using some secure method. This method is usually cumbersome or expensive (breaking a master key into multiple parts and sending each with a trusted courier for example) and not suitable for use on a larger scale. Once the master key has been securely exchanged, it can then be used to securely exchange subsequent keys with ease. This technique is usually termed key wrap. A common technique uses block ciphers and cryptographic hash functions.

A related method is to exchange a master key (sometimes termed a root key) and derive subsidiary keys as needed from that key and some other data (often referred to as diversification data). The most common use for this method is probably in smartcard-based cryptosystems, such as those found in banking cards. The bank or credit network embeds their secret key into the card's secure key storage during card production at a secured production facility. Then at the point of sale the card and card reader are both able to derive a common set of session keys based on the shared secret key and card-specific data (such as the card serial number). This method can also be used when keys must be related to each other (i.e., departmental keys are tied to divisional keys, and individual keys tied to departmental keys). However, tying keys to each other in this way increases the damage which may result from a security breach as attackers will learn something about more than one key. This reduces entropy, with regard to an attacker, for each key involved.

Key Storage

However distributed, keys must be stored securely to maintain communications security. Security is a big concern and hence there are various techniques in use to do so. Likely the most common is that an encryption application manages keys for the user and depends on an access password to control use of the key. Likewise, in the case of smartphone keyless access platforms, they keep all identifying door information off mobile phones and servers and encrypt all data, where just like low-tech keys, users give codes only to those they trust.

Key Use

The major issue is length of time a key is to be used, and therefore frequency of replacement. Because it increases any attacker's required effort, keys should be frequently changed. This also limits loss of information, as the number of stored encrypted messages which will become readable when a key is found will decrease as the frequency of key change increases. Historically, symmetric keys have been used for long periods in situations in which key exchange was very difficult or only possible intermittently. Ideally, the symmetric key should change with each message or interaction, so that only that message will become readable if the key is learned (*e.g.*, stolen, cryptanalyzed, or social engineered).

Challenges

Several challenges IT organizations face when trying to control and manage their encryption keys are:

1. Scalability: Managing a large number of encryption keys.

2. Security: Vulnerability of keys from outside hackers, malicious insiders.

3. Availability: Ensuring data accessibility for authorized users.

4. Heterogeneity: Supporting multiple databases, applications and standards.

5. Governance: Defining policy-driven access control and protection for data. Governance includes compliance with data protection requirements.

Compliance

Key management compliance refers to the oversight, assurance and capability of being able to demonstrate that keys are securely managed. This includes the following individual compliance domains:

- Physical security – The most visible form of compliance, which may include locked doors to secure system equipment and surveillance cameras. These safeguards can prevent unauthorized access to printed copies of key material and computer systems that run key management software.

- Logical security – Protects the organization against the theft or unauthorized access of information. This is where the use of cryptographic keys comes in by encrypting data, which is then rendered useless to those who do not have the key to decrypt it.

- Personnel security – This involves assigning specific roles or privileges to personnel to access information on a strict need-to-know basis. Background checks should be performed on new employees along with periodic role changes to ensure security.

Compliance can be achieved with respect to national and international data protection standards and regulations, such as Payment Card Industry Data Security Standard, Health Insurance Portability and Accountability Act, Sarbanes–Oxley Act, or General Data Protection Regulation.

Management and Compliance Systems

Key Management System

A key management system (KMS), also known as a cryptographic key management system (CKMS), is an integrated approach for generating, distributing and managing cryptographic keys for devices and applications. They may cover all aspects of security - from the secure generation of keys over the secure exchange of keys up to secure key handling and storage on the client. Thus, a KMS includes the backend functionality for key generation, distribution, and replacement as well as the client functionality for injecting keys, storing and managing keys on devices.

Standards-based Key Management

Many specific applications have developed their own key management systems with home grown protocols. However, as systems become more interconnected keys need to be shared between those different systems. To facilitate this, key management standards have evolved to define the protocols used to manage and exchange cryptographic keys and related information.

Key Management Interoperability Protocol (KMIP)

KMIP is an extensible key management protocol that has been developed by many organizations working within the OASIS standards body. The first version was released in 2010, and it has been further developed by an active technical committee.

The protocol allows for the creation of keys and their distribution among disparate software systems that need to utilize them. It covers the full key life cycle of both symmetric and asymmetric keys in a variety of formats, the wrapping of keys, provisioning schemes, and cryptographic operations as well as meta data associated with the keys.

The protocol is backed by an extensive series of test cases, and interoperability testing is performed between compliant systems each year.

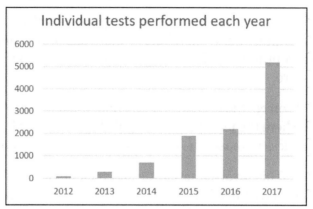

Individual interoperability tests performed by each server/client vendor combination since 2012.

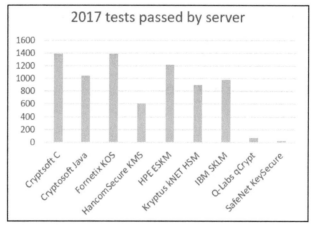

Results of 2017 OASIS KMIP interoperability testing.

Non-KMIP-Compliant Key Management

Open Source

- Barbican, the OpenStack security API.

- KeyBox - Web-based SSH access and key management.

- EPKS - Echo Public Key Share, system to share encryption keys online in a p2p community.

- Kmc-Subset137 - Key management system implementing UNISIG Subset-137 for ERTMS/ETCS railway application.

- privacyIDEA - Two factor management with support for managing SSH keys.

- StrongKey - Open source, last updated on Sourceforge in 2016. There is no more maintenance on this project according to its home page.

- Vault - Secret server from HashiCorp.

- Keeto

- NuCypher

Closed Source

- Amazon Web Service (AWS) Key Management Service (KMS)

- AppViewX CERT+ Certificate and Key Lifecycle Automation

- AppViewX SSH+ SSH Key Lifecycle Automation

- Bell ID Key Manager

- Cryptomathic CKMS

- Cryptsoft KMIP C and Java Servers

- Encryptionizer Key Manager (Windows only)

- Fornetix Key Orchestration

- Futurex Key Management

- Gazzang zTrustee

- HP Enterprise Secure Key Manager

- IBM Distributed Key Management System (DKMS)

- IBM Enterprise Key Management Foundation

- IBM Security Key Lifecycle Manager

- KeyNexus Enterprise on-premise

- Microsoft Azure Key Vault

- Oracle Key Vault

- Oracle Key Manager

- P6R KMIP Client SDK

- Porticor Virtual Private Data

- QuintessenceLabs qCrypt Key and Policy Manager

- RSA Data Protection Manager

- Gemalto's SafeNet KeySecure

- SSH Communications Security Universal SSH Key Manager

- Thales Key Management

- Townsend Security Alliance Key Manager

- Venafi Trust Protection Platform

- Vormetric Data Security Platform

KMS Security Policy

The security policy of a key management system provides the rules that are to be used to protect keys and metadata that the key management system supports. As defined by the National Institute of Standards and Technology NIST, the policy shall establish and specify rules for this information that will protect its:

- Confidentiality

- Integrity

- Availability

- Authentication of source

This protection covers the complete key life-cycle from the time the key becomes operational to its elimination.

Bring your own Encryption / Key

Bring your own encryption (BYOE)—also called bring your own key (BYOK)—refers to a cloud-computing security model to allow public-cloud customers to use their own encryption software and manage their own encryption keys. This security model is usually considered a marketing stunt, as critical keys are being handed over to third parties (cloud providers) and key owners are still left with the operational burden of generating, rotating and sharing their keys.

Public-key Infrastructure

A public-key infrastructure is a type of key management system that uses hierarchical digital certificates to provide authentication, and public keys to provide encryption. PKIs are used in World Wide Web traffic, commonly in the form of SSL and TLS.

Multicast Group Key Management

Group key management means managing the keys in a group communication. Most of the group communications use multicast communication so that if the message is sent once by the sender, it will be received by all the users. The main problem in multicast group communication is its security. In order to improve the security, various keys are given to the users. Using the keys, the users can encrypt their messages and send them secretly. IETF.org released RFC 4046, entitled Multicast Security (MSEC) Group Key Management Architecture, which discusses the challenges of group key management.

Key Distribution

In symmetric key cryptography, both parties must possess a secret key which they must exchange prior to using any encryption. Distribution of secret keys has been problematic until recently, because it involved face-to-face meeting, use of a trusted courier, or sending the key through an existing encryption channel. The first two are often impractical and always unsafe, while the third depends on the security of a previous key exchange.

In public key cryptography, the key distribution of public keys is done through public key servers. When a person creates a key-pair, they keep one key private and the other, known as the public-key, is uploaded to a server where it can be accessed by anyone to send the user a private, encrypted, message.

Secure Sockets Layer (SSL) uses Diffie–Hellman key exchange if the client does not have a public-private key pair and a published certificate in the public key infrastructure, and Public Key Cryptography if the user does have both the keys and the credential.

Key distribution is an important issue in wireless sensor network (WSN) design. There are many key distribution schemes in the literature that are designed to maintain an easy and at the same time secure communication among sensor nodes. The most accepted method of key distribution in WSNs is key predistribution, where secret keys are placed in sensor nodes before deployment. When the nodes are deployed over the target area, the secret keys are used to create the network.

Storage of Keys in the Cloud

Key distribution and key storage are more problematic in the cloud due to the transitory nature of the agents on it. Secret sharing can be used to store keys at many different servers on the cloud. In secret sharing, a secret is used as a seed to generate a number of distinct secrets, and the pieces are distributed so that some subset of the recipients can jointly authenticate themselves and use the secret information without learning what it is. But rather than store files on different servers, the key is parceled out and its secret shares stored at multiple locations in a manner that a subset of the shares can regenerate the key.

Secret sharing is used in cases where one wishes to distribute a secret among N shares so that $M < N$ of them (M of N) can regenerate the original secret, but no smaller group up to $M - 1$ can do so.

KERCKHOFF'S PRINCIPLE FOR CRYPTOSYSTEM

Kerckhoffs's principle (also called Kerckhoffs's desideratum, assumption, axiom, doctrine or law) of cryptography was stated by Netherlands born cryptographer Auguste Kerckhoffs in the 19th century: A cryptosystem should be secure even if everything about the system, except the key, is public knowledge.

Kerckhoffs's principle was reformulated (or possibly independently formulated) by American mathematician Claude Shannon as "the enemy knows the system", i.e., "one ought to design systems under the assumption that the enemy will immediately gain full familiarity with them". In that form, it is called Shannon's maxim. This concept is widely embraced by cryptographers, in contrast to "security through obscurity", which is not.

In 1883, Auguste Kerckhoffs wrote two journal articles on *La Cryptographie Militaire*, in which he stated six design principles for military ciphers. Translated from French, they are:

1. The system must be practically, if not mathematically, indecipherable;

2. It should not require secrecy, and it should not be a problem if it falls into enemy hands;

3. It must be possible to communicate and remember the key without using written notes, and correspondents must be able to change or modify it at will;

4. It must be applicable to telegraph communications;

5. It must be portable, and should not require several persons to handle or operate;

6. Lastly, given the circumstances in which it is to be used, the system must be easy to use and should not be stressful to use or require its users to know and comply with a long list of rules.

Some are no longer relevant given the ability of computers to perform complex encryption, but his second axiom, now known as Kerckhoffs's principle, is still critically important.

Kerckhoffs viewed cryptography as a rival to, and a better alternative than, steganographic encoding, which was common in the nineteenth century for hiding the meaning of military messages. One problem with encoding schemes is that they rely on humanly-held secrets such as "dictionaries" which disclose for example, the secret meaning of words. Steganographic-like dictionaries, once revealed, permanently compromise a corresponding encoding system. Another problem is that the risk of exposure increases as the number of users holding the secret(s) increases.

Nineteenth century cryptography in contrast used simple tables which provided for the transposition of alphanumeric characters, generally given row-column intersections which could be modified by keys which were generally short, numeric, and could be committed to human memory. The system was considered "indecipherable" because tables and keys do not convey meaning by themselves. Secret messages can be compromised only if a matching set of table, key, and message falls into enemy hands in a relevant time frame. Kerckhoffs viewed tactical messages as only having a few hours of relevance. Systems are not necessarily compromised, because their components (i.e. alphanumeric character tables and keys) can be easily changed.

Advantage of Secret Keys

Using secure cryptography is supposed to replace the difficult problem of keeping messages secure with a much more manageable one, keeping relatively small keys secure. A system that requires long-term secrecy for something as large and complex as the whole design of a cryptographic system obviously cannot achieve that goal. It only replaces one hard problem with another. However, if a system is secure even when the enemy knows everything except the key, then all that is needed is to manage keeping the keys secret.

There are a large number of ways the internal details of a widely used system could be discovered. The most obvious is that someone could bribe, blackmail, or otherwise threaten staff or customers into explaining the system. In war, for example, one side will probably capture some equipment and people from the other side. Each side will also use spies to gather information.

If a method involves software, someone could do memory dumps or run the software under the control of a debugger in order to understand the method. If hardware is being used, someone could buy or steal some of the hardware and build whatever programs or gadgets needed to test it. Hardware can also be dismantled so that the chip details can be examined under the microscope.

Maintaining Security

A generalization some make from Kerckhoffs's principle is: "The fewer and simpler the secrets that one must keep to ensure system security, the easier it is to maintain system security." Bruce Schneier ties it in with a belief that all security systems must be designed to fail as gracefully as possible:

> "Kerckhoffs's principle applies beyond codes and ciphers to security systems in general: every secret creates a potential failure point. Secrecy, in other words, is a prime cause of brittleness—and therefore something likely to make a system prone to catastrophic collapse. Conversely, openness provides ductility."

Any security system depends crucially on keeping some things secret. However, Kerckhoffs's principle points out that the things kept secret ought to be those least costly to change if inadvertently disclosed.

For example, a cryptographic algorithm may be implemented by hardware and software that is widely distributed among users. If security depends on keeping that secret, then disclosure leads to major logistic difficulties in developing, testing, and distributing implementations of a new algorithm – it is "brittle". On the other hand, if keeping the algorithm secret is not important, but only the keys used with the algorithm must be secret, then disclosure of the keys simply requires the simpler, less costly process of generating and distributing new keys.

Applications

In accordance with Kerckhoffs's principle, the majority of civilian cryptography makes use of publicly known algorithms. By contrast, ciphers used to protect classified government or military information are often kept secret. However, it should not be assumed that government/military ciphers must be kept secret to maintain security. It is possible that they are intended to be as cryptographically sound as public algorithms, and the decision to keep them secret is in keeping with a layered security posture.

Security through Obscurity

It is moderately common for companies, and sometimes even standards bodies as in the case of the CSS encryption on DVDs, to keep the inner workings of a system secret. Some argue this "security by obscurity" makes the product safer and less vulnerable to attack. A counter argument is that keeping the innards secret may improve security in the short term, but in the long run only systems that have been published and analyzed should be trusted.

Security through Obscurity Considered Dangerous

Hiding security vulnerabilities in algorithms, software, or hardware decreases the likelihood they will be repaired and increases the likelihood that they can and will be exploited. Discouraging or outlawing discussion of weaknesses and vulnerabilities is extremely dangerous and deleterious to the security of computer systems, the network, and its citizens.

Open Discussion Encourages Better Security

The long history of cryptography and cryptoanalysis has shown time and time again that open discussion and analysis of algorithms exposes weaknesses not thought of by the original authors, and thereby leads to better and more secure algorithms. "The system must not require secrecy and must be able to be stolen by the enemy without causing trouble."

ATTACKS ON CRYPTOSYSTEMS

In the present era, not only business but almost all the aspects of human life are driven by information. Hence, it has become imperative to protect useful information from malicious activities such as attacks. Let us consider the types of attacks to which information is typically subjected to.

Attacks are typically categorized based on the action performed by the attacker. An attack, thus, can be passive or active.

Passive Attacks

The main goal of a passive attack is to obtain unauthorized access to the information. For example, actions such as intercepting and eavesdropping on the communication channel can be regarded as passive attack.

These actions are passive in nature, as they neither affect information nor disrupt the communication channel. A passive attack is often seen as stealing information. The only difference in stealing physical goods and stealing information is that theft of data still leaves the owner in possession of that data. Passive information attack is thus more dangerous than stealing of goods, as information theft may go unnoticed by the owner.

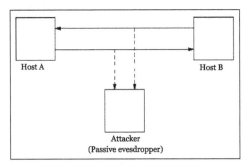

Active Attacks

An active attack involves changing the information in some way by conducting some process on the information. For example:

- Modifying the information in an unauthorized manner.

- Initiating unintended or unauthorized transmission of information.

- Alteration of authentication data such as originator name or timestamp associated with information.

- Unauthorized deletion of data.

- Denial of access to information for legitimate users (denial of service).

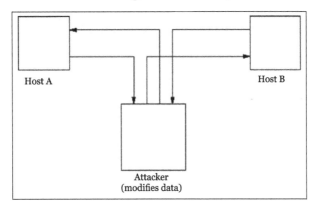

Cryptography provides many tools and techniques for implementing cryptosystems capable of preventing most of the attacks described above.

Assumptions of Attacker

Let us see the prevailing environment around cryptosystems followed by the types of attacks employed to break these systems.

Environment around Cryptosystem

While considering possible attacks on the cryptosystem, it is necessary to know the cryptosystems environment. The attacker's assumptions and knowledge about the environment decides his capabilities.

In cryptography, the following three assumptions are made about the security environment and attacker's capabilities.

Details of the Encryption Scheme

The design of a cryptosystem is based on the following two cryptography algorithms –

- Public Algorithms – With this option, all the details of the algorithm are in the public domain, known to everyone.

- Proprietary algorithms – The details of the algorithm are only known by the system designers and users.

In case of proprietary algorithms, security is ensured through obscurity. Private algorithms may not be the strongest algorithms as they are developed in-house and may not be extensively investigated for weakness.

Secondly, they allow communication among closed group only. Hence they are not suitable for modern communication where people communicate with large number of known or unknown entities. Also, according to Kerckhoff's principle, the algorithm is preferred to be public with strength of encryption lying in the key.

Thus, the first assumption about security environment is that the encryption algorithm is known to the attacker.

Availability of Ciphertext

We know that once the plaintext is encrypted into ciphertext, it is put on unsecure public channel (say email) for transmission. Thus, the attacker can obviously assume that it has access to the ciphertext generated by the cryptosystem.

Availability of Plaintext and Ciphertext

This assumption is not as obvious as other. However, there may be situations where an attacker can have access to plaintext and corresponding ciphertext. Some such possible circumstances are –

- The attacker influences the sender to convert plaintext of his choice and obtains the ciphertext.

- The receiver may divulge the plaintext to the attacker inadvertently. The attacker has access to corresponding ciphertext gathered from open channel.

- In a public-key cryptosystem, the encryption key is in open domain and is known to any potential attacker. Using this key, he can generate pairs of corresponding plaintexts and ciphertexts.

Cryptographic Attacks

The basic intention of an attacker is to break a cryptosystem and to find the plaintext from the ciphertext. To obtain the plaintext, the attacker only needs to find out the secret decryption key, as the algorithm is already in public domain.

Hence, he applies maximum effort towards finding out the secret key used in the cryptosystem. Once the attacker is able to determine the key, the attacked system is considered as broken or compromised.

Based on the methodology used, attacks on cryptosystems are categorized as follows –

- Ciphertext Only Attacks (COA) – In this method, the attacker has access to a set of ciphertext(s). He does not have access to corresponding plaintext. COA is said to be successful when the corresponding plaintext can be determined from a given set of ciphertext. Occasionally, the encryption key can be determined from this attack. Modern cryptosystems are guarded against ciphertext-only attacks.

- Known Plaintext Attack (KPA) – In this method, the attacker knows the plaintext for some parts of the ciphertext. The task is to decrypt the rest of the ciphertext using this information. This may be done by determining the key or via some other method. The best example of this attack is *linear cryptanalysis* against block ciphers.

- Chosen Plaintext Attack (CPA) – In this method, the attacker has the text of his choice encrypted. So he has the ciphertext-plaintext pair of his choice. This simplifies his task of determining the encryption key. An example of this attack is *differential cryptanalysis* applied against block ciphers as well as hash functions. A popular public key cryptosystem, RSA is also vulnerable to chosen-plaintext attacks.

- Dictionary Attack – This attack has many variants, all of which involve compiling a 'dictionary'. In simplest method of this attack, attacker builds a dictionary of ciphertexts and corresponding plaintexts that he has learnt over a period of time. In future, when an attacker gets the ciphertext, he refers the dictionary to find the corresponding plaintext.

- Brute Force Attack (BFA) – In this method, the attacker tries to determine the key by attempting all possible keys. If the key is 8 bits long, then the number of possible keys is 2^8 = 256. The attacker knows the ciphertext and the algorithm, now he attempts all the 256 keys one by one for decryption. The time to complete the attack would be very high if the key is long.

- Man in Middle Attack (MIM) – The targets of this attack are mostly public key cryptosystems where key exchange is involved before communication takes place.

  ○ Host A wants to communicate to host B, hence requests public key of B.

  ○ An attacker intercepts this request and sends his public key instead.

  ○ Thus, whatever host A sends to host B, the attacker is able to read.

  ○ In order to maintain communication, the attacker re-encrypts the data after reading with his public key and sends to B.

  ○ The attacker sends his public key as A's public key so that B takes it as if it is taking it from A.

- Side Channel Attack (SCA) – This type of attack is not against any particular type of cryptosystem or algorithm. Instead, it is launched to exploit the weakness in physical implementation of the cryptosystem.

- Timing Attacks – They exploit the fact that different computations take different times to compute on processor. By measuring such timings, it is be possible to know about a particular computation the processor is carrying out. For example, if the encryption takes a longer time, it indicates that the secret key is long.

- Power Analysis Attacks – These attacks are similar to timing attacks except that the amount of power consumption is used to obtain information about the nature of the underlying computations.

- Fault analysis Attacks – In these attacks, errors are induced in the cryptosystem and the attacker studies the resulting output for useful information.

Practicality of Attacks

The attacks on cryptosystems described here are highly academic, as majority of them come from the academic community. In fact, many academic attacks involve quite unrealistic assumptions about environment as well as the capabilities of the attacker. For example, in chosen-ciphertext attack, the attacker requires an impractical number of deliberately chosen plaintext-ciphertext pairs. It may not be practical altogether.

Nonetheless, the fact that any attack exists should be a cause of concern, particularly if the attack technique has the potential for improvement.

Adaptive Chosen-Ciphertext Attack

An adaptive chosen-ciphertext attack (abbreviated as CCA2) is an interactive form of chosen-ciphertext attack in which an attacker first sends a number of ciphertexts to be decrypted chosen adaptively, then uses the results to distinguish a target ciphertext without consulting the oracle on the challenge ciphertext, in an adaptive attack the attacker is further allowed adaptive queries to be asked after the target is revealed (but the target query is disallowed). It is extensing the indifferent (non-adaptive) chosen-ciphertext attack (CCA1) where the second stage of adaptive queries is not allowed. Charles Rackoff and Dan Simon defined CCA2 and suggested a system building on the non-adaptive CCA1 definition and system of Moni Naor and Moti Yung (which was the first treatment of chosen ciphertext attack immunity of public key systems).

In certain practical settings, the goal of this attack is to gradually reveal information about an encrypted message, or about the decryption key itself. For public-key systems, adaptive-chosen-ciphertexts are generally applicable only when they have the property of ciphertext malleability — that is, a ciphertext can be modified in specific ways that will have a predictable effect on the decryption of that message.

Practical Attacks

Adaptive-chosen-ciphertext attacks were perhaps considered to be a theoretical concern but not to be manifested in practice until 1998, when Daniel Bleichenbacher of Bell Laboratories (at the time) demonstrated a practical attack against systems using RSA encryption in concert with the PKCS#1 v1 encoding function, including a version of the Secure Socket Layer (SSL) protocol used by thousands of web servers at the time.

The Bleichenbacher attacks, also known as the million message attack, took advantage of flaws within the PKCS #1 function to gradually reveal the content of an RSA encrypted message. Doing this requires sending several million test ciphertexts to the decryption device (e.g., SSL-equipped web server). In practical terms, this means that an SSL session key can be exposed in a reasonable amount of time, perhaps a day or less.

With slight variations this vulnerability still exists in many modern servers, under the new name "Return Of Bleichenbacher's Oracle Threat" (ROBOT).

Preventing Attacks

In order to prevent adaptive-chosen-ciphertext attacks, it is necessary to use an encryption or encoding scheme that limits ciphertext malleability and a proof of security of the system. After the theoretical and foundation level development of CCA secure systems, a number of systems have been proposed in the Random Oracle model: the most common standard for RSA encryption is Optimal Asymmetric Encryption Padding (OAEP). Unlike improvised schemes such as the padding used in the early versions of PKCS#1, OAEP has been proven secure in the random oracle model, OAEP was incorporated into PKCS#1 as of version 2.0 published in 1998 as the now-recommended encoding scheme, with the older scheme still supported but not recommended for new applications. However, the golden standard for security is to show the system secure without relying on the Random Oracle idealization.

Mathematical Model

In complexity-theoretic cryptography, security against adaptive chosen-ciphertext attacks is commonly modeled using ciphertext indistinguishability (IND-CCA2).

Brute-force Attack

In cryptography, a brute-force attack consists of an attacker submitting many passwords or passphrases with the hope of eventually guessing correctly. The attacker systematically checks all possible passwords and passphrases until the correct one is found. Alternatively, the attacker can attempt to guess the key which is typically created from the password using a key derivation function. This is known as an exhaustive key search.

A brute-force attack is a cryptanalytic attack that can, in theory, be used to attempt to decrypt any encrypted data (except for data encrypted in an information-theoretically secure manner). Such an attack might be used when it is not possible to take advantage of other weaknesses in an encryption system (if any exist) that would make the task easier.

When password-guessing, this method is very fast when used to check all short passwords, but for longer passwords other methods such as the dictionary attack are used because a brute-force search takes too long. Longer passwords, passphrases and keys have more possible values, making them exponentially more difficult to crack than shorter ones.

Brute-force attacks can be made less effective by obfuscating the data to be encoded making it more difficult for an attacker to recognize when the code has been cracked or by making the attacker do more work to test each guess. One of the measures of the strength of an encryption system is how long it would theoretically take an attacker to mount a successful brute-force attack against it.

Brute-force attacks are an application of brute-force search, the general problem-solving technique of enumerating all candidates and checking each one.

Brute-force attacks work by calculating every possible combination that could make up a password and testing it to see if it is the correct password. As the password's length increases, the amount of time, on average, to find the correct password increases exponentially.

Theoretical Limits

The resources required for a brute-force attack grow exponentially with increasing key size, not linearly. Although U.S. export regulations historically restricted key lengths to 56-bit symmetric keys (e.g. Data Encryption Standard), these restrictions are no longer in place, so modern symmetric algorithms typically use computationally stronger 128- to 256-bit keys.

There is a physical argument that a 128-bit symmetric key is computationally secure against brute-force attack. The so-called Landauer limit implied by the laws of physics sets a lower limit on the energy required to perform a computation of $kT \cdot \ln 2$ per bit erased in a computation, where T is the temperature of the computing device in kelvins, k is the Boltzmann constant, and the natural logarithm of 2 is about 0.693. No irreversible computing device can use less energy than this, even in principle. Thus, in order to simply flip through the possible values for a 128-bit symmetric key (ignoring doing the actual computing to check it) would, theoretically, require $2^{128} - 1$ bit flips on a conventional processor. If it is assumed that the calculation occurs near room temperature (~300 K), the Von Neumann-Landauer Limit can be applied to estimate the energy required as ~10^{18} joules, which is equivalent to consuming 30 gigawatts of power for one year. This is equal to 30×10^9 W$\times 365 \times 24 \times 3600$ s $= 9.46 \times 10^{17}$ J or 262.7 TWh (more than 1% of the world energy production). The full actual computation – checking each key to see if a solution has been found – would consume many times this amount. Furthermore, this is simply the energy requirement for cycling through the key space; the actual time it takes to flip each bit is not considered, which is certainly greater than 0.

However, this argument assumes that the register values are changed using conventional set and clear operations which inevitably generate entropy. It has been shown that computational hardware can be designed not to encounter this theoretical obstruction, though no such computers are known to have been constructed.

Modern GPUs are well-suited to the repetitive tasks associated with hardware-based password cracking.

As commercial successors of governmental ASIC solutions have become available, also known as custom hardware attacks, two emerging technologies have proven their capability in the brute-force attack of certain ciphers. One is modern graphics processing unit (GPU) technology, the other is the field-programmable gate array (FPGA) technology. GPUs benefit from their wide availability and price-performance benefit, FPGAs from their energy efficiency per cryptographic operation. Both technologies try to transport the benefits of parallel processing to brute-force attacks. In case of GPUs some hundreds, in the case of FPGA some thousand processing units making them much better suited to cracking passwords than conventional processors. Various publications in the fields of cryptographic analysis have proved the energy efficiency of today's FPGA technology, for example, the COPACOBANA FPGA Cluster computer consumes the same energy as a single

PC (600 W), but performs like 2,500 PCs for certain algorithms. A number of firms provide hardware-based FPGA cryptographic analysis solutions from a single FPGA PCI Express card up to dedicated FPGA computers. WPA and WPA2 encryption have successfully been brute-force attacked by reducing the workload by a factor of 50 in comparison to conventional CPUs and some hundred in case of FPGAs.

A single COPACOBANA board boasting 6 Xilinx Spartans – a cluster is made up of 20 of these.

AES permits the use of 256-bit keys. Breaking a symmetric 256-bit key by brute force requires 2^{128} times more computational power than a 128-bit key. Fifty supercomputers that could check a billion billion (10^{18}) AES keys per second (if such a device could ever be made) would, in theory, require about 3×10^{51} years to exhaust the 256-bit key space.

An underlying assumption of a brute-force attack is that the complete keyspace was used to generate keys, something that relies on an effective random number generator, and that there are no defects in the algorithm or its implementation. For example, a number of systems that were originally thought to be impossible to crack by brute force have nevertheless been cracked because the key space to search through was found to be much smaller than originally thought, because of a lack of entropy in their pseudorandom number generators. These include Netscape's implementation of SSL and a Debian/Ubuntu edition of OpenSSL discovered in 2008 to be flawed. A similar lack of implemented entropy led to the breaking of Enigma's code.

Credential Recycling

Credential recycling refers to the hacking practice of re-using username and password combinations gathered in previous brute-force attacks. A special form of credential recycling is pass the hash, where unsalted hashed credentials are stolen and re-used without first being brute forced.

Unbreakable Codes

Certain types of encryption, by their mathematical properties, cannot be defeated by brute force. An example of this is one-time pad cryptography, where every cleartext bit has a corresponding key from a truly random sequence of key bits. A 140 character one-time-pad-encoded string subjected to a brute-force attack would eventually reveal every 140 character string possible, including the correct answer – but of all the answers given, there would be no way of knowing which was the correct one. Defeating such a system, as was done by the Venona project, generally relies not on pure cryptography, but upon mistakes in its implementation: the key pads not being truly random, intercepted keypads, operators making mistakes – or other errors.

Countermeasures

In case of an offline attack where the attacker has access to the encrypted material, one can try key combinations without the risk of discovery or interference. However database and directory administrators can take countermeasures against online attacks, for example by limiting the number of attempts that a password can be tried, by introducing time delays between successive attempts, increasing the answer's complexity (e.g. requiring a CAPTCHA answer or verification code sent via cellphone), and/or locking accounts out after unsuccessful logon attempts. Website administrators may prevent a particular IP address from trying more than a predetermined number of password attempts against any account on the site.

Reverse Brute-force Attack

In a reverse brute-force attack, a single (usually common) password is tested against multiple usernames or encrypted files. The process may be repeated for a select few passwords. In such a strategy, the attacker is generally not targeting a specific user.

Software that Performs Brute-force Attacks

- Aircrack-ng
- Cain and Abel
- Crack
- DaveGrohl
- Hashcat
- John the Ripper
- LophtCrack
- Ophcrack
- RainbowCrack

Meet-in-the-middle Attack

The meet-in-the-middle attack (MITM) is a generic space–time tradeoff cryptographic attack against encryption schemes which rely on performing multiple encryption operations in sequence. The MITM attack is the primary reason why Double DES is not used and why a Triple DES key (168-bit) can be bruteforced by an attacker with 2^{56} space and 2^{112} operations.

When trying to improve the security of a block cipher, a tempting idea is to encrypt the data several times using multiple keys. One might think this doubles or even n-tuples the security of the multiple-encryption scheme, depending on the number of times the data is encrypted, because an exhaustive search on all possible combination of keys (simple brute-force) would take $2^{n \cdot k}$ attempts if the data is encrypted with k-bit keys n times.

The MITM is a generic attack which weakens the security benefits of using multiple encryptions by storing intermediate values from the encryptions or decryptions and using those to improve the time required to brute force the decryption keys. This makes a Meet-in-the-Middle attack (MITM) a generic space–time tradeoff cryptographic attack.

The MITM attack attempts to find the keys by using both the range (ciphertext) and domain (plaintext) of the composition of several functions (or block ciphers) such that the forward mapping through the first functions is the same as the backward mapping (inverse image) through the last functions, quite literally *meeting* in the middle of the composed function. For example, although Double DES encrypts the data with two different 56-bit keys, Double DES can be broken with 2^{57} encryption and decryption operations.

The multidimensional MITM (MD-MITM) uses a combination of several simultaneous MITM attacks like described above, where the meeting happens in multiple positions in the composed function. Diffie and Hellman first proposed the meet-in-the-middle attack on a hypothetical expansion of a block cipher in 1977. Their attack used a space–time tradeoff to break the double-encryption scheme in only twice the time needed to break the single-encryption scheme.

In 2011, Bo Zhu and Guang Gong investigated the multidimensional meet-in-the-middle attack and presented new attacks on the block ciphers GOST, KTANTAN and Hummingbird-2.

Meet-in-the-middle (1D-MITM)

Assume someone wants to attack an encryption scheme with the following characteristics for a given plaintext P and ciphertext C:

$$C = ENC_{k_2}(ENC_{k_1}(P))$$
$$P = DEC_{k_1}(DEC_{k_2}(C))$$

Here ENC is the encryption function, DEC the decryption function defined as ENC^{-1} (inverse mapping) and k_1 and k_2 are two keys.

The naive approach at brute-forcing this encryption scheme is to decrypt the ciphertext with every possible k_2, and decrypt each of the intermediate outputs with every possible k_1, for a total of $2^{k_1} * 2^{k_2}$ (or $2^{k_1+k_2}$) operations.

The meet-in-the-middle attack uses a more efficient approach. By decrypting C with k_2, one obtains the following equivalence:

$$C = ENC_{k_2}(ENC_{k_1}(P))$$
$$DEC_{k_2}(C) = DEC_{k_2}(ENC_{k_2}[ENC_{k_1}(P)])$$
$$DEC_{k_2}(C) = ENC_{k_1}(P)$$

The attacker can compute $ENC_{k1}(P)$ for all values of k_1 and $DEC_{k2}(C)$ for all possible values of k_2, for a total of $2^{k_1} + 2^{k_2}$ (or 2^{k_1+1}, if k_1 and k_2 are the same size) operations. If the result from any of the $ENC_{k1}(P)$ operations matches a result from the $DEC_{k2}(C)$ operations, the pair of k_1 and k_2 is possibly the correct key. This potentially-correct key is called a *candidate key*. The attacker can determine which candidate key is correct by testing it with a second test-set of plaintext and ciphertext.

The MITM attack is one of the reasons why Data Encryption Standard (DES) was replaced with Triple DES and not Double DES. An attacker can use a MITM attack to bruteforce Double DES with 2^{57} operations and 2^{56} space, making it only a small improvement over DES. Triple DES uses a "triple length" (168-bit) key and is also vulnerable to a meet-in-the-middle attack in 2^{56} space and 2^{112} operations, but is considered secure due to the size of its keyspace.

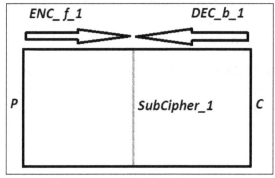

An illustration of 1D-MITM attack

MITM Algorithm

Compute the following:

- $SubCipher_1 = ENC_{f_1}(k_{f_1}, P), \forall k_{f_1} \in K:$

  and save each $SubCipher_1$ together with corresponding k_{f_1} in a set A

- $SubCipher_1 = DEC_{b_1}(k_{b_1}, C), \forall k_{b_1} \in K:$

  and compare each new $SubCipher_1$ with the set A

When a match is found, keep k_{f_1}, k_{b_1} as candidate key-pair in a table T. Test pairs in T on a new pair of (P, C) to confirm validity. If the key-pair does not work on this new pair, do MITM again on a new pair of (P, C).

MITM Complexity

If the keysize is k, this attack uses only 2^{k+1} encryptions (and decryptions) (and $O(2^k)$ memory in case a look-up table have been built for the set of forward computations) in contrast to the naive attack, which needs $2^{2 \cdot k}$ encryptions but $O(1)$ space.

Multidimensional MITM (MD-MITM)

While 1D-MITM can be efficient, a more sophisticated attack has been developed: multidimensional meet-in-the-middle attack, also abbreviated MD-MITM. This is preferred when the data has been encrypted using more than 2 encryptions with different keys. Instead of meeting in the middle (one place in the sequence), the MD-MITM attack attempts to reach several specific intermediate states using the forward and backward computations at several positions in the cipher.

Assume that the attack has to be mounted on a block cipher, where the encryption and decryption is defined as before:

$$C = ENC_{k_n}(ENC_{k_{n-1}}(...(ENC_{k_1}(P))...))$$

$$P = DEC_{k_1}(DEC_{k_2}(...(DEC_{k_n}(C))...))$$

Plaintext P is encrypted multiple times using a repetition of the same block cipher.

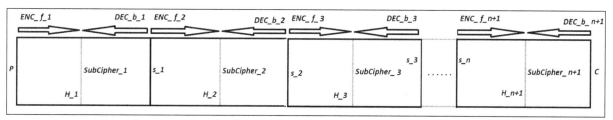

An illustration of MD-MITM attack.

The MD-MITM has been used for cryptanalysis of, among many, the GOST block cipher, where it has been shown that a 3D-MITM has significantly reduced the time complexity for an attack on it.

MD-MITM Algorithm

Compute the following:

- $SubCipher_1 = ENC_{f_1}(k_{f_1}, P)$ $\forall k_{f_1} \in K$

  and save each $SubCipher_1$ together with corresponding k_{f_1} in a set H_1.

- $SubCipher_{n+1} = DEC_{b_{n+1}}(k_{b_{n+1}}, C)$ $\forall k_{b_{n+1}} \in K$

  and save each $SubCipher_{n+1}$ together with corresponding $k_{b_{n+1}}$ in a set H_{n+1}.

For each possible guess on the intermediate state s_1 compute the following:

- $SubCipher_1 = DEC_{b_1}(k_{b_1}, s_1)$ $\forall k_{b_1} \in K$

  and for each match between this $SubCipher_1$ and the set H_1, save k_{b_1} and k_{f_1} in a new set T_1.

- $SubCipher_2 = ENC_{f_2}(k_{f_2}, s_1)$ $\forall k_{f_2} \in K$

  and save each $SubCipher_2$ together with corresponding k_{f_2} in a set H_2.

  For each possible guess on an intermediate state s_2 compute the following:

- $SubCipher_2 = DEC_{b_2}(k_{b_2}, s_2)$ $\forall k_{b_2} \in K$

  and for each match between this $SubCipher_2$ and the set H_2, check also whether it matches with T_1 and then save the combination of sub-keys together in a new set T_2.

For each possible guess on an intermediate state s_n compute the following:

- $SubCipher_n = DEC_{b_n}(k_{b_n}, s_n)$ $\forall k_{b_n} \in K$ and for each match between this $SubCipher_n$ and the set H_n, check also whether it matches with T_{n-1}, save k_{b_n} and k_{f_n} in a new set T_n.

- $SubCipher_{n+1} = ENC_{f_n+1}(k_{f_n+1}, s_n)$ $\forall k_{f_{n+1}} \in K$ and for each match between this $SubCipher_{n+1}$ and the set H_{n+1}, check also whether it matches with T_n. If this is the case then:

Use the found combination of sub-keys $(k_{f_1}, k_{b_1}, k_{f_2}, k_{b_2}, ..., k_{f_{n+1}}, k_{b_{n+1}})$ on another pair of plaintext/ciphertext to verify the correctness of the key.

Note the nested element in the algorithm. The guess on every possible value on s_j is done for each guess on the previous s_{j-1}. This make up an element of exponential complexity to overall time complexity of this MD-MITM attack.

MD-MITM Complexity

Time complexity of this attack without brute force, is $2^{|k_{f_1}|} + 2^{|k_{b_{n+1}}|} + 2^{|s_1|} \cdot (2^{|k_{b_1}|} + 2^{|k_{f_2}|} + 2^{|s_2|} \cdot (2^{|k_{b_2}|} + 2^{|k_{f_3}|} + \cdots))$.

Regarding the memory complexity, it is easy to see that $T_2, T_3, .., T_n$ are much smaller than the first built table of candidate values: T_1 as i increases, the candidate values contained in T_i must satisfy more conditions thereby fewer candidates will pass on to the end destination T_n.

An upper bound of the memory complexity of MD-MITM is then:

$$2^{|k_{f_1}|} + 2^{|k_{b_{n+1}}|} + 2^{|k|-|s_n|} \cdots$$

Here k denotes the length of the whole key (combined).

The data complexity depends on the probability that a wrong key may pass (obtain a false positive), which is $1/2^{|l|}$, where l is the intermediate state in the first MITM phase. The size of the intermediate state and the block size is often the same. Considering also how many keys that are left for testing after the first MITM-phase, it is $2^{|k|}/2^{|l|}$.

Therefore, after the first MITM phase, there are $2^{|k|-b} \cdot 2^{-b} = 2^{|k|-2b}$, where $|b|$ is the block size.

For each time the final candidate value of the keys are tested on a new plaintext/ciphertext-pair, the number of keys that will pass will be multiplied by the probability that a key may pass which is $1/2^{|b|}$.

The part of brute force testing (testing the candidate key on new (P,C) -pairs, have time complexity $2^{|k|-b} + 2^{|k|-2b} + 2^{|k|-3b} + 2^{|k|-4b} \cdots$, clearly for increasing multiples of b in the exponent, number tends to zero.

The conclusion on data complexity is by similar reasoning restricted by that around $\lceil |k|/n \rceil$ (P,C)-pairs.

This is a general description of how 2D-MITM is mounted on a block cipher encryption.

In two-dimensional MITM (2D-MITM) the method is to reach 2 intermediate states inside the multiple encryption of the plaintext.

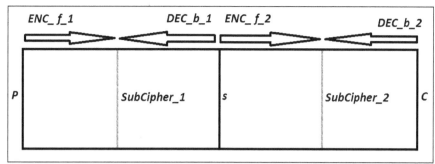

An illustration of 2D-MITM attack.

2D-MITM Algorithm

Compute the following:

- $SubCipher_1 = ENC_{f_1}(k_{f_1}, P)$ $\forall k_{f_1} \in K$

  and save each $SubCipher_1$ together with corresponding k_{f_1} in a set A

- $SubCipher_2 = DEC_{b_2}(k_{b_2}, C)$ $\forall k_{b_2} \in K$

  and save each $SubCipher_2$ together with corresponding k_{b_2} in a set B.

For each possible guess on an intermediate state s between $SubCipher_1$ and $SubCipher_2$ compute the following:

- $SubCipher_1 = DEC_{b_1}(k_{b_1}, s)$ $\forall k_{b_1} \in K$

  and for each match between this $SubCipher_1$ and the set A, save k_{b_1} and k_{f_1} in a new set T.

- $SubCipher_2 = ENC_{f_2}(k_{f_2}, s)$ $\forall k_{f_2} \in K$

  and for each match between this $SubCipher_2$ and the set B, check also whether it matches with T for if this is the case then:

Use the found combination of sub-keys $(k_{f_1}, k_{b_1}, k_{f_2}, k_{b_2})$ on another pair of plaintext/ciphertext to verify the correctness of the key.

2D-MITM Complexity

Time complexity of this attack without brute force, is:

$$2^{|k_{f_1}|} + 2^{|k_{b_2}|} + 2^{|s|} \cdot \left(2^{|k_{b_1}|} + 2^{|k_{f_2}|} \right),$$

where $|\cdot|$ denotes the length.

Main memory consumption is restricted by the construction of the sets A and B where T is much smaller than the others.

Biclique Attack

A biclique attack is a variant of the meet-in-the-middle (MITM) method of cryptanalysis. It utilizes a biclique structure to extend the number of possibly attacked rounds by the MITM attack. Since biclique cryptanalysis is based on MITM attacks, it is applicable to both block ciphers and (iterated) hash-functions. Biclique attacks are known for having broken both full AES and full IDEA, though only with slight advantage over brute force. It has also been applied to the KASUMI cipher and preimage resistance of the Skein-512 and SHA-2 hash functions.

The biclique attack is still the best publicly known single-key attack on AES. The computational complexity of the attack is $2^{126.1}$, $2^{189.7}$ and $2^{254.4}$ for AES128, AES192 and AES256, respectively. It is the only publicly known single-key attack on AES that attacks the full number of rounds. Previous attacks have attacked round reduced variants (typically variants reduced to 7 or 8 rounds).

As the computational complexity of the attack is $2^{126.1}$, it is a theoretical attack, which means the security of AES has not been broken, and the use of AES remains relatively secure. The biclique attack is nevertheless an interesting attack, which suggests a new approach to performing cryptanalysis on block ciphers. The attack has also rendered more information about AES, as it has brought into question the safety-margin in the number of rounds used therein.

The original MITM attack was first suggested by Diffie and Hellman in 1977, when they discussed the cryptanalytic properties of DES. They argued that the key-size was too small, and that reapplying DES multiple times with different keys could be a solution to the key-size; however, they advised against using double-DES and suggested triple-DES as a minimum, due to MITM attacks (MITM attacks can easily be applied to double-DES to reduce the security from 2^{56*2} to just $2*2^{56}$, since one can independently bruteforce the first and the second DES-encryption if they have the plain- and ciphertext).

Since Diffie and Hellman suggested MITM attacks, many variations have emerged that are useful in situations, where the basic MITM attack is inapplicable. The biclique attack variant was first suggested by Dmitry Khovratovich, Rechberger and Savelieva for use with hash-function cryptanalysis. However, it was Bogdanov, Khovratovich and Rechberger who showed how to apply the concept of bicliques to the secret-key setting including block-cipher cryptanalysis, when they published their attack on AES. Prior to this, MITM attacks on AES and many other block ciphers had received little attention, mostly due to the need for independent key bits between the two 'MITM subciphers' in order to facilitate the MITM attack — something that is hard to achieve with many modern key schedules, such as that of AES.

The Biclique

In a MITM attack, the keybits K_1 and K_2, belonging to the first and second subcipher, need to be independent; that is, they need to be independent of each other, else the matched intermediate values for the plain- and ciphertext cannot be computed independently in the MITM attack (there are variants of MITM attacks, where the blocks can have shared key-bits). This property is often hard to exploit over a larger number of rounds, due to the diffusion of the attacked cipher. Simply put: The more rounds you attack, the larger subciphers you will have. The larger subciphers you have, the fewer independent key-bits between the subciphers you will have to bruteforce independently. Of course, the actual number of independent key-bits in each subcipher depends on the diffusion properties of the key-schedule.

The way the biclique helps with tackling the above, is that it allows one to, for instance, attack 7 rounds of AES using MITM attacks, and then by utilizing a biclique structure of length 3 (i.e. it covers 3 rounds of the cipher), you can map the intermediate state at the start of round 7 to the end of the last round, e.g. 10 (if it is AES128), thus attacking the full number of rounds of the cipher, even if it was not possible to attack that amount of rounds with a basic MITM attack.

The meaning of the biclique is thus to build a structure effectively, which can map an intermediate value at the end of the MITM attack to the ciphertext at the end. Which ciphertext the intermediate state gets mapped to at the end, of course depends on the key used for the encryption. The key used to map the state to the ciphertext in the biclique, is based on the keybits bruteforced in the first and second subcipher of the MITM attack.

The essence of biclique attacks is thus, besides the MITM attack, to be able to build a biclique structure effectively, that depending on the keybits K_1 and K_2 can map a certain intermediate state to the corresponding ciphertext.

How to Build the Biclique

Bruteforce

Get 2^d intermediate states and 2^d ciphertexts, then compute the keys that maps between them. This requires 2^{2d} key-recoveries, since each intermediate state needs to be linked to all ciphertexts.

Independent Related-Key Differentials

Preliminary:

Remember that the function of the biclique is to map the intermediate values, S, to the ciphertext-values, C, based on the key $K[i,j]$ such that: $\forall i,j : S_j \xrightarrow[f]{K[i,j]} C_i$

Procedure:

Step one: An intermediate state(S_0), a ciphertext(C_0) and a key($K[0,0]$) is chosen such that: $S_0 \xrightarrow[f]{K[0,0]} C_o$, where f is the function that maps an intermediate state to a ciphertext using a given key. This is denoted as the base computation.

Step two: Two sets of related keys of size 2^d is chosen. The keys are chosen such that:

- The first set of keys are keys, which fulfills the following differential-requirements over f with respect to the base computation: $0 \xrightarrow[f]{\Delta_i^K} \Delta_i$

- The second set of keys are keys, which fulfills the following differential-requirements over f with respect to the base computation: $\nabla_j \xrightarrow[f]{\nabla_j^K} 0$

- The keys are chosen such that the trails of the Δ_i- and ∇_j-differentials are independent – i.e. they do not share any active non-linear components.

In other words: An input difference of o should map to an output difference of   under a key difference of Δ_i^K. All differences are in respect to the base computation. An input difference of ∇_j should map to an output difference of o under a key difference of ∇_j^K. All differences are in respect to the base computation.

Step three: Since the trails do not share any non-linear components (such as S-boxes), the trails can be combined to get:

$$0 \xrightarrow[f]{\Delta_i^K} \Delta_i \oplus \nabla_j \xrightarrow[f]{\nabla_j^K} 0 = \nabla_j \xrightarrow[f]{\Delta_i^K \oplus \nabla_j^K} \Delta_i$$

This conforms to the definitions of both the differentials from step 2.

It is trivial to see that the tuple $(S_0, C_0, K[0,0])$ from the base computation, also conforms by definition to both the differentials, as the differentials are in respect to the base computation. Substituting S_0, C_0 $K[0,0]$ into any of the two definitions, will yield $0 \xrightarrow[f]{0} 0$ since $\Delta_0 = 0, \nabla_0 = 0$ and $\Delta_0^K = 0$.

This means that the tuple of the base computation, can also be XOR'ed to the combined trails:

$$S_0 \oplus \nabla_j \xrightarrow[f]{K[0,0] \oplus \Delta_i^K \oplus \nabla_j^K} C_0 \oplus \Delta_i$$

Step four: It is trivial to see that:

$$S_j = S_0 \oplus \nabla_j$$

$$K[i,j] = K[0,0] \oplus \Delta_i^K \oplus \nabla_j^K$$

$$C_i = C_0 \oplus \Delta_i$$

If this is substituted into the above combined differential trails, the result will be:

$$S_j \xrightarrow[f]{K[i,j]} C_i$$

Which is the same as the definition, there was earlier had above for a biclique:

$$\forall i,j : S_j \xrightarrow[f]{K[i,j]} C_i$$

It is thus possible to create a biclique of size 2^{2d} (2^{2d} since all 2^d keys of the first set of keys, can be combined with the 2^d keys from the second set of keys). This means a biclique of size 2^{2d} can be created using only $2 * 2^d$ computations of the differentials Δ_i and ∇_j over f. If $\Delta_i \neq \nabla_j$ for $i+j>0$ then all of the keys $K[i,j]$ will also be different in the biclique.

This way is how the biclique is constructed in the leading biclique attack on AES. There are some practical limitations in constructing bicliques with this technique. The longer the biclique is, the more rounds the differential trails has to cover. The diffusion properties of the cipher, thus plays a crucial role in the effectiveness of constructing the biclique.

Biclique Cryptanalysis Procedure

Step one: The attacker groups all possible keys into key-subsets of size 2^{2d} for some d, where the key in a group is indexed as $K[i,j]$ in a matrix of size $2^d \times 2^d$. The attacker splits the cipher into two sub-ciphers, f and g (such that $E = f \circ g$), as in a normal MITM attack. The set of keys for each of the sub-ciphers is of cardinality 2^d, and is called $K[i,0]$ and $K[0,j]$. The combined key of the sub-ciphers is expressed with the aforementioned matrix $K[i,j]$.

Step two: The attacker builds a biclique for each group of 2^{2d} keys. The biclique is of dimension-d, since it maps 2^d internal states, S_j, to 2^d ciphertexts, C_i, using 2^{2d} keys. The section "How to build the biclique" suggests how to build the biclique using "Independent related-key differentials". The biclique is in that case built using the differentials of the set of keys, $K[i,0]$ and $K[0,j]$ belonging to the sub-ciphers.

Step three: The attacker takes the 2^d possible ciphertexts, C_i, and asks a decryption-oracle to provide the matching plaintexts, P_i.

Step four: The attacker chooses an internal state, S_j and the corresponding plaintext, P_i, and performs the usual MITM attack over f and g by attacking from the internal state and the plaintext.

Step five: Whenever a key-candidate is found that matches S_j with P_i, that key is tested on another plain-/ciphertext pair. If the key validates on the other pair, it is highly likely that it is the correct key.

The following example is based on the biclique attack on AES. The descriptions in the example uses the same terminology that the authors of the attack used (i.e. for variable names, etc). For simplicity it is the attack on the AES128 variant that is covered below. The attack consists of a 7-round MITM attack with the biclique covering the last 3 rounds.

Key Partitioning

The key-space is partitioned into 2^{112} groups of keys, where each group consist of 2^{16} keys. For each of the 2^{112} groups, a unique base-key $K[0,0]$ for the base-computation is selected. The base-key has two specific bytes set to zero, shown in the below table (which represents the key the same way AES does in a 4x4 matrix for AES128):

$$
\begin{bmatrix}
- & - & - & 0 \\
0 & - & - & - \\
- & - & - & - \\
- & - & - & -
\end{bmatrix}
$$

The remaining 14 bytes (112 bits) of the key is then enumerated. This yields 2^{112} unique base-keys; one for each group of keys. The ordinary 2^{16} keys in each group is then chosen with respect to their base-key. They are chosen such that they are nearly identical to the base-key. They only vary in 2 bytes (either the i's or the j's) of the below shown 4 bytes:

$$
\begin{bmatrix}
- & - & i & i \\
j & - & j & - \\
- & - & - & - \\
- & - & - & -
\end{bmatrix}
$$

This gives $2^8 K[i,0]$ and $2^8 K[0,j]$, which combined gives 2^{16} different keys, $K[i,j]$. These 2^{16} keys constitute the keys in the group for a respective base key.

Biclique Construction

2^{112} bicliques is constructed using the "Independent related-key differentials" technique. The requirement for using that technique, was that the forward- and backward-differential trails that need to be combined, did not share any active non-linear elements. How is it known that this is the case? Due to the way the keys in step 1 is chosen in relation to the base key, the differential trails Δ_i using the keys $K[i,0]$ never share any active S-boxes (which is the only non-linear component in AES), with the differential trails ∇_j using the key $K[0,j]$. It is therefore possible to XOR the differential trails and create the biclique.

MITM Attack

When the bicliques are created, the MITM attack can almost begin. Before doing the MITM attack, the 2^d intermediate values from the plaintext:

$$P_i \xrightarrow{\;K[i,0]\;} \xrightarrow[v_i]{\;\;\;\;} ,$$

the 2^d intermediate values from the ciphertext:

$$\xleftarrow[v_j]{\;\;\;\;} \xleftarrow{\;K[0,j]\;} S_j ,$$

and the corresponding intermediate states and sub-keys $K[i,0]$ or $K[0,j]$, are precomputed and stored, however.

Now the MITM attack can be carried out. In order to test a key $K[i,j]$, It is only necessary to recalculate the parts of the cipher, which is known will vary between $P_i \xrightarrow{\;K[i,0]\;} \xrightarrow[v_i]{\;\;}$ and $P_i \xrightarrow{\;K[i,j]\;} \xrightarrow[v_i]{\;\;}$. For the backward computation from S_j to $\xleftarrow[v_j]{\;\;}$, this is 4 S-boxes that needs to be recomputed. For the forwards computation from P_i to $\xrightarrow[v_i]{\;\;}$, it is just 3.

When the intermediate values match, a key-candidate $K[i,j]$ between P_i and S_j is found. The key-candidate is then tested on another plain-/ciphertext pair.

Results

This attack lowers the computational complexity of AES128 to $2^{126.18}$, which is 3–5 times faster than a bruteforce approach. The data complexity of the attack is 2^{88} and the memory complexity is 2^8.

Length Extension Attack

In cryptography and computer security, a length extension attack is a type of attack where an attacker can use Hash ($message_1$) and the length of $message_1$ to calculate Hash($message_1 \parallel message_2$) for an attacker-controlled $message_2$, without needing to know the content of $message_1$. Algorithms like MD5, SHA-1, and SHA-2 that are based on the Merkle–Damgård construction are susceptible to this kind of attack. The SHA-3 algorithm is not susceptible.

When a Merkle–Damgård based hash is misused as a message authentication code with construction H(*secret* ‖ *message*), and *message* and the length of *secret* is known, a length extension attack allows anyone to include extra information at the end of the message and produce a valid hash without knowing the secret. Note that since HMAC doesn't use this construction, HMAC hashes are not prone to length extension attacks.

The vulnerable hashing functions work by taking the input message, and using it to transform an internal state. After all of the input has been processed, the hash digest is generated by outputting the internal state of the function. It is possible to reconstruct the internal state from the hash digest, which can then be used to process the new data. In this way, one may extend the message and compute the hash that is a valid signature for the new message.

Example:

A server for delivering waffles of a specified type to a specific user at a location could be implemented to handle requests of the given format.

```
Original Data: count=10&lat=37.351&user_id=1&long=-119.827&waffle=eggo
```

```
Original Signature: 6d5f807e23db210bc254a28be2d6759a0f5f5d99
```

The server would perform the request given (to deliver ten waffles of type eggo to the given location for user 1) only if the signature is valid for the user. The signature used here is a MAC, signed with a key not known to the attacker. (This example is also vulnerable to a replay attack, by sending the same request and signature a second time.)

It is possible for an attacker to modify the request, in this example switching the requested waffle from "eggo" to "liege." This can be done by taking advantage of a flexibility in the message format if duplicate content in the query string gives preference to the latter value. This flexibility does not indicate an exploit in the message format, because the message format was never designed to be cryptographically secure in the first place, without the signature algorithm to help it.

```
Desired New Data: count=10&lat=37.351&user_id=1&long=-119.827&waffle=eggo&waffle=liege
```

In order to sign this new message, typically the attacker would need to know the key the message was signed with, and generate a new signature by generating a new MAC. However, with a length extension attack, it is possible to feed the hash (the signature given above) into the state of the hashing function, and continue where the original request had left off, so long as you know the length of the original request. In this request, the original key's length was 14 bytes, which could be determined by trying forged requests with various assumed lengths, and checking which length results in a request that the server accepts as valid.

The message as fed into the hashing function is often padded, as many algorithms can only work on input messages whose lengths are a multiple of some given size. The content of this padding is always specified by the hash function used. The attacker must include all of these padding bits in their forged message before the internal states of their message and the original will line up. Thus, the attacker constructs a slightly different message using these padding rules:

```
New Data: count=10&lat=37.351&user_id=1&long=-119.827&waffle=eggo\x80\x00\x00

          \x00\x00\x00\x00\x00\x00\x00\x00\x00\x00\x00\x00\x00\x00\x00\x00
```

```
\x00\x00\x00\x00\x00\x00\x00\x00\x00\x00\x00\x00\x00\x00\x00\x00\x00

\x00\x00\x00\x00\x00\x00\x00\x00\x00\x00\x00\x00\x00\x00\x00\x00\x00

\x00\x00\x02\x28&waffle=liege
```

This message includes all of the padding that was appended to the original message inside of the hash function before their payload (in this case, a 0x80 followed by a number of 0x00s and a message length, 0x228 = 552 = (14+55)*8, which is the length of the key plus the original message, appended at the end). The attacker knows that the state behind the hashed key/message pair for the original message is identical to that of new message up to the final "&." The attacker also knows the hash digest at this point, which means they know the internal state of the hashing function at that point. It is then trivial to initialize a hashing algorithm at that point, input the last few characters, and generate a new digest which can sign their new message without the original key.

```
New Signature: 0e41270260895979317fff3898ab85668953aaa2
```

By combining the new signature and new data into a new request, the server will see the forged request as a valid request due to the signature being the same as it would have been generated if the password was known.

Man-in-the-middle Attack

In cryptography and computer security, a man-in-the-middle attack (MITM) is an attack where the attacker secretly relays and possibly alters the communications between two parties who believe they are directly communicating with each other. One example of a MITM attack is active eavesdropping, in which the attacker makes independent connections with the victims and relays messages between them to make them believe they are talking directly to each other over a private connection, when in fact the entire conversation is controlled by the attacker. The attacker must be able to intercept all relevant messages passing between the two victims and inject new ones. This is straightforward in many circumstances; for example, an attacker within reception range of an unencrypted wireless access point (Wi-Fi) could insert themselves as a man-in-the-middle.

As it aims to circumvent mutual authentication, a MITM attack can succeed only when the attacker impersonates each endpoint sufficiently well to satisfy their expectations. Most cryptographic protocols include some form of endpoint authentication specifically to prevent MITM attacks. For example, TLS can authenticate one or both parties using a mutually trusted certificate authority.

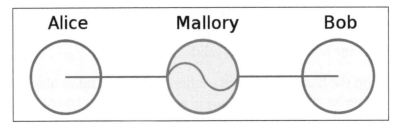

An illustration of the man-in-the-middle attack.

Suppose Alice wishes to communicate with Bob. Meanwhile, Mallory wishes to intercept the conversation to eavesdrop and optionally to deliver a false message to Bob.

First, Alice asks Bob for his public key. If Bob sends his public key to Alice, but Mallory is able to intercept it, an MITM attack can begin. Mallory sends Alice a forged message that appears to originate from Bob, but instead includes Mallory's public key.

Alice, believing this public key to be Bob's, encrypts her message with Mallory's key and sends the enciphered message back to Bob. Mallory again intercepts, deciphers the message using her private key, possibly alters it if she wants, and re-enciphers it using the public key she intercepted from Bob when he originally tried to send it to Alice. When Bob receives the newly enciphered message, he believes it came from Alice.

1. Alice sends a message to Bob, which is intercepted by Mallory:

   Alice *"Hi Bob, it's Alice. Give me your key."* → Mallory Bob

2. Mallory relays this message to Bob; Bob cannot tell it is not really from Alice:

   Alice Mallory *"Hi Bob, it's Alice. Give me your key."* → Bob

3. Bob responds with his encryption key:

   Alice Mallory ← *[Bob's key]* Bob

4. Mallory replaces Bob's key with her own, and relays this to Alice, claiming that it is Bob's key:

   Alice ← *[Mallory's key]* Mallory Bob

5. Alice encrypts a message with what she believes to be Bob's key, thinking that only Bob can read it:

   Alice *"Meet me at the bus stop!"* *[encrypted with Mallory's key]* → Mallory Bob

6. However, because it was actually encrypted with Mallory's key, Mallory can decrypt it, read it, modify it (if desired), re-encrypt with Bob's key, and forward it to Bob:

   Alice Mallory *"Meet me at the van down by the river!"* *[encrypted with Bob's key]* → Bob

7. Bob thinks that this message is a secure communication from Alice.

This example shows the need for Alice and Bob to have some way to ensure that they are truly each using each other's public keys, rather than the public key of an attacker. Otherwise, such attacks are generally possible, in principle, against any message sent using public-key technology. A variety of techniques can help defend against MITM attacks.

Defense and Detection

MITM attacks can be prevented or detected by two means: authentication and tamper detection. Authentication provides some degree of certainty that a given message has come from a legitimate source. Tamper detection merely shows evidence that a message may have been altered.

Authentication

All cryptographic systems that are secure against MITM attacks provide some method of authentication for messages. Most require an exchange of information (such as public keys) in addition to the message over a secure channel. Such protocols, often using key-agreement protocols, have been developed with different security requirements for the secure channel, though some have attempted to remove the requirement for any secure channel at all.

A public key infrastructure, such as Transport Layer Security, may harden Transmission Control Protocol against MITM attacks. In such structures, clients and servers exchange certificates which are issued and verified by a trusted third party called a certificate authority (CA). If the original key to authenticate this CA has not been itself the subject of a MITM attack, then the certificates issued by the CA may be used to authenticate the messages sent by the owner of that certificate. Use of mutual authentication, in which both the server and the client validate the other's communication, covers both ends of a MITM attack, though the default behavior of most connections is to only authenticate the server.

Attestments, such as verbal communications of a shared value (as in ZRTP), or recorded attestments such as audio/visual recordings of a public key hash are used to ward off MITM attacks, as visual media is much more difficult and time-consuming to imitate than simple data packet communication. However, these methods require a human in the loop in order to successfully initiate the transaction.

In a corporate environment, successful authentication (as indicated by the browser's green padlock) does not always imply secure connection with the remote server. Corporate security policies might contemplate the addition of custom certificates in workstations' web browsers in order to be able to inspect encrypted traffic. As a consequence, a green padlock does not indicate that the client has successfully authenticated with the remote server but just with the corporate server/ proxy used for SSL/TLS inspection.

HTTP Public Key Pinning (HPKP), sometimes called "certificate pinning," helps prevent a MITM attack in which the certificate authority itself is compromised, by having the server provide a list of "pinned" public key hashes during the first transaction. Subsequent transactions then require one or more of the keys in the list must be used by the server in order to authenticate that transaction.

DNSSEC extends the DNS protocol to use signatures to authenticate DNS records, preventing simple MITM attacks from directing a client to a malicious IP address.

Tamper Detection

Latency examination can potentially detect the attack in certain situations, such as with long calculations that lead into tens of seconds like hash functions. To detect potential attacks, parties check for discrepancies in response times. For example: Say that two parties normally take a certain amount of time to perform a particular transaction. If one transaction, however, were to take an abnormal length of time to reach the other party, this could be indicative of a third party's interference inserting additional latency in the transaction.

Quantum Cryptography, in theory, provides tamper-evidence for transactions through the no-cloning theorem. Protocols based on quantum cryptography typically authenticate part or all of their classical communication with an unconditionally secure authentication scheme e.g. Wegman-Carter authentication.

Forensic Analysis

Captured network traffic from what is suspected to be an attack can be analyzed in order to determine whether or not there was an attack and determine the source of the attack, if any. Important evidence to analyze when performing network forensics on a suspected attack includes:

- IP address of the server

- DNS name of the server

- X.509 certificate of the server

  - Is the certificate self signed?

  - Is the certificate signed by a trusted CA?

  - Has the certificate been revoked?

  - Has the certificate been changed recently?

  - Do other clients, elsewhere on the Internet, also get the same certificate?

Notable Instances

A notable non-cryptographic MITM attack was perpetrated by a Belkin wireless network router in 2003. Periodically, it would take over an HTTP connection being routed through it: this would fail to pass the traffic on to destination, but instead itself responded as the intended server. The reply it sent, in place of the web page the user had requested, was an advertisement for another Belkin product. After an outcry from technically literate users, this 'feature' was removed from later versions of the router's firmware.

In 2011, a security breach of the Dutch certificate authority DigiNotar resulted in the fraudulent issuing of certificates. Subsequently, the fraudulent certificates were used to perform MITM attacks.

In 2013, the Nokia's Xpress Browser was revealed to be decrypting HTTPS traffic on Nokia's proxy servers, giving the company clear text access to its customers' encrypted browser traffic. Nokia responded by saying that the content was not stored permanently, and that the company had organizational and technical measures to prevent access to private information.

In 2017, Equifax withdrew its mobile phone apps following concern about MITM vulnerabilities.

Other notable real-life implementations include the following:

- DSniff – the first public implementation of MITM attacks against SSL and SSH

- Fiddler2 HTTP(S) diagnostic tool

- NSA impersonation of Google

- Superfish malware

- Forcepoint Content Gateway – used to perform inspection of SSL traffic at the proxy

- Comcast uses MITM attacks to inject JavaScript code to 3rd party web pages, showing their own ads and messages on top of the pages.

Coppersmith's Attack

Coppersmith's attack describes a class of cryptographic attacks on the public-key cryptosystem RSA based on the Coppersmith method. Particular applications of the Coppersmith method for attacking RSA include cases when the public exponent e is small or when partial knowledge of the secret key is available.

RSA Basics

The public key in the RSA system is a tuple of integers (N, e), where N is the product of two primes p and q. The secret key is given by an integer d satisfying $ed \equiv 1 (\mod(p-1)(q-1))$; equivalently, the secret key may be given by $d_p \equiv d(\mod p-1)$ and $d_q \equiv d(\mod q-1)$ if the Chinese remainder theorem is used to improve the speed of decryption. Encryption of a message M produces the ciphertext $C \equiv M^e (\mod N)$ which can be decrypted using d by computing $C^d \equiv M(\mod N)$.

Low Public Exponent Attack

In order to reduce encryption or signature-verification time, it is useful to use a small public exponent (e). In practice, common choices for e are 3, 17 and 65537 $(2^{16}+1)$. These values for e are Fermat primes, sometimes referred to as F_0, F_2 and F_4 respectively $(F_x = 2^{2^x}+1)$. They are chosen because they make the modular exponentiation operation faster. Also, having chosen such e, it is simpler to test whether $\gcd(e, p-1) = 1$ and $\gcd(e, q-1) = 1$ while generating and testing the primes in step 1 of the key generation. Values of p or q that fail this test can be rejected there and then. (Even better: if e is prime and greater than 2 then the test $p \mod e \neq 1$ can replace the more expensive test $\gcd(p-1, e) = 1$.)

If the public exponent is small and the plaintext m is very short, then the RSA function may be easy to invert which makes certain attacks possible. Padding schemes ensure that messages have full lengths but additionally choosing public exponent $e = 2^{16}+1$ is recommended. When this value is used, signature-verification requires 17 multiplications, as opposed to about 25 when a random e of similar size is used. Unlike low private exponent, attacks that apply when a small e is used are far from a total break which would recover the secret key d. The most powerful attacks on low public exponent RSA are based on the following theorem which is due to Don Coppersmith.

Coppersmith Method

Theorem (Coppersmith):

Let N be an integer and $f \in \mathbb{Z}[x]$ be a monic polynomial of degree d over the integers. Set $X = N^{\frac{1}{d}-\epsilon}$

for $\frac{1}{d} > \epsilon > 0$. Then, given $\langle N, f \rangle$ attacker, Eve, can efficiently find all integers $x_0 < X$ satisfying

$f(x_0) \equiv 0 \pmod{N}$. The running time is dominated by the time it takes to run the LLL algorithm on a lattice of dimension $\mathrm{O}(w)$ with $w = \min\left\{\dfrac{1}{\epsilon}, \log_2 N\right\}$.

This theorem states the existence of an algorithm which can efficiently find all roots of f modulo N that are smaller than. $X = N^{\frac{1}{d}}$. As X gets smaller, the algorithm's runtime will decrease. This theorem's strength is the ability to find all small roots of polynomials modulo a composite N.

Håstad's Broadcast Attack

The simplest form of Håstad's attack is presented to ease understanding. The general case uses the Coppersmith method.

Suppose one sender sends the same message M in encrypted form to a number of people $P_1; P_2; \ldots; P_k$, each using the same small public exponent e, say $e = 3$, and different moduli $\langle N_i, e \rangle$. A simple argument shows that as soon as $k \geq 3$ ciphertexts are known, the message M is no longer secure: Suppose Eve intercepts $C_1, C_2,$ and C_3, where $C_i \equiv M^3 \pmod{N_i}$. We may assume $\gcd(N_i, N_j) = 1$ for all i, j (otherwise, it is possible to compute a factor of one of the N_i's by computing $\gcd(N_i, N_j)$.) By the Chinese Remainder Theorem, she may compute $C \in \mathbb{Z}^*_{N_1 N_2 N_3}$ such that $C \equiv C_i \pmod{N_i}$. Then $C \equiv M^3 \pmod{N_1 N_2 N_3}$; however, since $M < N_i$ for all i', we have $M^3 < N_1 N_2 N_3$. Thus $C = M^3$ holds over the integers, and Eve can compute the cube root of C to obtain.

For larger values of e more ciphertexts are needed, particularly, e ciphertexts are sufficient.

Generalizations

Håstad also showed that applying a linear-padding to M prior to encryption does not protect against this attack. Assume the attacker learns that $C_i = f_i(M)^e$ for $1 \leq i \leq k$ and some linear function f_i, i.e., Bob applies a pad to the message M prior to encrypting it so that the recipients receive slightly different messages. For instance, if M is m bits long, Bob might encrypt $M_i = i 2^m + M$ and send this to the i-th recipient.

If a large enough group of people is involved, the attacker can recover the plaintext M_i from all the ciphertext with similar methods. In more generality, Håstad proved that a system of univariate equations modulo relatively prime composites, such as applying any fixed polynomial $g_i(M) \equiv 0 \pmod{N_i}$, could be solved if sufficiently many equations are provided. This attack suggests that randomized padding should be used in RSA encryption.

Theorem (Håstad):

Suppose $N_1, \ldots, N_k$ are relatively prime integers and set $N_{\min} = \min_i\{N_i\}$. Let $g_i(x) \in \mathbb{Z} / N_i[x]$ be k polynomials of maximum degree q. Suppose there exists a unique $M < N_{\min}$ satisfying $g_i(M) \equiv 0 \pmod{N_i}$ for all $i \in \{1, \ldots, k\}$. Furthermore, suppose $k > q$. There is an efficient algorithm which, given $\langle N_i, g_i(x) \rangle$ for all i, computes M.

Proof:

Since the N_i are relatively prime the Chinese Remainder Theorem might be used to compute co-efficients T_i satisfying $T_i \equiv 1 (\mathrm{mod}\, N_i)$ and $T_i \equiv 0 (\mathrm{mod}\, N_j)$ for all $i \neq j$. Setting $g(x) = \sum T_i \cdot g_i(x)$ we know that $g(M) \equiv 0 (\mathrm{mod}\, \prod N_i)$. Since the T_i are nonzero we have that $g(x)$ is also non-zero. The degree of $g(x)$ is at most q. By Coppersmith's Theorem, we may compute all integer roots x_0 satisfying $g(x_0) \equiv 0 (\mathrm{mod}\, \prod N_i)$ and $|x_0| < (\prod N_i)^{\frac{1}{q}}$. However, we know that $M < N_{\min} < (\prod N_i)^{\frac{1}{k}} < (\prod N_i)^{\frac{1}{q}}$, so M is among the roots found by Coppersmith's theorem.

This theorem can be applied to the problem of broadcast RSA in the following manner: Suppose the -th plaintext is padded with a polynomial $f_i(x)$, so that $g_i = (f_i(x))^{e_i} - C_i \,\mathrm{mod}\, N_i$. Then $g_i(M) \equiv 0\,\mathrm{mod}\,N_i$ is true, and Coppersmith's method can be used. The attack succeeds once $k > \max_i(e_i \cdot \deg f_i)$, where k is the number of messages. The original result used Håstad's variant instead of the full Coppersmith method. As a result, it required $k = O(q^2)$ messages, where $q = \max_i(e_i \deg f_i)$.

Franklin-Reiter Related-message Attack

Franklin-Reiter identified a new attack against RSA with public exponent $e = 3$. If two messages differ only by a known fixed difference between the two messages and are RSA encrypted under the same RSA modulus N, then it is possible to recover both of them.

Let $\langle N; e_i \rangle$ be Alice's public key. Suppose $M_1; M_2 \in \mathbb{Z}_N$ are two distinct messages satisfying $M_1 \equiv f(M_2)(\mathrm{mod}\, N)$ for some publicly known polynomial $f \in \mathbb{Z}_N[x]$. To send M_1 and M_2 to Alice, Bob may naively encrypt the messages and transmit the resulting ciphertexts $C_1; C_2$. Eve can easily recover $M_1; M_2$ given $C_1; C_2$, by using the following theorem.

Theorem (Franklin-Reiter):

Set $e = 3$ and let $\langle N, e \rangle$ be an RSA public key. Let $M_1 \neq M_2 \in \mathbb{Z}_N^*$ satisfy $M_1 \equiv f(M_2)(\mathrm{mod}\, N)$ for some linear polynomial $f = ax + b \in \mathbb{Z}_N[x]$ with $b \neq 0$. Then, given $\langle N, e, C_1, C_2, f \rangle$, attacker, Eve, can recover M_1, M_2 in time quadratic in $\log_2 N$.

For an arbitrary e (rather than restricting to $e = 3$) the time required is quadratic in e and $\log_2 N$.

Proof:

Since $C_1 \equiv M_1^e(\mathrm{mod}\, N)$, we know that M_2 is a root of the polynomial $g_1(x) = f(x)^e - C_1 \in \mathbb{Z}_N[x]$. Similarly, M_2 is a root of $g_2(x) = x^e - C_2 \in \mathbb{Z}_N[x]$. The linear factor $x - M_2$ divides both polynomials. Therefore, Eve calculates the greatest common divisor (gcd) of g_1 and   , if the gcd turns out to be linear, M_2 is found. The *gcd* can be computed in quadratic time in e and $\log_2 N$ using the Euclidean algorithm.

Coppersmith's Short-pad Attack

Like Håstad's and Franklin-Reiter's attack, this attack exploits a weakness of RSA with public exponent $e = 3$. Coppersmith showed that if randomized padding suggested by Håstad is used improperly then RSA encryption is not secure.

Suppose Bob sends a message M to Alice using a small random padding before encrypting it. An attacker, Eve, intercepts the ciphertext and prevents it from reaching its destination. Bob decides to resend M to Alice because Alice did not respond to his message. He randomly pads M again and transmits the resulting ciphertext. Eve now has two ciphertexts corresponding to two encryptions of the same message using two different random pads.

Even though Eve does not know the random pad being used, she still can recover the message M by using the following theorem, if the random padding is too short.

Theorem (Coppersmith):

Let $\langle N, e \rangle$ be a public RSA key where N is n-bits long. Set $m = \left\lfloor \dfrac{n}{e^2} \right\rfloor$. Let $M \in \mathbb{Z}_N^*$ be a message of length at most $n - m$ bits. Define $M_1 = 2^m M + r_1$ and $M_2 = 2^m M + r_2$, where r_1 and r_2 are distinct integers with $0 \le r_1, r_2 < 2^m$. If Eve is given $\langle N, e \rangle$ and the encryptions C_1, C_2 of M_1, M_2 (but is not given r_1 or r_2), she can efficiently recover M.

Proof:

Define $g_1(x, y) = x^e - C_1$ and $g_2(x, y) = (x + y)^e - C_2$. We know that when $y = r_2 - r_1$, these polynomials have $x = M_1$ as a common root. In other words, $\Delta = r_2 - r_1$ is a root of the resultant $h(y) = \text{res}_x(g_1, g_2) \in \mathbb{Z}_N[y]$. Furthermore, $|\Delta| < 2^m < N^{\frac{1}{e^2}}$. Hence, Δ is a small root of h modulo N, and Eve can efficiently find it using the Coppersmith method. Once Δ is known, the Franklin-Reiter attack can be used to recover M_2 and consequently M.

Wiener's Attack

The Wiener's attack, named after cryptologist Michael J. Wiener, is a type of cryptographic attack against RSA. The attack uses the continued fraction method to expose the private key d when d is small.

Fictional characters Alice and Bob are people who want to communicate securely. More specifically, Alice wants to send a message to Bob which only Bob can read. First Bob chooses two primes p and q. Then he calculates the RSA modulus $N = pq$. This RSA modulus is made public together with the encryption exponent e. N and e form the public key pair (e,N). By making this information public, anyone can encrypt messages to Bob. The decryption exponent d satisfies $ed = 1 \bmod \lambda(N)$, where $\lambda(N)$ denotes the Carmichael function, though sometimes $\varphi(N)$, the Euler's phi function, is used (this is the order of the multiplicative group $\mathbb{Z}_N^*$, which is not necessarily a cyclic group). The encryption exponent e and $\lambda(N)$ also must be relatively prime so that there is a modular inverse. The factorization of N and the private key d are kept secret, so that only Bob can decrypt the message. We denote the private key pair as *(d, N)*. The encryption of the message M is given by $C \equiv M^e \bmod N$ and the decryption of cipher text C is given by $C^d \equiv (M^e)^d \equiv M^{(ed)} \equiv M \bmod N$ (using Fermat's little theorem).

Using the Euclidean algorithm, one can efficiently recover the secret key d if one knows the factorization of N. By having the secret key d, one can efficiently factor the modulus of N.

Small Private Key

In the RSA cryptosystem, Bob might tend to use a small value of d, rather than a large random number to improve the RSA decryption performance. However, Wiener's attack shows that choosing a small value for d will result in an insecure system in which an attacker can recover all secret information, i.e., break the RSA system. This break is based on Wiener's Theorem, which holds for small values of d. Wiener has proved that the attacker may efficiently find d when $d < \frac{1}{3} N^{\frac{1}{4}}$.

Some countermeasures against his attack that allow fast decryption. Two techniques are described as follows.

Choosing large public key: Replace e by e', where $e' = e + k \cdot \lambda(N)$ for some large of. When k is large enough, i.e. $e' > N^{\frac{3}{2}}$, then Wiener's attack can not be applied regardless of how small d is.

Using the Chinese Remainder Theorem: Suppose one chooses d such that both $d_p = d \bmod (p-1)$ and $d_q = d \bmod (q-1)$ are small but d itself is not, then a fast decryption of C can be done as follows:

1. First compute $M_p \equiv C^{d_p} \bmod p$ and $M_q \equiv C^{d_q} \bmod q$.

2. Use the Chinese Remainder Theorem to compute the unique value of $M \in \mathbb{Z}_N$ which satisfies $M \equiv M_p \bmod p$ and $M \equiv M_q \bmod q$. The result of M satisfies $M \equiv C^d \bmod N$ as needed. The point is that Wiener's attack does not apply here because the value of $d \bmod \lambda(N)$ can be large.

How Wiener's Attack Works

Note that

$$\lambda(N) = \mathrm{lcm}(p-1, q-1) = \frac{(p-1)(q-1)}{G} = \frac{\varphi(N)}{G}$$

where $G = \gcd(p-1, q-1)$.

Since,

$$ed \equiv 1 \left(\bmod \lambda(N) \right),$$

there exists an integer K such that:

$$ed = K \times \lambda(N) + 1$$

$$ed = \frac{K}{G}(p-1)(q-1)+1$$

Defining $k = \dfrac{K}{\gcd(K,G)}$ and $g = \dfrac{G}{\gcd(K,G)}$, and substituting into the above gives:

$$ed = \frac{k}{g}(p-1)(q-1)+1.$$

Divided by dpq:

$$\frac{e}{pq} = \frac{k}{dg}(1-\delta), \text{ where } \delta = \frac{p+q-1-\frac{g}{k}}{pq}.$$

So, $\dfrac{e}{pq}$ is slightly smaller than $\dfrac{k}{dg}$, and the former is composed entirely of public information.

However, a method of checking a guess is still required. Assuming that $ed > pq$ (a reasonable assumption unless G is large) the last equation above may be written as:

$$edg = k(p-1)(q-1)+g$$

By using simple algebraic manipulations and identities, a guess can be checked for accuracy.

Wiener's Theorem

Let $N = pq$ with $q < p < 2q$. Let $d < \dfrac{1}{3}N^{\frac{1}{4}}$.

Given $\langle N,e \rangle$ with $ed \equiv 1 \,(\mathrm{mod}\ \lambda(N))$, the attacker can efficiently recover d.

Example:

Suppose that the public keys are $\langle N,e \rangle = \langle 90581, 17993 \rangle$

The attack shall determine d.

By using Wiener's Theorem and continued fractions to approximate d, first we try to find the continued fractions expansion of $\dfrac{e}{N}$. Note that this algorithm finds fractions in their lowest terms. We know that:

$$\frac{e}{N} = \frac{17993}{90581} = \cfrac{1}{5+\cfrac{1}{29+\ldots+\cfrac{1}{3}}} = [0,5,29,4,1,3,2,4,3]$$

According to the continued fractions expansion of $\dfrac{e}{N}$, all convergents $\dfrac{k}{d}$ are:

$$\frac{k}{d} = 0, \frac{1}{5}, \frac{29}{146}, \frac{117}{589}, \frac{146}{735}, \frac{555}{2794}, \frac{1256}{6323}, \frac{5579}{28086}, \frac{17993}{90581}$$

We can verify that the first convergent does not produce a factorization of N. However, the convergent $\frac{1}{5}$ yields:

$$\varphi(N) = \frac{ed-1}{k} = \frac{17993 \times 5 - 1}{1} = 89964$$

Now, if we solve the equation:

$$x^2 - \left((N - \varphi(N)) + 1\right)x + N = 0$$

$$x - \left((90581 - 89964) + 1\right)x + 90581 = 0$$

$$x^2 - (618)x + 90581 = 0$$

then we find the roots which are $x = 379; 239$. Therefore we have found the factorization:

$$N = 90581 = 379 \times 239 = p \times q.$$

Notice that, for the modulus $N = 90581$, Wiener's Theorem will work if:

$$d < \frac{N^{\frac{1}{4}}}{3} \approx 5.7828 \cdot$$

Proof of Wiener's Theorem

The proof is based on approximations using continued fractions.

Since $ed = 1 \bmod \lambda(N)$, there exists a k such that $ed - k\lambda(N) = 1$. Therefore

$$\left| \frac{e}{\lambda(N)} - \frac{k}{d} \right| = \frac{1}{d\lambda(N)}.$$

Let $G = \gcd(p-1, q-1)$, note that if $\varphi(N)$ is used instead of $\lambda(N)$, then the proof can be replaced with $G = 1$ and $\varphi(N)$ replaced with $\lambda(N)$.

Then multiplying by —,

$$\left| \frac{e}{\varphi(N)} - \frac{k}{Gd} \right| = \frac{1}{d\varphi(N)}$$

Hence, $\frac{k}{Gd}$ is an approximation of $\frac{e}{\varphi(N)}$. Although the attacker does not know $\varphi(N)$, he may use N to approximate it. Indeed, since

$\varphi(N) = N - p - q + 1$ and $p + q - 1 < 3\sqrt{N}$, we have:

$$\left| p + q - 1 \right| < 3\sqrt{N}$$

$$|N - \varphi(N)| < 3\sqrt{N}$$

Using N in place of $\varphi(N)$ we obtain:

$$\left| \frac{e}{N} - \frac{k}{Gd} \right| = \left| \frac{edG - kN}{NGd} \right|$$

$$= \left| \frac{edG - k\varphi(N) - kN + k\varphi(N)}{NGd} \right|$$

$$= \left| \frac{1 - k(N - \varphi(N))}{NGd} \right|$$

$$\leq \left| \frac{3k\sqrt{N}}{NGd} \right| = \frac{3k\sqrt{N}}{\sqrt{N}\sqrt{N}Gd} \leq \frac{3k}{d\sqrt{N}}$$

Now, $k\lambda(N) = ed - 1 < ed$, so $k\lambda(N) < ed$. Since $e < \lambda(N)$, so $k\lambda(N) < ed < \lambda(N)d$, then we obtain:

$$k\lambda(N) < \lambda(N)d$$

$$k < d$$

Since $k < d$ and $d < \frac{1}{3}N^{\frac{1}{4}}$. Hence we obtain:

$$\left| \frac{e}{N} - \frac{k}{Gd} \right| \leq \frac{1}{dN^{\frac{1}{4}}}$$

Since $d < \frac{1}{3}N^{\frac{1}{4}}, 2d < 3d$, then $2d < 3d < N^{-}$, we obtain:

$$2d < N^{\frac{1}{4}}, \text{ so } \frac{1}{2d} > \frac{1}{N^{\frac{1}{4}}}$$

From above two equations, we can conclude that:

$$\left| \frac{e}{N} - \frac{k}{Gd} \right| \leq \frac{3k}{d\sqrt{N}} < \frac{1}{d \cdot 2d} = \frac{1}{2d^2}$$

If $\left| x - \frac{a}{b} \right| < \frac{1}{2b^2}$, then $\frac{a}{b}$ is a convergent of x, thus $\frac{k}{d}$ appears among the convergents of $\frac{e}{N}$. Therefore the algorithm will indeed eventually find $\frac{k}{Gd}$.

Birthday Attack in Cryptography

Birthday attack is a type of cryptographic attack that belongs to a class of brute force attacks. It exploits the mathematics behind the birthday problem in probability theory. The success of this attack largely depends upon the higher likelihood of collisions found between random attack attempts and a fixed degree of permutations, as described in the birthday paradox problem.

Birthday Paradox Problem

Let us consider the example of a classroom of 30 students and a teacher. The teacher wishes to find pairs of students that have the same birthday. Hence the teacher asks for everyone's birthday to find such pairs. Intuitively this value may seem small. For example, if the teacher fixes a particular date say October 10, then the probability that at least one student is born on that day is $1 - (364/365)^{30}$ which is about 7.9%. However, the probability that at least one student have same birthday as any other student is around 70% using the following formula:

```
1 - 365!/((365 - n!) * (365ⁿ))  (substituting n = 70 here)
```

Derivation of The Above Term

Assumptions

1. Assuming a non leap year (hence 365 days).

2. Assuming that a person has equally likely chance of being born on any day of the year.

Let us consider n = 2.

P(Two people have the same birthday) = 1 – P(Two people having different birthday)

$$= 1 - (365*365)*(364*365)$$

$$= 1 - 1*(364/365)$$

$$= 1 - 364/365$$

$$= 1/365.$$

So for n people the probability that all of them have different birthday is:

P(N people having different birthdays) = $(365/365)*(365-1/365)*(365-2/365)*...(365-n+1)/365$.

$$= 365!/((365-n)! * 365ⁿ)$$

Hash Function

A hash function H is a transformation that takes a variable sized input mand returns a fixed size string called as hash value(h = H(m)). Hash functions chosen in cryptography must satisfy the following requirements:

- The input is of variable length,

- The output has a fixed length,

- H(x) is relatively easy to compute for any given x,

- H(x) is one-way,

- H(x) is collision-free.

A hash function H is said to be one-way if it is hard to invert, where "hard to invert" means that given a hash value h, it is computationally infeasible to find some input x such that H(x) = h.

If, given a message x, it is computationally infeasible to find a message y not equal to x such that H(x) = H(y) then H is said to be a weakly collision-free hash function.

A strongly collision-free hash function H is one for which it is computationally infeasible to find any two messages x and y such that H(x) = H(y).

Let $H: M \Rightarrow \{0, 1\}^n$ be a hash function ($|M| \gg 2^n$)

Following is a generic algorithm to find a collision in time $O(2^{n/2})$ hashes.

Algorithm:

1. Choose $2^{n/2}$ random messages in M: $m_1, m_2, m_{n/2}$

2. For i = 1, 2,..., $2^{n/2}$ compute ti = $H(m_i) \Rightarrow \{0, 1\}n$

3. Look for a collision ($t_i = t_j$). If not found, go back to step 1

We consider the following experiment. From a set of H values we choose n values uniformly at random thereby allowing repetitions. Let p(n; H) be the probability that during this experiment at least one value is chosen more than once. This probability can be approximated as:

$$p(n; H) = 1 - (\ (365\text{-}1)/365) * (365\text{-}2)/365) * ...(365\text{-}n\text{+}1/365))$$

$$p(n; H) = e^{-n(n-1)/(2H)} = e^{-n^2/(2H)}$$

Digital Signature Susceptibility

Digital signatures can be susceptible to birthday attack. A message m is typically signed by first computing H(m), where H is cryptographic hash function, and then using some secret key to sign H(m). Suppose Alice want to trick Bob into signing a fraudulent contract. Alice prepare a fair contract m and fraudulent one m'. She then finds a number of positions where m can be changed without changing the meaning, such as inserting commas, empty lines, one versus two spaces after a sentence, replacing synonyms etc. By combining these changes she can create a huge number of variations on m which are all fair contracts.

Similarly, Alice can also make some of these changes on m' to take it even more closer towards m, that is H(m) = H(m'). Hence, Alice can now present the fair version m to Bob for signing. After Bob has signed, Alice takes the signature and attaches to it the fraudulent contract. This signature proves that Bob has signed the fraudulent contract.

To avoid such an attack the output of hash function should be a very long sequence of bits such that birthday attack now becomes computationally infeasible.

References

- Cryptosystems, cryptography: tutorialspoint.com, Retrieved 3 February, 2019

- Keane, J. (13 January 2016). "Why stolen laptops still cause data breaches, and what's being done to stop them". Pcworld. IDG Communications, Inc. Retrieved 8 May 2018

- Decryption: defit.org, Retrieved 13 March, 2019

- Bek, E. (19 May 2016). "Protect Your Company from Theft: Self Encrypting Drives". Western Digital Blog. Western Digital Corporation. Retrieved 8 May2018

- Birthday-attack-in-cryptography: geeksforgeeks.org, Retrieved 1 January, 2019

- Pressestelle Ruhr-Universität Bochum - Online-Redaktion. "Startseite - Ruhr-Universität Bochum" (in German). Crypto.rub.de. Retrieved 2013-08-06

- Attacks-on-cryptosystems, cryptography: tutorialspoint.com, Retrieved 9 July, 2019

- "Security Policy and Key Management: Centrally Manage Encryption Key". Slideshare.net. 2012-08-13. Retrieved 2013-08-06

- Cracking DES – Secrets of Encryption Research, Wiretap Politics & Chip Design. Electronic Frontier Foundation. ISBN 1-56592-520-3

- Bellovin, Steven; Bush, Randy (February 2002), Security Through Obscurity Considered Dangerous, Internet Engineering Task Force (IETF), retrieved December 1, 2018

- Imad Khaled Salah; Abdullah Darwish; Saleh Oqeili (2006). "Mathematical Attacks on RSA Cryptosystem". Journal of Computer Science. 2 (8): 665–671. Doi:10.3844/jcssp.2006.665.671

Cryptographic Algorithms and Keys

Cryptographic algorithms are sets of well-defined mathematical instructions which are used to encrypt or decrypt data. Cryptographic keys refer to a string of data which is used to lock or unlock cryptographic functions. The chapter closely examines the key concepts of cryptographic algorithms and keys to provide an extensive understanding of the subject.

CRYPTOGRAPHIC ALGORITHM

Cryptographic algorithms are used for important tasks such as data encryption, authentication, and digital signatures, but one problem has to be solved to enable these algorithms: binding cryptographic keys to machine or user identities. Public key infrastructure (PKI) systems are built to bridge useful identities (email addresses, Domain Name System addresses, etc.) and the cryptographic keys used to authenticate or encrypt data passing among these identities.

Cryptographic algorithms are being applied in an increasing number of devices to satisfy their high security requirements. Many of these devices require high-speed operation and include specialized hardware encryption and/or decryption circuits for the selected cryptographic algorithm. A unique characteristic of these circuits is their very high sensitivity to faults. Unlike ordinary arithmetic/logic circuits such as adders and multipliers, even a single data bit fault in an encryption or decryption circuit will, in most cases, spread quickly and result in a totally scrambled output (an almost random pattern). There is, therefore, a need to prevent such faults or, at the minimum, be able to detect them.

Cryptographic algorithms are the most frequently used privacy protection method in the IoT domain. Many cryptographic tools have been applied in practice. Unfortunately, traditional encryption mechanisms with overly computational complexity cannot meet the new requirements for smart applications, especially for those systems that consist of many resource-constraint devices. Consequently, how to develop lightweight yet effective encryption algorithms is of significant practical value.

Homomorphic encryption (HE), as a method of performing calculations on encrypted information, has received increasing attention in recent years. The key function of it is to protect sensitive information from being exposed when performing computations on encrypted data. For example, Abdallah et al. developed a lightweight HE-based privacy protection data aggregation method for smart grids that can avoid involving the smart meter when aggregate readings are performed. Another work by Talpur et al. proposed an IoT network architecture based on HE technology for healthcare monitoring systems. Despite the great potential of HE methods, computational expense may restrict the application of this method.

Zero-knowledge proof is another cryptographic method that allows one party to prove something to other parties, without conveying additional information.

CUSTOM BUILDING CRYPTOGRAPHY ALGORITHMS

Cryptography is a very straightforward concept which deals with manipulating the strings (or text) to make them unreadable for the intermediate person. It has a very effective way to encrypt or decrypts the text coming from the other parties. Some of the examples are, Caesar Cipher, Viginere Cipher, Columner Cipher, DES, AES and the list continues. To develop custom cryptography algorithm, hybrid encryption algorithms can be used.

Hybrid Encryption is a concept in cryptography which combines/merge one/two cryptography algorithms to generate more effective encrypted text.

FibBil Cryptography Algorithm

Problem Statement:

Program to generate an encrypted text, by computing Fibonacci Series, adding the terms of Fibonacci Series with each plaintext letter, until the length of the key.

Algorithm:

For Encryption: Take an input plain text and key from the user, reverse the plain text and concatenate the plain text with the key, Copy the string into an array. After copying, separate the array elements into two parts, EvenArray, and OddArray in which even index of an array will be placed in EvenArray and same for OddArray. Start generating the Fibonacci Series F(i) up-to-the length of the key$_j$ such that c=i+j where c is cipher text with mod 26. Append all the cth elements in a CipherString and, so Encryption Done. When sum up concept is use, it highlights of implementing Caesar Cipher.

For Decryption: Vice Versa of the Encryption Algorithm.

Example for the Algorithm

Input: hello

Key: abcd

Output: riobkxezg

Reverse the input, olleh, append this with the key i.e. ollehabcd.

EvenString: leac

OddString: olhbd

As key length is 4, 4 times loop will be generated including FibNum 0, which is ignored.

For EvenArray Ciphers
FibNum: 1
In Even Array for l and FibNum 1 cip is k
In Even Array for e and FibNum 1 cip is d
In Even Array for a and FibNum 1 cip is z
In Even Array for c and FibNum 1 cip is b
FibNum: 2
In Even Array for l and FibNum 2 cip is j
In Even Array for e and FibNum 2 cip is c
In Even Array for a and FibNum 2 cip is y
In Even Array for c and FibNum 2 cip is a
FibNum: 3 (Final Computed letters)
In Even Array for l and FibNum 3 cip is i
In Even Array for e and FibNum 3 cip is b
In Even Array for a and FibNum 3 cip is x
In Even Array for c and FibNum 3 cip is z

For OddArray Ciphers
FibNum: 1
In Odd Array for o and FibNum 1 cip is p
In Odd Array for l and FibNum 1 cip is m
In Odd Array for h and FibNum 1 cip is i
In Odd Array for b and FibNum 1 cip is c
In Odd Array for d and FibNum 1 cip is e
FibNum: 2
In Odd Array for o and FibNum 2 cip is q
In Odd Array for l and FibNum 2 cip is n
In Odd Array for h and FibNum 2 cip is j
In Odd Array for b and FibNum 2 cip is d
In Odd Array for d and FibNum 2 cip is f
FibNum: 3 (Final Computed letters)
In Odd Array for o and FibNum 3 cip is r
In Odd Array for l and FibNum 3 cip is o
In Odd Array for h and FibNum 3 cip is k
In Odd Array for b and FibNum 3 cip is e

In Odd Array for d and FibNum 3 cip is g

Arrange EvenArrayCiphers and OddArrayCiphers in their index order, so final String Cipher will be, riobkxezg

Program

```java
import java.util.*;

import java.lang.*;


class GFG {


    public static void main(String[] args)

    {

        String pass = "hello";

        String key = "abcd";

        System.out.println(encryptText(pass, key));

    }

    public static String encryptText(String password, String key)

    {

        int a = 0, b = 1, c = 0, m = 0, k = 0, j = 0;

        String cipher = "", temp = "";


        // Declare a password string

        StringBuffer pw = new StringBuffer(password);


        // Reverse the String

        pw = pw.reverse();

        pw = pw.append(key);


        // For future Purpose

        temp = pw.toString();

        char stringArray[] = temp.toCharArray();

        String evenString = "", oddString = "";
```

```
// Declare EvenArray for storing
// even index of stringArray
char evenArray[];


// Declare OddArray for storing
// odd index of stringArray
char oddArray[];


// Storing the positions in their respective arrays
for (int i = 0; i < stringArray.length; i++) {
    if (i % 2 == 0) {
        oddString = oddString + Character.toString(stringArray[i]);
    }
    else {
        evenString = evenString + Character.toString(stringArray[i]);
    }
}
evenArray = new char[evenString.length()];
oddArray = new char[oddString.length()];


// Generate a Fibonacci Series
// Upto the Key Length
while (m <= key.length()) {
    // As it always starts with 1
    if (m == 0)
        m = 1;


    else {


        // Logic For Fibonacci Series
        a = b;
        b = c;
```

```
c = a + b;

for (int i = 0; i < evenString.length(); i++) {

    // Caesar Cipher Algorithm Start for even positions

    int p = evenString.charAt(i);

    int cip = 0;

    if (p == '0' || p == '1' || p == '2' || p == '3' || p == '4'

        || p == '5' || p == '6'

        || p == '7' || p == '8' || p == '9') {

        cip = p - c;

        if (cip < '0')

            cip = cip + 9;

    }

    else {

        cip = p - c;

        if (cip < 'a') {

            cip = cip + 26;

        }

    }

    evenArray[i] = (char)cip;

    /* Caesar Cipher Algorithm End*/

}

for (int i = 0; i < oddString.length(); i++) {

    // Caesar Cipher Algorithm Start for odd positions

    int p = oddString.charAt(i);

    int cip = 0;

    if (p == '0' || p == '1' || p == '2' || p == '3' || p == '4'

        || p == '5' || p == '6'

        || p == '7' || p == '8' || p == '9') {

        cip = p + c;

        if (cip > '9')

            cip = cip - 9;

    }
```

```
            else {

                cip = p + c;

                if (cip > 'z') {

                    cip = cip - 26;

                }

            }

            oddArray[i] = (char)cip;

            // Caesar Cipher Algorithm End

        }


        m++;

    }

}


// Storing content of even and
// odd array to the string array
for (int i = 0; i < stringArray.length; i++) {

    if (i % 2 == 0) {

        stringArray[i] = oddArray[k];

        k++;

    }

    else {

        stringArray[i] = evenArray[j];

        j++;

    }

}
// Generating a Cipher Text
// by stringArray (Caesar Cipher)
for (char d : stringArray) {

    cipher = cipher + d;

}
```

```
    // Return the Cipher Text

    return cipher;

  }

}
```

Output

```
riobkxezg
```

SYMMETRIC-KEY ALGORITHM

Symmetric-key algorithms are algorithms for cryptography that use the same cryptographic keys for both encryption of plaintext and decryption of ciphertext. The keys may be identical or there may be a simple transformation to go between the two keys. The keys, in practice, represent a shared secret between two or more parties that can be used to maintain a private information link. This requirement that both parties have access to the secret key is one of the main drawbacks of symmetric key encryption, in comparison to public-key encryption (also known as asymmetric key encryption).

Types

Symmetric-key encryption can use either stream ciphers or block ciphers.

- Stream ciphers encrypt the digits (typically bytes), or letters (in substitution ciphers) of a message one at a time. An example is the Vigenere Cipher.

- Block ciphers take a number of bits and encrypt them as a single unit, padding the plaintext so that it is a multiple of the block size. Blocks of 64 bits were commonly used. The Advanced Encryption Standard (AES) algorithm approved by NIST in December 2001, and the GCM block cipher mode of operation use 128-bit blocks.

Implementations

Examples of popular symmetric-key algorithms include Twofish, Serpent, AES (Rijndael), Blowfish, CAST5, Kuznyechik, RC4, DES, 3DES, Skipjack, Safer+/++ (Bluetooth), and IDEA.

Cryptographic Primitives based on Symmetric Ciphers

Symmetric ciphers are commonly used to achieve other cryptographic primitives than just encryption.

Encrypting a message does not guarantee that this message is not changed while encrypted. Hence often a message authentication code is added to a ciphertext to ensure that changes to the ciphertext will be noted by the receiver. Message authentication codes can be constructed from symmetric ciphers (e.g. CBC-MAC).

However, symmetric ciphers cannot be used for non-repudiation purposes except by involving additional parties.

Another application is to build hash functions from block ciphers.

Construction of Symmetric Ciphers

Many modern block ciphers are based on a construction proposed by Horst Feistel. Feistel's construction makes it possible to build invertible functions from other functions that are themselves not invertible.

Security of Symmetric Ciphers

Symmetric ciphers have historically been susceptible to known-plaintext attacks, chosen-plaintext attacks, differential cryptanalysis and linear cryptanalysis. Careful construction of the functions for each round can greatly reduce the chances of a successful attack.

Key Establishment

Symmetric-key algorithms require both the sender and the recipient of a message to have the same secret key. All early cryptographic systems required one of those people to somehow receive a copy of that secret key over a physically secure channel.

Nearly all modern cryptographic systems still use symmetric-key algorithms internally to encrypt the bulk of the messages, but they eliminate the need for a physically secure channel by using Diffie–Hellman key exchange or some other public-key protocol to securely come to agreement on a fresh new secret key for each message (forward secrecy).

Key Generation

When used with asymmetric ciphers for key transfer, pseudorandom key generators are nearly always used to generate the symmetric cipher session keys. However, lack of randomness in those generators or in their initialization vectors is disastrous and has led to cryptanalytic breaks in the past. Therefore, it is essential that an implementation uses a source of high entropy for its initialization.

Reciprocal Cipher

A reciprocal cipher is a cipher where, just as one enters the plaintext into the cryptography system to get the ciphertext, one could enter the ciphertext into the same place in the system to get the plaintext. A reciprocal cipher is also sometimes referred as self-reciprocal cipher. Examples of reciprocal ciphers include:

- Beaufort cipher
- Enigma machine
- ROT13

- XOR cipher

- Vatsyayana cipher

Stream Ciphers

A stream cipher is a symmetric key cipher where plaintext digits are combined with a pseudo-random cipher digit stream (keystream). In a stream cipher, each plaintext digit is encrypted one at a time with the corresponding digit of the keystream, to give a digit of the ciphertext stream. Since encryption of each digit is dependent on the current state of the cipher, it is also known as *state cipher*. In practice, a digit is typically a bit and the combining operation an exclusive-or (XOR).

The pseudorandom keystream is typically generated serially from a random seed value using digital shift registers. The seed value serves as the cryptographic key for decrypting the ciphertext stream. Stream ciphers represent a different approach to symmetric encryption from block ciphers. Block ciphers operate on large blocks of digits with a fixed, unvarying transformation. This distinction is not always clear-cut: in some modes of operation, a block cipher primitive is used in such a way that it acts effectively as a stream cipher. Stream ciphers typically execute at a higher speed than block ciphers and have lower hardware complexity. However, stream ciphers can be susceptible to serious security problems if used incorrectly; in particular, the same starting state (seed) must never be used twice.

Loose Inspiration from the One-time Pad

Stream ciphers can be viewed as approximating the action of a proven unbreakable cipher, the one-time pad (OTP), sometimes known as the Vernam cipher. A one-time pad uses a keystream of completely random digits. The keystream is combined with the plaintext digits one at a time to form the ciphertext. This system was proved to be secure by Claude E. Shannon in 1949. However, the keystream must be generated completely at random with at least the same length as the plaintext and cannot be used more than once. This makes the system cumbersome to implement in many practical applications, and as a result the one-time pad has not been widely used, except for the most critical applications. Key generation, distribution and management are critical for those applications.

A stream cipher makes use of a much smaller and more convenient key such as 128 bits. Based on this key, it generates a pseudorandom keystream which can be combined with the plaintext digits in a similar fashion to the one-time pad. However, this comes at a cost. The keystream is now pseudorandom and so is not truly random. The proof of security associated with the one-time pad no longer holds. It is quite possible for a stream cipher to be completely insecure.

Types

A stream cipher generates successive elements of the keystream based on an internal state. This state is updated in essentially two ways: if the state changes independently of the plaintext or ciphertext messages, the cipher is classified as a synchronous stream cipher. By contrast, self-synchronising stream ciphers update their state based on previous ciphertext digits.

Synchronous Stream Ciphers

Lorenz SZ cipher machine as used by the German military during World War II.

In a synchronous stream cipher a stream of pseudo-random digits is generated independently of the plaintext and ciphertext messages, and then combined with the plaintext (to encrypt) or the ciphertext (to decrypt). In the most common form, binary digits are used (bits), and the keystream is combined with the plaintext using the exclusive or operation (XOR). This is termed a binary additive stream cipher.

In a synchronous stream cipher, the sender and receiver must be exactly in step for decryption to be successful. If digits are added or removed from the message during transmission, synchronisation is lost. To restore synchronisation, various offsets can be tried systematically to obtain the correct decryption. Another approach is to tag the ciphertext with markers at regular points in the output.

If, however, a digit is corrupted in transmission, rather than added or lost, only a single digit in the plaintext is affected and the error does not propagate to other parts of the message. This property is useful when the transmission error rate is high; however, it makes it less likely the error would be detected without further mechanisms. Moreover, because of this property, synchronous stream ciphers are very susceptible to active attacks: if an attacker can change a digit in the ciphertext, he might be able to make predictable changes to the corresponding plaintext bit; for example, flipping a bit in the ciphertext causes the same bit to be flipped in the plaintext.

Self-synchronizing Stream Ciphers

Another approach uses several of the previous N ciphertext digits to compute the keystream. Such schemes are known as self-synchronizing stream ciphers, asynchronous stream ciphers or ciphertext autokey (CTAK). The idea of self-synchronization was patented in 1946, and has the advantage that the receiver will automatically synchronise with the keystream generator after receiving N ciphertext digits, making it easier to recover if digits are dropped or added to the message stream. Single-digit errors are limited in their effect, affecting only up to N plaintext digits.

An example of a self-synchronising stream cipher is a block cipher in cipher feedback (CFB) mode.

Based on Linear-feedback Shift Registers

Binary stream ciphers are often constructed using linear-feedback shift registers (LFSRs) because they can be easily implemented in hardware and can be readily analysed mathematically. The use of LFSRs on their own, however, is insufficient to provide good security. Various schemes have been proposed to increase the security of LFSRs.

Non-linear Combining Functions

Because LFSRs are inherently linear, one technique for removing the linearity is to feed the outputs of several parallel LFSRs into a non-linear Boolean function to form a *combination generator*. Various properties of such a *combining function* are critical for ensuring the security of the resultant scheme, for example, in order to avoid correlation attacks.

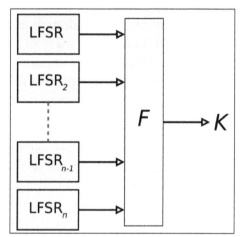

One approach is to use n LFSRs in parallel, their outputs combined using an n-input binary Boolean function (F).

Clock-controlled Generators

Normally LFSRs are stepped regularly. One approach to introducing non-linearity is to have the LFSR clocked irregularly, controlled by the output of a second LFSR. Such generators include the stop-and-go generator, the alternating step generator and the shrinking generator.

An alternating step generator comprises three LFSRs, which we will call LFSR0, LFSR1 and LFSR2 for convenience. The output of one of the registers decides which of the other two is to be used; for instance if LFSR2 outputs a 0, LFSR0 is clocked, and if it outputs a 1, LFSR1 is clocked instead. The output is the exclusive OR of the last bit produced by LFSR0 and LFSR1. The initial state of the three LFSRs is the key.

The stop-and-go generator (Beth and Piper, 1984) consists of two LFSRs. One LFSR is clocked if the output of a second is a 1, otherwise it repeats its previous output. This output is then (in some versions) combined with the output of a third LFSR clocked at a regular rate.

The shrinking generator takes a different approach. Two LFSRs are used, both clocked regularly. If the output of the first LFSR is 1, the output of the second LFSR becomes the output of the generator. If the first LFSR outputs 0, however, the output of the second is discarded, and no bit is output by the generator. This mechanism suffers from timing attacks on the second generator, since the speed of the output is variable in a manner that depends on the second generator's state. This can be alleviated by buffering the output.

Filter Generator

Another approach to improving the security of an LFSR is to pass the entire state of a single LFSR into a non-linear *filtering function.*

Other Designs

Instead of a linear driving device, one may use a nonlinear update function. For example, Klimov and Shamir proposed triangular functions (T-functions) with a single cycle on n-bit words.

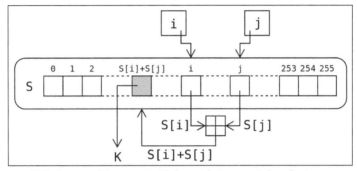

RC4 is one of the most widely used stream cipher designs.

Security

For a stream cipher to be secure, its keystream must have a large period and it must be impossible to recover the cipher's key or internal state from the keystream. Cryptographers also demand that the keystream be free of even subtle biases that would let attackers distinguish a stream from random noise, and free of detectable relationships between keystreams that correspond to related keys or related cryptographic nonces. That should be true for all keys (there should be no weak keys), even if the attacker can know or choose some plaintext or ciphertext.

As with other attacks in cryptography, stream cipher attacks can be certificational so they are not necessarily practical ways to break the cipher but indicate that the cipher might have other weaknesses.

Securely using a secure synchronous stream cipher requires that one never reuse the same keystream twice. That generally means a different nonce or key must be supplied to each invocation of the cipher. Application designers must also recognize that most stream ciphers provide not authenticity but privacy: encrypted messages may still have been modified in transit.

Short periods for stream ciphers have been a practical concern. For example, 64-bit block ciphers like DES can be used to generate a keystream in output feedback (OFB) mode. However, when not using full feedback, the resulting stream has a period of around 2^{32} blocks on average; for many applications, the period is far too low. For example, if encryption is being performed at a rate of 8 megabytes per second, a stream of period 2^{32} blocks will repeat after about a half an hour.

Some applications using the stream cipher RC4 are attackable because of weaknesses in RC4's key setup routine; new applications should either avoid RC4 or make sure all keys are unique and ideally unrelated (such as generated by a well-seeded CSPRNG or a cryptographic hash function) and that the first bytes of the keystream are discarded.

Usage

Stream ciphers are often used for their speed and simplicity of implementation in hardware, and in applications where plaintext comes in quantities of unknowable length like a secure wireless connection. If a block cipher (not operating in a stream cipher mode) were to be used in this type of application, the designer would need to choose either transmission efficiency or implementation complexity, since block ciphers cannot directly work on blocks shorter than their block size. For example, if a 128-bit block cipher received separate 32-bit bursts of plaintext, three quarters of the data transmitted would be padding. Block ciphers must be used in ciphertext stealing or residual block termination mode to avoid padding, while stream ciphers eliminate this issue by naturally operating on the smallest unit that can be transmitted (usually bytes).

Another advantage of stream ciphers in military cryptography is that the cipher stream can be generated in a separate box that is subject to strict security measures and fed to other devices such as a radio set, which will perform the xor operation as part of their function. The latter device can then be designed and used in less stringent environments.

ChaCha is becoming the most widely used stream cipher in software; others include: RC4, A5/1, A5/2, Chameleon, FISH, Helix, ISAAC, MUGI, Panama, Phelix, Pike, SEAL, SOBER, SOBER-128, and WAKE.

Feistel Cipher

In cryptography, a Feistel cipher is a symmetric structure used in the construction of block ciphers, named after the German-born physicist and cryptographer Horst Feistel who did pioneering research while working for IBM (USA); it is also commonly known as a Feistel network. A large proportion of block ciphers use the scheme, including the Data Encryption Standard (DES). The Feistel structure has the advantage that encryption and decryption operations are very similar, even identical in some cases, requiring only a reversal of the key schedule. Therefore, the size of the code or circuitry required to implement such a cipher is nearly halved.

A Feistel network is an iterated cipher with an internal function called a round function.

Feistel networks were first seen commercially in IBM's Lucifer cipher, designed by Horst Feistel and Don Coppersmith in 1973. Feistel networks gained respectability when the U.S. Federal Government adopted the DES (a cipher based on Lucifer, with changes made by the NSA). Like other components of the DES, the iterative nature of the Feistel construction makes implementing the cryptosystem in hardware easier (particularly on the hardware available at the time of DES's design).

Theoretical Work

Many modern and also some old symmetric block ciphers are based on Feistel networks (e.g. GOST 28147-89 block cipher), and the structure and properties of Feistel ciphers have been extensively explored by cryptographers. Specifically, Michael Luby and Charles Rackoff analyzed the Feistel cipher construction, and proved that if the round function is a cryptographically secure pseudorandom function, with K_i used as the seed, then 3 rounds are sufficient to make the block cipher a pseudorandom permutation, while 4 rounds are sufficient to make it a "strong" pseudorandom permutation (which means that it remains pseudorandom even to an adversary who gets oracle access to its inverse permutation).

Because of this very important result of Luby and Rackoff, Feistel ciphers are sometimes called Luby–Rackoff block ciphers. Further theoretical work has generalized the construction somewhat, and given more precise bounds for security.

Construction Details

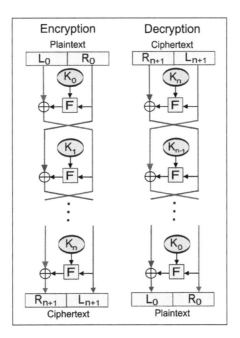

Let F be the round function and let $K_0, K_1, \ldots, K_n$ be the sub-keys for the rounds $0, 1, \ldots, n$ respectively.

Then the basic operation is as follows:

Split the plaintext block into two equal pieces, (L_0, R_0).

For each round $i = 0, 1, \ldots, n$, compute:

$$L_{i+1} = R_i$$

$$R_{i+1} = L_i \oplus F(R_i, K_i)$$

Where $\oplus$ means XOR. Then the ciphertext is (R_{n+1}, L_{n+1}).

Decryption of a ciphertext (R_{n+1}, L_{n+1}) is accomplished by computing for $i = n, n-1, \ldots, 0$

$$R_i = L_{i+1}$$

$$L_i = R_{i+1} \oplus F(L_{i+1}, K_i)$$

Then (L_0, R_0) is the plaintext again.

One advantage of the Feistel model compared to a substitution–permutation network is that the round function F does not have to be invertible.

The diagram illustrates both encryption and decryption. Note the reversal of the subkey order for decryption; this is the only difference between encryption and decryption.

Unbalanced Feistel Cipher

Unbalanced Feistel ciphers use a modified structure where L_0 and R_0 are not of equal lengths. The Skipjack cipher is an example of such a cipher. The Texas Instruments digital signature transponder uses a proprietary unbalanced Feistel cipher to perform challenge–response authentication.

The Thorp shuffle is an extreme case of an unbalanced Feistel cipher in which one side is a single bit. This has better provable security than a balanced Feistel cipher but requires more rounds.

Other Uses

The Feistel construction is also used in cryptographic algorithms other than block ciphers. For example, the optimal asymmetric encryption padding (OAEP) scheme uses a simple Feistel network to randomize ciphertexts in certain asymmetric key encryption schemes.

A generalized Feistel algorithm can be used to create strong permutations on small domains of size not a power of two.

Feistel Networks as a Design Component

Whether the entire cipher is a Feistel cipher or not, Feistel-like networks can be used as a component of a cipher's design. For example, MISTY1 is a Feistel cipher using a three-round Feistel network in its round function, Skipjack is a modified Feistel cipher using a Feistel network in its G permutation, and Threefish (part of Skein) is a non-Feistel block cipher that uses a Feistel-like MIX function.

List of Feistel Ciphers

Feistel or modified Feistel:

• Blowfish	• KASUMI	• RC5
• Camellia	• LOKI97	• Simon
• CAST-128	• Lucifer	• TEA
• DES	• MARS	• Triple DES
• FEAL	• MAGENTA	• Twofish
• GOST 28147-89	• MISTY1	• XTEA
• ICE		

Generalised Feistel:

• CAST-256	• RC6
• CLEFIA	• Skipjack
• MacGuffin	• SMS4
• RC2	

RSA ALGORITHM IN CRYPTOGRAPHY

```python
# Write Python3 code here
from decimal import Decimal


def gcd(a,b):
    if b==0:
        return a
    else:
        return gcd(b,a%b)
p = int(input('Enter the value of p = '))
q = int(input('Enter the value of q = '))
no = int(input('Enter the value of text = '))
n = p*q
t = (p-1)*(q-1)


for e in range(2,t):
    if gcd(e,t)== 1:
        break



for i in range(1,10):
    x = 1 + i*t
    if x % e == 0:
        d = int(x/e)
        break
```

```
ctt = Decimal(0)

ctt =pow(no,e)

ct = ctt % n


dtt = Decimal(0)

dtt = pow(ct,d)

dt = dtt % n


print('n = '+str(n)+' e = '+str(e)+' t = '+str(t)+' d = '+str(d)+' cipher text =
'+str(ct)+' decrypted text = '+str(dt))
```

RSA algorithm is asymmetric cryptography algorithm. Asymmetric actually means that it works on two different keys i.e. Public Key and Private Key. As the name describes that the Public Key is given to everyone and Private key is kept private.

An Example of Asymmetric Cryptography

1. A client (for example browser) sends its public key to the server and requests for some data.

2. The server encrypts the data using client's public key and sends the encrypted data.

3. Client receives this data and decrypts it.

Since this is asymmetric, nobody else except browser can decrypt the data even if a third party has public key of browser.

The idea of RSA is based on the fact that it is difficult to factorize a large integer. The public key consists of two numbers where one number is multiplication of two large prime numbers. And private key is also derived from the same two prime numbers. So if somebody can factorize the large number, the private key is compromised. Therefore encryption strength totally lies on the key size and if we double or triple the key size, the strength of encryption increases exponentially. RSA keys can be typically 1024 or 2048 bits long, but experts believe that 1024 bit keys could be broken in the near future. But till now it seems to be an infeasible task.

Let us learn the mechanism behind RSA algorithm.

Generating Public Key

```
Select two prime no's. Suppose P = 53 and Q = 59.

Now First part of the Public key  : n = P*Q = 3127.

We also need a small exponent say e :

But e Must be

     An integer.
```

```
Not be a factor of n.

1 < e < Φ(n) [Φ(n) is discussed below],

Let us now consider it to be equal to 3.
```

```
Our Public Key is made of n and e
```

Generating Private Key

```
We need to calculate Φ(n) :

Such that Φ(n) = (P-1)(Q-1)

        so,  Φ(n) = 3016
```

```
Now calculate Private Key, d :

d = (k*Φ(n) + 1) / e for some integer k

For k = 2, value of d is 2011.
```

Now we are ready with our – Public Key (n = 3127 and e = 3) and Private Key(d = 2011)

Now we will encrypt "HI" :

```
Convert letters to numbers : H  = 8 and I = 9

Thus Encrypted Data c = 89ᵉ mod n.

Thus our Encrypted Data comes out to be 1394
```

```
Now we will decrypt 1394 :
```

```
Decrypted Data = cᵈ mod n.

Thus our Encrypted Data comes out to be 89
```

```
8 = H and I = 9 i.e. "HI".
```

Below is C implementation of RSA algorithm for small values:

```c
// C program for RSA asymmetric cryptographic
// algorithm. For demonstration values are
// relatively small compared to practical
// application
#include<stdio.h>
```

```c
#include<math.h>


// Returns gcd of a and b
int gcd(int a, int h)
{
    int temp;
    while (1)
    {
        temp = a%h;
        if (temp == 0)
          return h;
        a = h;
        h = temp;
    }
}


// Code to demonstrate RSA algorithm
int main()
{
    // Two random prime numbers
    double p = 3;
    double q = 7;

    // First part of public key:
    double n = p*q;

    // Finding other part of public key.
    // e stands for encrypt
    double e = 2;
    double phi = (p-1)*(q-1);
    while (e < phi)
    {
```

```c
    // e must be co-prime to phi and
    // smaller than phi.
    if (gcd(e, phi)==1)
        break;
    else
        e++;
}


// Private key (d stands for decrypt)
// choosing d such that it satisfies
// d*e = 1 + k * totient
int k = 2;   // A constant value
double d = (1 + (k*phi))/e;


// Message to be encrypted
double msg = 20;


printf("Message data = %lf", msg);


// Encryption c = (msg ^ e) % n
double c = pow(msg, e);
c = fmod(c, n);
printf("\nEncrypted data = %lf", c);


// Decryption m = (c ^ d) % n
double m = pow(c, d);
m = fmod(m, n);
printf("\nOriginal Message Sent = %lf", m);


    return 0;
}
// This code is contributed by Akash Sharan.
```

Output

```
Message data = 12.000000

Encrypted data = 3.000000

Original Message Sent = 12.000000
```

ALGORITHM FOR DYNAMIC TIME OUT TIMER CALCULATION

Calculating Time out timer (TOT) at transport layer is tricky as propagation delay is not constant i.e. path may change continuously and traffic is dynamic. So, static TOT cannot be used at TCP. And unnecessarily retransmitting the same data packet multiple times may cause congestion. Solution for this is we need dynamic TOT which can adjust to changes in round trip time (RTT).

Algorithm for Dynamic TOT Calculation

1. Basic algorithm

2. Jacobson's algorithm

3. Karn's modification

Basic Algorithm

```
We assume initial round trip time i.e PRTT.

On sending out each packet TOT = 2 * PRTT.

The next round trip time is calculated using
```

$$PRTT_{n+1} = \alpha\, PRTT_n + (1 - \alpha)\, ARTT_n$$

```
where PRTT = predicted round trip time

     ARTT = actual round trip time

     α = smoothing factor such that 0<= α <=1
```

Example – Let $PRTT_1$ = 10ms and α = 0.5

```
TOT = 2 * PRTT₁ = 20ms

Let ARTT₁ = 15ms

Then,

PRTT₂ = (0.5 * 10) + (0.5 * 15) = 12.5ms

TOT = 2 * 12.5 = 25ms
```

```
Let ARTT₂ = 20ms
```

$$PRTT_3 = (0.5 * 12.5) + (0.5 * 20) = 16.25ms$$

```
TOT = 2 * 16.25 = 32.5ms
```

```
And so on TOT is calculated.
```

Advantages

- Better than static TOT.

- TOT is flexible to dynamic round trip time.

- It takes into consideration all packets to derive new PRTT.

Disadvantages

- TOT = 2 * PRTT is used to allow a grace time for returning acknowledgement.

- It is wasteful.

Jacobson's Algorithm

Calculates TOT value more intuitively than basic algorithm.

```
We assume initial round trip time i.e. PRTT.
```

$$PRTT_{n+1} = \alpha\ PRTT_n + (1 - \alpha)ARTT_n$$

$$PD_{n+1} = \alpha\ PD_n + (1 - \alpha)AD_n$$

$$where\ AD_n = |PRTT_n - ARTT_n|$$

```
AD = Actual deviation
```

```
PD = predicted deviation
```

```
On sending out each packet, TOT = (4 * PD) + PRTT.
```

Example:

```
Iteration 1
```

$$Given\ \alpha = 0.5,\ PRTT_1 = 10ms,\ PD_1 = 5ms\ and\ ARTT_1 = 20ms$$

```
TOT = (4 * 5) + 10 = 30ms
```

```
AD1 = |10 - 20| = 10ms
```

```
Iteration 2
```

$$PRTT_2 = \alpha\ PRTT1 + (1 - \alpha)ARTT_1$$

$$= (0.5 * 10) + (0.5 * 20) = 15ms$$

$$PD_2 = \alpha\ PD_1 + (1 - \alpha)AD_1$$
$$= (0.5 * 5) + (0.5 * 10) = 7.5ms$$

$$TOT = (4 * 7.5) + 15 = 45ms$$

Given $ARTT_2 = 30ms$

$$AD_2 = |15 - 30| = 15ms$$

Iteration 3

$$PRTT_3 = \alpha\ PRTT_2 + (1 - \alpha)ARTT_2$$
$$= (0.5 * 15) + (0.5 * 30) = 22.5ms$$

$$PD_3 = \alpha\ PD_2 + (1 - \alpha)AD_2$$
$$= (0.5 * 7.5) + (0.5 * 15) = 11.25ms$$

$$TOT = (4 * 11.25) + 22.5 = 67.5ms$$

Given $ARTT_3 = 10ms$

$$AD_2 = |22.5 - 10| = 12.5ms$$

And so on TOT is calculated.

Problem with Basic and Jacobson's Algorithm

In both, $PRTT_{n+1} = \alpha\ PRTT_n + (1 - \alpha)ARTT_n$ i.e both depend on previous segment ARTT. But if initial time out timer times out then what next TOT will be chosen since the acknowledgement is delayed i.e its coming after time out so ARTT is not available.

Karn's Modification

Whenever the timer times out do not apply either of Basic or Jacobson algorithm as ARTT is not available instead double the time out timer(TOT) whenever the timer times out and a retransmission is made.

ONE TIME PASSWORD ALGORITHM IN CRYPTOGRAPHY

Authentication is the process of identifying and validating an individual is the rudimentary step before granting access to any protected service (such as a personal account). Authentication has been built into the cyber security standards and offers to prevent unauthorized access to safeguarded resources. Authentication mechanisms today create a double layer gateway prior to unlocking any protected information.

This double layer of security, termed as two factor authentication, creates a pathway that requires validation of credentials (username/email and password) followed by creation and validation of the One Time Password (OTP). The OTP is a numeric code that is randomly and uniquely generated during each authentication event. This adds an additional layer of security, as the password generated is fresh set of digits each time an authentication is attempted and it offers the quality of being unpredictable for the next created session.

The two main methods for delivery of the OTP is:

- SMS Based: This is quite straightforward. It is the standard procedure for delivering the OTP via a text message after regular authentication is successful. Here, the OTP is generated on the server side and delivered to the authenticator via text message. It is the most common method of OTP delivery that is encountered across services.

- Application Based: This method of OTP generation is done on the user side using a specific smartphone application that scans a QR code on the screen. The application is responsible for the unique OTP digits. This reduces wait time for the OTP as well as reduces security risk as compared to the SMS based delivery.

The most common way for the generation of OTP defined by The Initiative For Open Authentication (OATH) is the Time Based One Time Passwords (TOTP), which is a Time Synchronized OTP. In these OTP systems, time is the cardinal factor to generate the unique password.

The password generated is created using the current time and it also factors in a secret key. An example of this OTP generation is the Time Based OTP Algorithm (TOTP) described as follows:

- Backend server generates the secret key.

- The server shares secret key with the service generating the OTP.

- A hash based message authentication code (HMAC) is generated using the obtained secret key and time. This is done using the cryptographic SHA-1 algorithm. Since both the server and the device requesting the OTP, have access to time, which is obviously dynamic, it is taken as a parameter in the algorithm. Here, the Unix timestamp is considered which is independent of time zone i.e. time is calculated in seconds starting from January First 1970. Let us consider "0215a7d8c15b492e21116482b6d34fc4e1a9f6ba" as the generated string from the HMAC-SHA1 algorithm.

- The code generated is 20 bytes long and is thus truncated to the desired length suitable for the user to enter. Here dynamic truncation is used. For the 20-byte code "0215a7d8c-15b492e21116482b6d34fc4e1a9f6ba", each character occupies 4 bits. The entire string is taken as 20 individual one byte sting.

0	1	2	3	4	5	6	7	8	9	10	11	12	13	14	15	16	17	18	19
02	15	a7	d8	c1	5b	49	2e	21	11	64	82	b6	d3	4f	c4	e1	a9	f6	ba

We look at the last character, here a. The decimal value of which is taken to determine the offset from which to begin truncation. Starting from the offset value, 10 the next 31 bits are read to obtain the string "6482b6d3". The last thing left to do, is to take our hexadecimal numerical value, and convert it to decimal, which gives 1686288083.

All we need now are the last desired length of OTP digits of the obtained decimal string, zero-padded if necessary. This is easily accomplished by taking the decimal string, modulo 10 ^ number of digits required in OTP. We end up with "288083" as our TOTP code.

- A counter is used to keep track of the time elapsed and generate a new code after a set interval of time.

- OTP generated is delivered to user by the methods described above.

Apart from the time-based method described above, there also exist certain mathematical algorithms for OTP generation for example a one-way function that creates a subsequent OTP from the previously created OTP.

The two factor authentication system is an effective strategy that exploits the authentication principles of "something that you know" and "something that you have". The dynamic nature of the latter principle implemented by the One Time Password Algorithm is crucial to security and offers an effective layer of protection against malicious attackers. The unpredictability of the OTP presents a hindrance in peeling off the layers that this method of cryptography has to offer.

CRYPTOGRAPHIC HASH FUNCTION

A cryptographic hash function (CHF) is a hash function that is suitable for use in cryptography. It is a mathematical algorithm that maps data of arbitrary size (often called the "message") to a bit string of a fixed size (the "hash value", "hash", or "message digest") and is a one-way function, that is, a function which is practically infeasible to invert. Ideally, the only way to find a message that produces a given hash is to attempt a brute-force search of possible inputs to see if they produce a match, or use a rainbow table of matched hashes. Cryptographic hash functions are a basic tool of modern cryptography.

The ideal cryptographic hash function has the following main properties:
- It is deterministic, meaning that the same message always results in the same hash.
- It is quick to compute the hash value for any given message.
- It is infeasible to generate a message that yields a given hash value.
- It is infeasible to find two different messages with the same hash value.
- A small change to a message should change the hash value so extensively that the new hash value appears uncorrelated with the old hash value (avalanche effect).

Cryptographic hash functions have many information-security applications, notably in digital signatures, message authentication codes (MACs), and other forms of authentication. They can also be used as ordinary hash functions, to index data in hash tables, for fingerprinting, to detect duplicate data or uniquely identify files, and as checksums to detect accidental data corruption. Indeed, in information-security contexts, cryptographic hash values are sometimes called (*digital*) *fingerprints, checksums,* or just *hash values,* even though all these terms stand for more general functions with rather different properties and purposes.

Properties

Most cryptographic hash functions are designed to take a string of any length as input and produce a fixed-length hash value.

A cryptographic hash function must be able to withstand all known types of cryptanalytic attack. In theoretical cryptography, the security level of a cryptographic hash function has been defined using the following properties:

- Pre-image resistance

  Given a hash value h it should be difficult to find any message m such that $h = \text{hash}(m)$. This concept is related to that of a one-way function. Functions that lack this property are vulnerable to preimage attacks.

- Second pre-image resistance

  Given an input m_1, it should be difficult to find a different input m_2 such that $\text{hash}(m_1) = \text{hash}(m_2)$. Functions that lack this property are vulnerable to second-preimage attacks.

- Collision resistance

  It should be difficult to find two different messages m_1 and m_2 such that $\text{hash}(m_1) = \text{hash}(m_2)$. Such a pair is called a cryptographic hash collision. This property is sometimes referred to as *strong collision resistance.* It requires a hash value at least twice as long as that required for pre-image resistance; otherwise collisions may be found by a birthday attack.

Collision resistance implies second pre-image resistance, but does not imply pre-image resistance. The weaker assumption is always preferred in theoretical cryptography, but in practice, a hash-function which is only second pre-image resistant is considered insecure and is therefore not recommended for real applications.

Informally, these properties mean that a malicious adversary cannot replace or modify the input data without changing its digest. Thus, if two strings have the same digest, one can be very confident that they are identical. Second pre-image resistance prevents an attacker from crafting a document with the same hash as a document the attacker cannot control. Collision resistance prevents an attacker from creating two distinct documents with the same hash.

A function meeting these criteria may still have undesirable properties. Currently popular cryptographic hash functions are vulnerable to *length-extension* attacks: given $\text{hash}(m)$ and $\text{len}(m)$ but not m, by choosing a suitable m' an attacker can calculate $\text{hash}(m \parallel m')$, where $\parallel$ denotes concatenation. This property can be used to break naive authentication schemes based on hash functions. The HMAC construction works around these problems.

In practice, collision resistance is insufficient for many practical uses. In addition to collision resistance, it should be impossible for an adversary to find two messages with substantially similar digests; or to infer any useful information about the data, given only its digest. In particular, a hash function should behave as much as possible like a random function (often called a random oracle in proofs of security) while still being deterministic and efficiently computable. This rules out functions like the SWIFFT function, which can be rigorously proven to be collision resistant assuming that certain problems on ideal lattices are computationally difficult, but as a linear function, does not satisfy these additional properties.

Checksum algorithms, such as CRC32 and other cyclic redundancy checks, are designed to meet much weaker requirements, and are generally unsuitable as cryptographic hash functions. For example, a CRC was used for message integrity in the WEP encryption standard, but an attack was readily discovered which exploited the linearity of the checksum.

Degree of Difficulty

In cryptographic practice, "difficult" generally means "almost certainly beyond the reach of any adversary who must be prevented from breaking the system for as long as the security of the system is deemed important". The meaning of the term is therefore somewhat dependent on the application since the effort that a malicious agent may put into the task is usually proportional to his expected gain. However, since the needed effort usually multiplies with the digest length, even a thousand-fold advantage in processing power can be neutralized by adding a few dozen bits to the latter.

For messages selected from a limited set of messages, for example passwords or other short messages, it can be feasible to invert a hash by trying all possible messages in the set. Because cryptographic hash functions are typically designed to be computed quickly, special key derivation functions that require greater computing resources have been developed that make such brute force attacks more difficult.

In some theoretical analyses "difficult" has a specific mathematical meaning, such as "not solvable in asymptotic polynomial time". Such interpretations of difficulty are important in the study of provably secure cryptographic hash functions but do not usually have a strong connection to practical security. For example, an exponential time algorithm can sometimes still be fast enough to make a feasible attack. Conversely, a polynomial time algorithm (e.g., one that requires n^{20} steps for n-digit keys) may be too slow for any practical use.

An illustration of the potential use of a cryptographic hash is as follows: Alice poses a tough math problem to Bob and claims she has solved it. Bob would like to try it himself, but would yet like to be sure that Alice is not bluffing. Therefore, Alice writes down her solution, computes its hash and tells Bob the hash value (whilst keeping the solution secret). Then, when Bob comes up with the solution himself a few days later, Alice can prove that she had the solution earlier by revealing it and having Bob hash it and check that it matches the hash value given to him before. (This is an example of a simple commitment scheme; in actual practice, Alice and Bob will often be computer programs, and the secret would be something less easily spoofed than a claimed puzzle solution).

Applications

Verifying the Integrity of Messages and Files

An important application of secure hashes is verification of message integrity. Comparing message digests (hash digests over the message) calculated before, and after, transmission can determine whether any changes have been made to the message or file.

MD5, SHA1, or SHA2 hash digests are sometimes published on websites or forums to allow verification of integrity for downloaded files, including files retrieved using file sharing such as mirroring. This practice establishes a chain of trust so long as the hashes are posted on a site authenticated by HTTPS. Using a cryptographic hash and a chain of trust prevents malicious changes to the file to go undetected. Other error detecting codes such as cyclic redundancy checks only prevent against non-malicious alterations of the file.

Signature Generation and Verification

Almost all digital signature schemes require a cryptographic hash to be calculated over the message. This allows the signature calculation to be performed on the relatively small, statically sized hash digest. The message is considered authentic if the signature verification succeeds given the signature and recalculated hash digest over the message. So the message integrity property of the cryptographic hash is used to create secure and efficient digital signature schemes.

Password Verification

Password verification commonly relies on cryptographic hashes. Storing all user passwords as cleartext can result in a massive security breach if the password file is compromised. One way to reduce this danger is to only store the hash digest of each password. To authenticate a user, the password presented by the user is hashed and compared with the stored hash. A password reset method is required when password hashing is performed; original passwords cannot be recalculated from the stored hash value.

Standard cryptographic hash functions are designed to be computed quickly, and, as a result, it is possible to try guessed passwords at high rates. Common graphics processing units can try billions of possible passwords each second. Password hash functions that perform Key stretching – such as PBKDF2, scrypt or Argon2 – commonly use repeated invocations of a cryptographic hash to increase the time (and in some cases computer memory) required to perform brute force attacks on stored password hash digests. A password hash requires the use of a large random, non-secret salt value which can be stored with the password hash. The salt randomizes the output of the password hash, making it impossible for an adversary to store tables of passwords and precomputed hash values to which the password hash digest can be compared.

The output of a password hash function can also be used as a cryptographic key. Password hashes are therefore also known as Password Based Key Derivation Functions (PBKDFs).

Proof-of-work

A proof-of-work system (or protocol, or function) is an economic measure to deter denial-of-service attacks and other service abuses such as spam on a network by requiring some work from the service requester, usually meaning processing time by a computer. A key feature of these schemes is their asymmetry: the work must be moderately hard (but feasible) on the requester side but easy to check for the service provider. One popular system – used in Bitcoin mining and Hashcash – uses partial hash inversions to prove that work was done, to unlock a mining reward in Bitcoin and as a good-will token to send an e-mail in Hashcash. The sender is required to find a message whose hash value begins with a number of zero bits. The average work that sender needs to perform in order to find a valid message is exponential in the number of zero bits required in the hash value, while the recipient can verify the validity of the message by executing a single hash function. For instance, in Hashcash, a sender is asked to generate a header whose 160 bit SHA-1 hash value has the first 20 bits as zeros. The sender will on average have to try 2^{19} times to find a valid header.

File or Data Identifier

A message digest can also serve as a means of reliably identifying a file; several source code management systems, including Git, Mercurial and Monotone, use the sha1sum of various types of content (file content, directory trees, ancestry information, etc.) to uniquely identify them. Hashes are used to identify files on peer-to-peer filesharing networks. For example, in an ed2k link, an MD4-variant hash is combined with the file size, providing sufficient information for locating file sources, downloading the file and verifying its contents. Magnet links are another example. Such file hashes are often the top hash of a hash list or a hash tree which allows for additional benefits.

One of the main applications of a hash function is to allow the fast look-up of a data in a hash table. Being hash functions of a particular kind, cryptographic hash functions lend themselves well to this application too.

However, compared with standard hash functions, cryptographic hash functions tend to be much more expensive computationally. For this reason, they tend to be used in contexts where it is necessary for users to protect themselves against the possibility of forgery (the creation of data with the same digest as the expected data) by potentially malicious participants.

Hash Functions based on Block Ciphers

There are several methods to use a block cipher to build a cryptographic hash function, specifically a one-way compression function.

The methods resemble the block cipher modes of operation usually used for encryption. Many well-known hash functions, including MD4, MD5, SHA-1 and SHA-2 are built from block-cipher-like components designed for the purpose, with feedback to ensure that the resulting function is not invertible. SHA-3 finalists included functions with block-cipher-like components (e.g., Skein, BLAKE) though the function finally selected, Keccak, was built on a cryptographic sponge instead.

A standard block cipher such as AES can be used in place of these custom block ciphers; that might be useful when an embedded system needs to implement both encryption and hashing with minimal code size or hardware area. However, that approach can have costs in efficiency and security. The ciphers in hash functions are built for hashing: they use large keys and blocks, can efficiently change keys every block, and have been designed and vetted for resistance to related-key attacks. General-purpose ciphers tend to have different design goals. In particular, AES has key and block sizes that make it nontrivial to use to generate long hash values; AES encryption becomes less efficient when the key changes each block; and related-key attacks make it potentially less secure for use in a hash function than for encryption.

Hash Function Design

Merkle–Damgård Construction

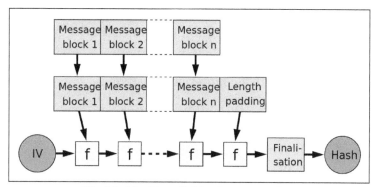

The Merkle–Damgård hash construction.

A hash function must be able to process an arbitrary-length message into a fixed-length output. This can be achieved by breaking the input up into a series of equal-sized blocks, and operating on them in sequence using a one-way compression function. The compression function can either be specially designed for hashing or be built from a block cipher. A hash function built with the Merkle–Damgård construction is as resistant to collisions as is its compression function; any collision for the full hash function can be traced back to a collision in the compression function.

The last block processed should also be unambiguously length padded; this is crucial to the security of this construction. This construction is called the Merkle–Damgård construction. Most common classical hash functions, including SHA-1 and MD5, take this form.

Wide Pipe vs. Narrow Pipe

A straightforward application of the Merkle–Damgård construction, where the size of hash output is equal to the internal state size (between each compression step), results in a narrow-pipe hash design. This design causes many inherent flaws, including length-extension, multicollisions, long message attacks, generate-and-paste attacks, and also cannot be parallelized. As a result, modern hash functions are built on wide-pipe constructions that have a larger internal state size – which range from tweaks of the Merkle–Damgård construction to new constructions such as the sponge construction and HAIFA construction. None of the entrants in the NIST hash function competition use a classical Merkle–Damgård construction.

Meanwhile, truncating the output of a longer hash, such as used in SHA-512/256, also defeats many of these attacks.

Use in Building other Cryptographic Primitives

Hash functions can be used to build other cryptographic primitives. For these other primitives to be cryptographically secure, care must be taken to build them correctly.

Message authentication codes (MACs) (also called keyed hash functions) are often built from hash functions. HMAC is such a MAC.

Just as block ciphers can be used to build hash functions, hash functions can be used to build block ciphers. Luby-Rackoff constructions using hash functions can be provably secure if the underlying hash function is secure. Also, many hash functions (including SHA-1 and SHA-2) are built by using a special-purpose block cipher in a Davies–Meyer or other construction. That cipher can also be used in a conventional mode of operation, without the same security guarantees.

Pseudorandom number generators (PRNGs) can be built using hash functions. This is done by combining a (secret) random seed with a counter and hashing it.

Some hash functions, such as Skein, Keccak, and RadioGatún output an arbitrarily long stream and can be used as a stream cipher, and stream ciphers can also be built from fixed-length digest hash functions. Often this is done by first building a cryptographically secure pseudorandom number generator and then using its stream of random bytes as keystream. SEAL is a stream cipher that uses SHA-1 to generate internal tables, which are then used in a keystream generator more or less unrelated to the hash algorithm. SEAL is not guaranteed to be as strong (or weak) as SHA-1. Similarly, the key expansion of the HC-128 and HC-256 stream ciphers makes heavy use of the SHA-256 hash function.

Concatenation

Concatenating outputs from multiple hash functions provides collision resistance as good as the strongest of the algorithms included in the concatenated result. For example, older versions of Transport Layer Security (TLS) and Secure Sockets Layer (SSL) use concatenated MD5 and SHA-1 sums. This ensures that a method to find collisions in one of the hash functions does not defeat data protected by both hash functions.

For Merkle–Damgård construction hash functions, the concatenated function is as collision-resistant as its strongest component, but not more collision-resistant. Antoine Joux observed that 2-collisions lead to n-collisions: if it is feasible for an attacker to find two messages with the same MD5 hash, the attacker can find as many messages as the attacker desires with identical MD5 hashes with no greater difficulty. Among the n messages with the same MD5 hash, there is likely to be a collision in SHA-1. The additional work needed to find the SHA-1 collision (beyond the exponential birthday search) requires only polynomial time.

Cryptographic Hash Algorithms

MD5

MD5 was designed by Ronald Rivest in 1991 to replace an earlier hash function MD4, and was specified in 1992 as RFC 1321. Collisions against MD5 can be calculated within seconds which makes the algorithm unsuitable for most use cases where a cryptographic hash is required. MD5 produces a digest of 128 bits (16 bytes).

SHA-1

SHA-1 was developed as part of the U.S. Government's Capstone project. The original specification – now commonly called SHA-0 – of the algorithm was published in 1993 under the title Secure Hash Standard, FIPS PUB 180, by U.S. government standards agency NIST (National Institute of Standards and Technology). It was withdrawn by the NSA shortly after publication and was superseded by the revised version, published in 1995 in FIPS PUB 180-1 and commonly designated SHA-1. Collisions against the full SHA-1 algorithm can be produced using the shattered attack and the hash function should be considered broken. SHA-1 produces a hash digest of 160 bits (20 bytes).

Documents may refer to SHA-1 as just "SHA", even though this may conflict with the other Standard Hash Algorithms such as SHA-0, SHA-2 and SHA-3.

RIPEMD-160

RIPEMD (RACE Integrity Primitives Evaluation Message Digest) is a family of cryptographic hash functions developed in Leuven, Belgium, by Hans Dobbertin, Antoon Bosselaers and Bart Preneel at the COSIC research group at the Katholieke Universiteit Leuven, and first published in 1996. RIPEMD was based upon the design principles used in MD4, and is similar in performance to the more popular SHA-1. RIPEMD-160 has however not been broken. As the name implies, RIPEMD-160 produces a hash digest of 160 bits (20 bytes).

bcrypt

bcrypt is a password hashing function designed by Niels Provos and David Mazières, based on the Blowfish cipher, and presented at USENIX in 1999. Besides incorporating a salt to protect against rainbow table attacks, bcrypt is an adaptive function: over time, the iteration count can be increased to make it slower, so it remains resistant to brute-force search attacks even with increasing computation power.

Whirlpool

In computer science and cryptography, Whirlpool is a cryptographic hash function. It was designed by Vincent Rijmen and Paulo S. L. M. Barreto, who first described it in 2000. Whirlpool is based on a substantially modified version of the Advanced Encryption Standard (AES). Whirlpool produces a hash digest of 512 bits (64 bytes).

SHA-2

SHA-2 (Secure Hash Algorithm 2) is a set of cryptographic hash functions designed by the United States National Security Agency (NSA), first published in 2001. They are built using the Merkle–Damgård structure, from a one-way compression function itself built using the Davies–Meyer structure from a (classified) specialized block cipher.

SHA-2 basically consists of two hash algorithms: SHA-256 and SHA-512. SHA-224 is a variant of SHA-256 with different starting values and truncated output. SHA-384 and the lesser known SHA-512/224 and SHA-512/256 are all variants of SHA-512. SHA-512 is more secure than SHA-256 and is commonly faster than SHA-256 on 64 bit machines such as AMD64.

The output size in bits is given by the extension to the "SHA" name, so SHA-224 has an output size of 224 bits (28 bytes), SHA-256 produces 32 bytes, SHA-384 produces 48 bytes and finally SHA-512 produces 64 bytes.

SHA-3

SHA-3 (Secure Hash Algorithm 3) was released by NIST on August 5, 2015. SHA-3 is a subset of the broader cryptographic primitive family Keccak. The Keccak algorithm is the work of Guido Bertoni, Joan Daemen, Michael Peeters, and Gilles Van Assche. Keccak is based on a sponge construction which can also be used to build other cryptographic primitives such as a stream cipher. SHA-3 provides the same output sizes as SHA-2: 224, 256, 384 and 512 bits.

Configurable output sizes can also be obtained using the SHAKE-128 and SHAKE-256 functions. Here the -128 and -256 extensions to the name imply the security strength of the function rather than the output size in bits.

BLAKE2

An improved version of BLAKE called BLAKE2 was announced in December 21, 2012. It was created by Jean-Philippe Aumasson, Samuel Neves, Zooko Wilcox-O'Hearn, and Christian Winnerlein with the goal to replace widely used, but broken MD5 and SHA-1 algorithms. When run on 64-bit x64 and ARM architectures, BLAKE2b is faster than SHA-3, SHA-2, SHA-1, and MD5. Although BLAKE nor BLAKE2 have not been standardized as SHA-3 it has been used in many protocols including the Argon2 password hash for the high efficiency that it offers on modern CPUs. As BLAKE was a candidate for SHA-3, BLAKE and BLAKE2 both offer the same output sizes as SHA-3 – including a configurable output size.

Attacks on Cryptographic Hash Algorithms

There is a long list of cryptographic hash functions but many have been found to be vulnerable and should not be used. For instance, NIST selected 51 hash functions as candidates for round 1 of the SHA-3 hash competition, of which 10 were considered broken and 16 showed significant weaknesses and therefore didn't make it to the next round.

Even if a hash function has never been broken, a successful attack against a weakened variant may undermine the experts' confidence. For instance, in August 2004 collisions were found in several then-popular hash functions, including MD5. These weaknesses called into question the security of stronger algorithms derived from the weak hash functions—in particular, SHA-1 (a strengthened version of SHA-0), RIPEMD-128, and RIPEMD-160 (both strengthened versions of RIPEMD).

On 12 August 2004, Joux, Carribault, Lemuet, and Jalby announced a collision for the full SHA-0 algorithm. Joux et al. accomplished this using a generalization of the Chabaud and Joux attack. They found that the collision had complexity 2^{51} and took about 80,000 CPU hours on a supercomputer with 256 Itanium 2 processors—equivalent to 13 days of full-time use of the supercomputer.

In February 2005, an attack on SHA-1 was reported that would find collision in about 2^{69} hashing operations, rather than the 2^{80} expected for a 160-bit hash function. In August 2005, another attack on SHA-1 was reported that would find collisions in 2^{63} operations. Other theoretical weaknesses of SHA-1 have been known: and in February 2017 Google announced a collision in SHA-1. Security researchers recommend that new applications can avoid these problems by using later members of the SHA family, such as SHA-2, or using techniques such as randomized hashing that do not require collision resistance.

A successful, practical attack broke MD5 used within certificates for Transport Layer Security in 2008.

Many cryptographic hashes are based on the Merkle–Damgård construction. All cryptographic hashes that directly use the full output of a Merkle–Damgård construction are vulnerable against length extension attacks. This makes the MD5, SHA-1, RIPEMD-160, Whirlpool and the SHA-256 / SHA-512 hash algorithms all vulnerable against this specific attack. SHA-3, BLAKE2 and the truncated SHA-2 variants are not vulnerable against this type of attack.

BLOCK CIPHERS

In cryptography, a block cipher is a deterministic algorithm operating on fixed-length groups of bits, called *blocks*, with an unvarying transformation that is specified by a symmetric key. Block ciphers operate as important elementary components in the design of many cryptographic protocols, and are widely used to implement encryption of bulk data.

The modern design of block ciphers is based on the concept of an iterated product cipher. Claude Shannon analyzed product ciphers and suggested them as a means of effectively improving security by combining simple operations such as substitutions and permutations. Iterated product ciphers carry out encryption in multiple rounds, each of which uses a different subkey derived from the original key. One widespread implementation of such ciphers, named a Feistel network after Horst Feistel, is notably implemented in the DES cipher. Many other realizations of block ciphers, such as the AES, are classified as substitution–permutation networks.

The publication of the DES cipher by the United States National Bureau of Standards (subsequently the U.S. National Institute of Standards and Technology, NIST) in 1977 was fundamental in the public understanding of modern block cipher design. It also influenced the academic development of cryptanalytic attacks. Both differential and linear cryptanalysis arose out of studies on the DES design. As of 2016 there is a palette of attack techniques against which a block cipher must be secure, in addition to being robust against brute-force attacks.

Even a secure block cipher is suitable only for the encryption of a single block under a fixed key. A multitude of modes of operation have been designed to allow their repeated use in a secure way, commonly to achieve the security goals of confidentiality and authenticity. However, block ciphers may also feature as building blocks in other cryptographic protocols, such as universal hash functions and pseudo-random number generators.

A block cipher consists of two paired algorithms, one for encryption, E, and the other for decryption, D. Both algorithms accept two inputs: an input block of size n bits and a key of size k bits; and both yield an n-bit output block. The decryption algorithm D is defined to be the inverse function of encryption, i.e., $D = E^{-1}$. More formally, a block cipher is specified by an encryption function:

$$E_K(P) := E(K,P) : \{0,1\}^k \times \{0,1\}^n \rightarrow \{0,1\}^n,$$

which takes as input a key K of bit length k, called the *key size*, and a bit string P of length n, called the *block size*, and returns a string C of n bits. P is called the plaintext, and C is termed the ciphertext. For each K, the function $E_K(P)$ is required to be an invertible mapping on $\{0,1\}^n$. The inverse for E is defined as a function:

$$E_K^{-1}(C) := D_K(C) = D(K,C): \{0,1\}^k \times \{0,1\}^n \rightarrow \{0,1\}^n,$$

taking a key K and a ciphertext C to return a plaintext value P, such that

$$\forall K: D_K(E_K(P)) = P.$$

For example, a block cipher encryption algorithm might take a 128-bit block of plaintext as input, and output a corresponding 128-bit block of ciphertext. The exact transformation is controlled using a second input – the secret key. Decryption is similar: the decryption algorithm takes, in this example, a 128-bit block of ciphertext together with the secret key, and yields the original 128-bit block of plain text.

For each key K, E_K is a permutation (a bijective mapping) over the set of input blocks. Each key selects one permutation from the set of $(2^n)!$ possible permutations.

Design

Iterated Block Ciphers

Most block cipher algorithms are classified as iterated block ciphers which means that they transform fixed-size blocks of plaintext into identical size blocks of ciphertext, via the repeated application of an invertible transformation known as the round function, with each iteration referred to as a round.

Usually, the round function R takes different *round keys* K_i as second input, which are derived from the original key:

$$M_i = R_{K_i}(M_{i-1})$$

Here M_0 is the plaintext and M_r the ciphertext, with r being the number of rounds.

Frequently, key whitening is used in addition to this. At the beginning and the end, the data is modified with key material (often with XOR, but simple arithmetic operations like adding and subtracting are also used):

$$M_0 = M \oplus K_0$$

$$M_i = R_{K_i}(M_{i-1}); i = 1\ldots r$$

$$C = M_r \oplus K_{r+1}$$

Given one of the standard iterated block cipher design schemes, it is fairly easy to construct a block cipher that is cryptographically secure, simply by using a large number of rounds. However, this will make the cipher inefficient. Thus, efficiency is the most important additional design criterion for professional ciphers. Further, a good block cipher is designed to avoid side-channel attacks, such as input-dependent memory accesses that might leak secret data via the cache state or the execution time. In addition, the cipher should be concise, for small hardware and software implementations. Finally, the cipher should be easily cryptanalyzable, such that it can be shown how many rounds the cipher needs to be reduced to, so that the existing cryptographic attacks would work – and, conversely, that it can be shown that the number of actual rounds is large enough to protect against them.

Substitution–permutation Networks

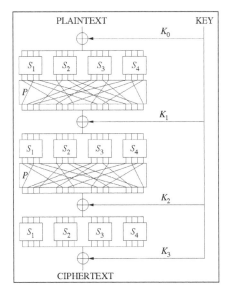

A sketch of a substitution–permutation network with 3 rounds, encrypting a plaintext block of 16 bits into a ciphertext block of 16 bits. The S-boxes are the S_i, the P-boxes are the same P, and the round keys are the K_i.

One important type of iterated block cipher known as a substitution–permutation network (SPN) takes a block of the plaintext and the key as inputs, and applies several alternating rounds consisting of a substitution stage followed by a permutation stage—to produce each block of ciphertext output. The non-linear substitution stage mixes the key bits with those of the plaintext, creating Shannon's confusion. The linear permutation stage then dissipates redundancies, creating diffusion.

A *substitution box (S-box)* substitutes a small block of input bits with another block of output bits. This substitution must be one-to-one, to ensure invertibility (hence decryption). A secure S-box will have the property that changing one input bit will change about half of the output bits on average, exhibiting what is known as the avalanche effect—i.e. it has the property that each output bit will depend on every input bit.

A *permutation box (P-box)* is a permutation of all the bits: it takes the outputs of all the S-boxes of one round, permutes the bits, and feeds them into the S-boxes of the next round. A good P-box has the property that the output bits of any S-box are distributed to as many S-box inputs as possible.

At each round, the round key (obtained from the key with some simple operations, for instance, using S-boxes and P-boxes) is combined using some group operation, typically XOR.

Decryption is done by simply reversing the process (using the inverses of the S-boxes and P-boxes and applying the round keys in reversed order).

Feistel Ciphers

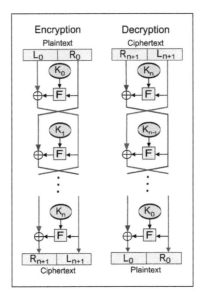

Many block ciphers, such as DES and Blowfish utilize structures known as *Feistel ciphers*.

In a *Feistel cipher*, the block of plain text to be encrypted is split into two equal-sized halves. The round function is applied to one half, using a subkey, and then the output is XORed with the other half. The two halves are then swapped.

Let F be the round function and let $K_0, K_1, \ldots, K_n$ be the sub-keys for the rounds $0, 1, \ldots, n$ respectively.

Then the basic operation is as follows:

Split the plaintext block into two equal pieces, (L_0, R_0)

For each round $i = 0, 1, \ldots, n$, compute

$$L_{i+1} = R_i$$

$$R_{i+1} = L_i \oplus \text{F}(R_i, K_i).$$

Then the ciphertext is (R_{n+1}, L_{n+1}).

Decryption of a ciphertext (R_{n+1}, L_{n+1}) is accomplished by computing for $i = n, n-1, \ldots, 0$

$$R_i = L_{i+1}$$

$$L_i = R_{i+1} \oplus \text{F}(L_{i+1}, K_i).$$

Then (L_0, R_0) is the plaintext again.

One advantage of the Feistel model compared to a substitution–permutation network is that the round function F does not have to be invertible.

Lai–Massey Ciphers

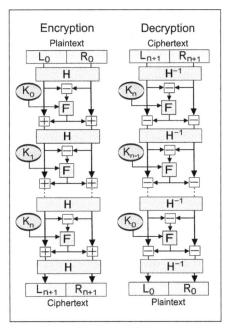

The Lai–Massey scheme. The archetypical cipher utilizing it is IDEA.

The Lai–Massey scheme offers security properties similar to those of the Feistel structure. It also shares its advantage that the round function F does not have to be invertible. Another similarity is that is also splits the input block into two equal pieces. However, the round function is applied to the difference between the two, and the result is then added to both half blocks.

Let F be the round function and H a half-round function and let $K_0, K_1, \ldots, K_n$ be the sub-keys for the rounds $i = 0, 1, \ldots, n$ respectively.

Then the basic operation is as follows:

Split the plaintext block into two equal pieces, (L_0, R_0)

For each round $i = 0, 1, \ldots, n$, compute

$$(L'_{i+1}, R'_{i+1}) = \mathrm{H}(L'_i + T_i, R'_i + T_i)$$

where $T_i = \mathrm{F}(L'_i - R'_i, K_i)$ and $(L'_0, R'_0) = \mathrm{H}(L_0, R_0)$

Then the ciphertext is $(L_{n+1}, R_{n+1}) = (L'_{n+1}, R'_{n+1})$.

Decryption of a ciphertext (L_{n+1}, R_{n+1}) is accomplished by computing for $i = n, n-1, \ldots, 0$

$$(L'_i, R'_i) = \mathrm{H}^{-1}(L'_{i+1} - T_i, R'_{i+1} - T_i)$$

where $T_i = \mathrm{F}(L'_{i+1} - R'_{i+1}, K_i)$ and $(L'_{n+1}, R'_{n+1}) = \mathrm{H}^{-1}(L_{n+1}, R_{n+1})$

Then $(L_0, R_0) = (L_0', R_0')$ is the plaintext again.

Operations

ARX (Add–Rotate–XOR)

Many modern block ciphers and hashes are ARX algorithms—their round function involves only three operations: modular addition, rotation with fixed rotation amounts, and XOR (ARX). Examples include ChaCha20, Speck, XXTEA, and BLAKE. Many authors draw an ARX network, a kind of data flow diagram, to illustrate such a round function.

These ARX operations are popular because they are relatively fast and cheap in hardware and software, and also because they run in constant time, and are therefore immune to timing attacks. The rotational cryptanalysis technique attempts to attack such round functions.

Other Operations

Other operations often used in block ciphers include data-dependent rotations as in RC5 and RC6, a substitution box implemented as a lookup table as in Data Encryption Standard and Advanced Encryption Standard, a permutation box, and multiplication as in IDEA.

Modes of Operation

Insecure encryption of an image as a result of Electronic Codebook (ECB) mode encoding.

A block cipher by itself allows encryption only of a single data block of the cipher's block length. For a variable-length message, the data must first be partitioned into separate cipher blocks. In the simplest case, known as the Electronic Codebook (ECB) mode, a message is first split into separate blocks of the cipher's block size (possibly extending the last block with padding bits), and then each block is encrypted and decrypted independently. However, such a naive method is generally insecure because equal plaintext blocks will always generate equal ciphertext blocks (for the same key), so patterns in the plaintext message become evident in the ciphertext output.

To overcome this limitation, several so called block cipher modes of operation have been designed and specified in national recommendations such as NIST 800-38A and BSI TR-02102 and international standards such as ISO/IEC 10116. The general concept is to use randomization of the plaintext data based on an additional input value, frequently called an initialization vector, to create what is termed probabilistic encryption. In the popular cipher block chaining (CBC) mode, for encryption to be secure the initialization vector passed along with the plaintext message must be a random or pseudo-random value, which is added in an exclusive-or manner to the first plaintext block before it is being encrypted. The resultant ciphertext block is then used as the new initialization vector for the next plaintext block. In the cipher feedback (CFB) mode, which emulates a self-synchronizing stream cipher, the initialization vector is first encrypted and then added to the plaintext block. The output feedback (OFB) mode repeatedly encrypts the initialization vector to create a key stream for the emulation of a synchronous stream cipher. The newer counter (CTR) mode similarly creates a key stream, but has the advantage of only needing unique and not (pseudo-)random values as initialization vectors; the needed randomness is derived internally by using the initialization vector as a block counter and encrypting this counter for each block.

From a security-theoretic point of view, modes of operation must provide what is known as semantic security. Informally, it means that given some ciphertext under an unknown key one cannot practically derive any information from the ciphertext (other than the length of the message) over what one would have known without seeing the ciphertext. It has been shown that all of the modes with the exception of the ECB mode, provide this property under so-called chosen plaintext attacks.

Padding

Some modes such as the CBC mode only operate on complete plaintext blocks. Simply extending the last block of a message with zero-bits is insufficient since it does not allow a receiver to easily distinguish messages that differ only in the amount of padding bits. More importantly, such a simple solution gives rise to very efficient padding oracle attacks. A suitable padding scheme is therefore needed to extend the last plaintext block to the cipher's block size. While many popular schemes described in standards and in the literature have been shown to be vulnerable to padding oracle attacks, a solution which adds a one-bit and then extends the last block with zero-bits, standardized as "padding method 2" in ISO/IEC 9797-1, has been proven secure against these attacks.

Brute-force Attacks

This property results in the cipher's security degrading quadratically, and needs to be taken into account when selecting a block size. There is a trade-off though as large block sizes can result in the algorithm becoming inefficient to operate. Earlier block ciphers such as the DES have typically selected a 64-bit block size, while newer designs such as the AES support block sizes of 128 bits or more, with some ciphers supporting a range of different block sizes.

Provable Security

When a block cipher is used in a given mode of operation, the resulting algorithm should ideally be about as secure as the block cipher itself. ECB emphatically lacks this property: regardless of how secure the underlying block cipher is, ECB mode can easily be attacked. On the other hand, CBC mode can be proven to be secure under the assumption that the underlying block cipher is likewise secure. Note, however, that making statements like this requires formal mathematical definitions for what it means for an encryption algorithm or a block cipher to "be secure".

This general approach to cryptography – proving higher-level algorithms (such as CBC) are secure under explicitly stated assumptions regarding their components (such as a block cipher) – is known as provable security.

Standard Model

Informally, a block cipher is secure in the standard model if an attacker cannot tell the difference between the block cipher (equipped with a random key) and a random permutation.

To be a bit more precise, let E be an n-bit block cipher. We imagine the following game:

- The person running the game flips a coin.

    ○ If the coin lands on heads, he chooses a random key K and defines the function $f = E_K$.

    ○ If the coin lands on tails, he chooses a random permutation π on the set of n-bit strings, and defines the function $f = \pi$.

- The attacker chooses an n-bit string X, and the person running the game tells him the value of $f(X)$.

- Step 2 is repeated a total of q times. (Each of these q interactions is a *query*.)

- The attacker guesses how the coin landed. He wins if his guess is correct.

The attacker, which we can model as an algorithm, is called an *adversary*. The function f (which the adversary was able to query) is called an *oracle*.

Note that an adversary can trivially ensure a 50% chance of winning simply by guessing at random (or even by, for example, always guessing "heads"). Therefore, let $P_E(A)$ denote the probability that the adversary A wins this game against E, and define the *advantage* of A as $2(P_E(A) - 1/2)$. It follows that if A guesses randomly, its advantage will be 0; on the other hand, if A always wins, then its advantage is 1. The block cipher E is a *pseudo-random permutation* (PRP) if no adversary has an advantage significantly greater than 0, given specified restrictions on q and the adversary's running time. If in Step 2 above adversaries have the option of learning $f^{-1}(X)$ instead of $f(X)$ (but still have only small advantages) then E is a *strong* PRP (SPRP). An adversary is *non-adaptive* if it chooses all q values for X before the game begins (that is, it does not use any information gleaned from previous queries to choose each X as it goes).

These definitions have proven useful for analyzing various modes of operation. For example, one can define a similar game for measuring the security of a block cipher-based encryption algorithm, and then try to show (through a reduction argument) that the probability of an adversary winning this new game is not much more than $P_E(A)$ for some A. (The reduction typically provides limits on q and the running time of A.) Equivalently, if $P_E(A)$ is small for all relevant A, then no attacker has a significant probability of winning the new game. This formalizes the idea that the higher-level algorithm inherits the block cipher's security.

Practical Evaluation

Block ciphers may be evaluated according to multiple criteria in practice. Common factors include:

- Key parameters, such as its key size and block size, both of which provide an upper bound on the security of the cipher.

- The *estimated security level*, which is based on the confidence gained in the block cipher design after it has largely withstood major efforts in cryptanalysis over time, the design's mathematical soundness, and the existence of practical or certificational attacks.

- The cipher's *complexity* and its suitability for implementation in hardware or software. Hardware implementations may measure the complexity in terms of gate count or energy consumption, which are important parameters for resource-constrained devices.

- The cipher's *performance* in terms of processing throughput on various platforms, including its memory requirements.

- The *cost* of the cipher, which refers to licensing requirements that may apply due to intellectual property rights.

- The *flexibility* of the cipher, which includes its ability to support multiple key sizes and block lengths.

Tweakable Block Ciphers

M. Liskov, R. Rivest, and D. Wagner have described a generalized version of block ciphers called "tweakable" block ciphers. A tweakable block cipher accepts a second input called the tweak along with its usual plaintext or ciphertext input. The tweak, along with the key, selects the permutation computed by the cipher. If changing tweaks is sufficiently lightweight (compared with a usually fairly expensive key setup operation), then some interesting new operation modes become possible. The disk encryption theory article describes some of these modes.

Format-preserving Encryption

Block ciphers traditionally work over a binary alphabet. That is, both the input and the output are binary strings, consisting of n zeroes and ones. In some situations, however, one may wish to have a block cipher that works over some other alphabet; for example, encrypting 16-digit credit card numbers in such a way that the ciphertext is also a 16-digit number might facilitate adding an encryption layer to legacy software. This is an example of *format-preserving encryption*. More generally, format-preserving encryption requires a keyed permutation on some finite language. This makes format-preserving encryption schemes a natural generalization of (tweakable) block ciphers. In contrast, traditional encryption schemes, such as CBC, are not permutations because the same plaintext can encrypt to multiple different ciphertexts, even when using a fixed key.

Relation to Other Cryptographic Primitives

Block ciphers can be used to build other cryptographic primitives, such as those below. For these other primitives to be cryptographically secure, care has to be taken to build them the right way.

- Stream ciphers can be built using block ciphers. OFB-mode and CTR mode are block modes that turn a block cipher into a stream cipher.

- Cryptographic hash functions can be built using block ciphers.

- Cryptographically secure pseudorandom number generators (CSPRNGs) can be built using block ciphers.

- Secure pseudorandom permutations of arbitrarily sized finite sets can be constructed with block ciphers.

- Message authentication codes (MACs) are often built from block ciphers. CBC-MAC, OMAC and PMAC are such MACs.

- Authenticated encryption is also built from block ciphers. It means to both encrypt and MAC at the same time. That is to both provide confidentiality and authentication. CCM, EAX, GCM and OCB are such authenticated encryption modes.

Just as block ciphers can be used to build hash functions, hash functions can be used to build block ciphers. Examples of such block ciphers are SHACAL, BEAR and LION.

CRYPTOGRAPHIC KEY

A cryptographic key is a string of bits used by a cryptographic algorithm to transform plain text into cipher text or vice versa. This key remains private and ensures secure communication.

A cryptographic key is the core part of cryptographic operations. Many cryptographic systems include pairs of operations, such as encryption and decryption. A key is a part of the variable data that is provided as input to a cryptographic algorithm to execute this sort of operation. In a properly designed cryptographic scheme, the security of the scheme is dependent on the security of the keys used.

Cryptographic keys are symmetric or asymmetric. Symmetric encryption requires only one key, which is used to encrypt and decrypt data. Asymmetric encryption uses two different keys: one for encryption and one for decryption. A certificate authority (CA) provides public/private key pairs using the public key infrastructure. The digital certificate registration authority process begins before the user's digital certificate status is communicated to the CA.

Cryptographic keys may be further indexed by the purposes for which they are used, which can include data encryption and decryption, digital signature verification, digital signature creation, message authentication, key transport and key wrapping.

KEY SIZE

In cryptography, key size or key length is the number of bits in a key used by a cryptographic algorithm (such as a cipher).

Key length defines the upper-bound on an algorithm's security (i.e., a logarithmic measure of the fastest known attack against an algorithm, relative to the key length), since the security of all algorithms can be violated by brute-force attacks. Ideally, key length would coincide with the lower-bound on an algorithm's security. Indeed, most symmetric-key algorithms are designed to have security equal to their key length. However, after design, a new attack might be discovered. For instance, Triple DES was designed to have a 168 bit key, but an attack of complexity 2^{112} is now known (i.e., Triple DES has 112 bits of security). Nevertheless, as long as the relation between key length and security is sufficient for a particular application, then it doesn't matter if key length and security coincide. This is important for asymmetric-key algorithms, because no such algorithm is known to satisfy this property; elliptic curve cryptography comes the closest with an effective security of roughly half its key length.

Significance

Keys are used to control the operation of a cipher so that only the correct key can convert encrypted text (ciphertext) to plaintext. Many ciphers are actually based on publicly known algorithms or are open source and so it is only the difficulty of obtaining the key that determines security of the system, provided that there is no analytic attack (i.e., a 'structural weakness' in the algorithms or protocols used), and assuming that the key is not otherwise available (such as via theft, extortion, or compromise of computer systems). The widely accepted notion that the security of the system should depend on the key alone has been explicitly formulated by Auguste Kerckhoffs and Claude Shannon; the statements are known as Kerckhoffs' principle and Shannon's Maxim respectively.

A key should therefore be large enough that a brute-force attack (possible against any encryption algorithm) is infeasible – i.e., would take too long to execute. Shannon's work on information theory showed that to achieve so called *perfect secrecy*, the key length must be at least as large as the message and only used once (this algorithm is called the One-time pad). In light of this, and the practical difficulty of managing such long keys, modern cryptographic practice has discarded the notion of perfect secrecy as a requirement for encryption, and instead focuses on *computational security*, under which the computational requirements of breaking an encrypted text must be infeasible for an attacker.

Key Size and Encryption System

Encryption systems are often grouped into families. Common families include symmetric systems (e.g. AES) and asymmetric systems (e.g. RSA); they may alternatively be grouped according to the central algorithm used (e.g. elliptic curve cryptography).

As each of these is of a different level of cryptographic complexity, it is usual to have different key sizes for the same level of security, depending upon the algorithm used. For example, the security available with a 1024-bit key using asymmetric RSA is considered approximately equal in security to an 80-bit key in a symmetric algorithm.

The actual degree of security achieved over time varies, as more computational power and more powerful mathematical analytic methods become available. For this reason cryptologists tend to look at indicators that an algorithm or key length shows signs of potential vulnerability, to move to longer key sizes or more difficult algorithms. For example, as of May 2007, a 1039 bit integer was factored with the special number field sieve using 400 computers over 11 months. The factored number was of a special form; the special number field sieve cannot be used on RSA keys. The computation is roughly equivalent to breaking a 700 bit RSA key. However, this might be an advance warning that 1024 bit RSA used in secure online commerce should be deprecated, since they may become breakable in the near future.

The 2015 Logjam attack revealed additional dangers in using Diffie-Helman key exchange when only one or a few common 1024-bit or smaller prime moduli are in use. This common practice allows large amounts of communications to be compromised at the expense of attacking a small number of primes.

Brute-force Attack

Even if a symmetric cipher is currently unbreakable by exploiting structural weaknesses in its algorithm, it is possible to run through the entire space of keys in what is known as a *brute-force attack*. Since longer symmetric keys require exponentially more work to brute force search, a sufficiently long symmetric key makes this line of attack impractical.

With a key of length n bits, there are 2^n possible keys. This number grows very rapidly as n increases. The large number of operations (2^{128}) required to try all possible 128-bit keys is widely considered out of reach for conventional digital computing techniques for the foreseeable future. However, experts anticipate alternative computing technologies that may have processing power superior to current computer technology. If a suitably sized quantum computer capable of running Grover's algorithm reliably becomes available, it would reduce a 128-bit key down to 64-bit security, roughly a DES equivalent. This is one of the reasons why AES supports a 256-bit key length.

Symmetric Algorithm Key Lengths

US Government export policy has long restricted the 'strength' of cryptography that can be sent out of the country. For many years the limit was 40 bits. Today, a key length of 40 bits offers little protection against even a casual attacker with a single PC, a predictable and inevitable consequence of governmental restrictions limiting key length. In response, by the year 2000, most of the major US restrictions on the use of strong encryption were relaxed. However, not all regulations have been removed, and encryption registration with the U.S. Bureau of Industry and Security is still required to export "mass market encryption commodities, software and components with encryption exceeding 64 bits" (75 FR 36494).

IBM's Lucifer cipher was selected in 1974 as the base for what would become the Data Encryption Standard. Lucifer's key length was reduced from 128 bits to 56 bits, which the NSA and NIST argued was sufficient. The NSA has major computing resources and a large budget; some cryptographers including Whitfield Diffie and Martin Hellman complained that this made the cipher so weak that NSA computers would be able to break a DES key in a day through brute force parallel computing. The NSA disputed this, claiming brute forcing DES would take them something like 91 years. However, by the late 90s, it became clear that DES could be cracked in a few days' time-frame with custom-built hardware such as could be purchased by a large corporation or government. 56 bits was considered insufficient length for symmetric algorithm keys; DES has been replaced in many applications by Triple DES, which has 112 bits of security when used 168-bit keys (triple key). In 2002, Distributed.net and its volunteers broke a 64-bit RC5 key after several years effort, using about seventy thousand (mostly home) computers.

The Advanced Encryption Standard published in 2001 uses key sizes of 128 bits, 192 or 256 bits. Many observers consider 128 bits sufficient for the foreseeable future for symmetric algorithms of AES's quality until quantum computers become available. However, as of 2015, the U.S. National

Security Agency has issued guidance that it plans to switch to quantum computing resistant algorithms and now requires 256-bit AES keys for data classified up to Top Secret.

In 2003, the U.S. National Institute for Standards and Technology, NIST proposed phasing out 80-bit keys by 2015. At 2005, 80-bit keys were allowed only until 2010.

Since 2015, NIST guidance says that "the use of keys that provide less than 112 bits of security strength for key agreement is now disallowed." NIST approved symmetric encryption algorithms include three-key Triple DES, and AES. Approvals for two-key Triple DES and Skipjack were withdrawn in 2015; the NSA's Skipjack algorithm used in its Fortezza program employs 80-bit keys.

Asymmetric Algorithm Key Lengths

The effectiveness of public key cryptosystems depends on the intractability (computational and theoretical) of certain mathematical problems such as integer factorization. These problems are time consuming to solve, but usually faster than trying all possible keys by brute force. Thus, asymmetric algorithm keys must be longer for equivalent resistance to attack than symmetric algorithm keys. As of 2002, an asymmetric key length of 1024 bits was generally considered by cryptology experts to be the minimum necessary for the RSA encryption algorithm.

As of 2003 RSA Security claims that 1024-bit RSA keys are equivalent in strength to 80-bit symmetric keys, 2048-bit RSA keys to 112-bit symmetric keys and 3072-bit RSA keys to 128-bit symmetric keys. RSA claims that 1024-bit keys are likely to become crackable some time between 2006 and 2010 and that 2048-bit keys are sufficient until 2030. The NIST recommends 2048-bit keys for RSA. An RSA key length of 3072 bits should be used if security is required beyond 2030. NIST key management guidelines further suggest that 15360-bit RSA keys are equivalent in strength to 256-bit symmetric keys.

The Finite Field Diffie-Hellman algorithm has roughly the same key strength as RSA for the same key sizes. The work factor for breaking Diffie-Hellman is based on the discrete logarithm problem, which is related to the integer factorization problem on which RSA's strength is based. Thus, a 3072-bit Diffie-Hellman key has about the same strength as a 3072-bit RSA key.

One of the asymmetric algorithm types, elliptic curve cryptography, or ECC, appears to be secure with shorter keys than other asymmetric key algorithms require. NIST guidelines state that ECC keys should be twice the length of equivalent strength symmetric key algorithms. So, for example, a 224-bit ECC key would have roughly the same strength as a 112-bit symmetric key. These estimates assume no major breakthroughs in solving the underlying mathematical problems that ECC is based on. A message encrypted with an elliptic key algorithm using a 109-bit long key has been broken by brute force.

The NSA previously specified that "Elliptic Curve Public Key Cryptography using the 256-bit prime modulus elliptic curve as specified in FIPS-186-2 and SHA-256 are appropriate for protecting classified information up to the SECRET level. Use of the 384-bit prime modulus elliptic curve and SHA-384 are necessary for the protection of TOP SECRET information." In 2015 the NSA announced that it plans to transition from Elliptic Curve Cryptography to new algorithms that are resistant to attack by future quantum computers. In the interim it recommends the larger 384-bit curve for all classified information.

Effect of Quantum Computing Attacks on Key Strength

The two best known quantum computing attacks are based on Shor's algorithm and Grover's algorithm. Of the two, Shor's offers the greater risk to current security systems.

Derivatives of Shor's algorithm are widely conjectured to be effective against all mainstream public-key algorithms including RSA, Diffie-Hellman and elliptic curve cryptography. According to Professor Gilles Brassard, an expert in quantum computing: "The time needed to factor an RSA integer is the same order as the time needed to use that same integer as modulus for a single RSA encryption. In other words, it takes no more time to break RSA on a quantum computer (up to a multiplicative constant) than to use it legitimately on a classical computer." The general consensus is that these public key algorithms are insecure at any key size if sufficiently large quantum computers capable of running Shor's algorithm become available. The implication of this attack is that all data encrypted using current standards based security systems such as the ubiquitous SSL used to protect e-commerce and Internet banking and SSH used to protect access to sensitive computing systems is at risk. Encrypted data protected using public-key algorithms can be archived and may be broken at a later time.

Mainstream symmetric ciphers (such as AES or Twofish) and collision resistant hash functions (such as SHA) are widely conjectured to offer greater security against known quantum computing attacks. They are widely thought most vulnerable to Grover's algorithm. Bennett, Bernstein, Brassard, and Vazirani proved in 1996 that a brute-force key search on a quantum computer cannot be faster than roughly $2^{n/2}$ invocations of the underlying cryptographic algorithm, compared with roughly 2^n in the classical case. Thus in the presence of large quantum computers an n-bit key can provide at least $n/2$ bits of security. Quantum brute force is easily defeated by doubling the key length, which has little extra computational cost in ordinary use. This implies that at least a 256-bit symmetric key is required to achieve 128-bit security rating against a quantum computer. As mentioned above, the NSA announced in 2015 that it plans to transition to quantum-resistant algorithms.

According to NSA "A sufficiently large quantum computer, if built, would be capable of undermining all widely-deployed public key algorithms used for key establishment and digital signatures. It is generally accepted that quantum computing techniques are much less effective against symmetric algorithms than against current widely used public key algorithms. While public key cryptography requires changes in the fundamental design to protect against a potential future quantum computer, symmetric key algorithms are believed to be secure provided a sufficiently large key size is used. In the longer term, NSA looks to NIST to identify a broadly accepted, standardized suite of commercial public key algorithms that are not vulnerable to quantum attacks.

As of 2016, the NSA's Commercial National Security Algorithm Suite includes:

Algorithm	Usage
RSA 3072-bit or larger	Key Establishment, Digital Signature
Diffie-Hellman (DH) 3072-bit or larger	Key Establishment
ECDH with NIST P-384	Key Establishment

ECDSA with NIST P-384	Digital Signature
SHA-384	Integrity
AES-256	Confidentiality

KEY STRETCHING

In cryptography, key stretching techniques are used to make a possibly weak key, typically a password or passphrase, more secure against a brute-force attack by increasing the resources (time and possibly space) it takes to test each possible key. Passwords or passphrases created by humans are often short or predictable enough to allow password cracking, and key stretching is intended to make such attacks more difficult by complicating a basic step of trying a single password candidate. Because a key generation function must be deterministic so that the weak key always generates the same stretched key (called an enhanced key), the stretching of the key does not alter the entropy of the key-space, only complicates the method of computing the enhanced key. Attacks on unsalted key stretching functions exist called rainbow tables. Salting the key is the process of appending a long, random string to the weak key. This is done so that precomputed hashes of either short keys or password lists cannot be used in authentication schemes that require the hash to be presented or to reverse hashes into their original pass-phrases which may be used to compromise users on other services using the same pass-phrase.

Key stretching techniques generally work as follows. The initial key is fed into an algorithm that outputs an enhanced key. The enhanced key should be of sufficient size to make it infeasible to break by brute force (e.g. 128 bits). The overall algorithm used should be secure in the sense that there should be no known way of taking a shortcut that would make it possible to calculate the enhanced key with less processor work and memory used than by using the key stretching algorithm itself.

The key stretching process leaves the attacker with two options: either try every possible combination of the enhanced key (infeasible if the enhanced key is long enough), or else try likely combinations of the initial key. In the latter approach, if the initial key is a password or a passphrase, then the attacker would first try every word in a dictionary or common password list and then try all character combinations for longer passwords. Key stretching does not prevent this approach, but the attacker has to spend much more resources (time and/or memory used) on each attempt, which may easily make this approach infeasible as well.

If the attacker uses the same class of hardware as the user, each guess will take the similar amount of time to process as it took the user (for example, one second). Even if the attacker has much greater computing resources than the user, the key stretching will still slow the attacker down while not seriously affecting the usability of the system for any legitimate user, since the user's computer only has to compute the stretching function once upon the user entering their password, whereas the attacker must compute it for every guess in the attack.

There are several ways to perform key stretching. One way is to apply a cryptographic hash function or a block cipher repeatedly in a loop. E.g., in applications where the key is used for a cipher, the key schedule in the cipher may be modified so that it takes a specific length of time to perform. Another way is to use cryptographic hash functions that have large memory requirements – these can be effective in frustrating attacks by memory-bound adversaries.

A related technique, salting, protects against attacks that take advantage of certain time–memory tradeoffs (which often utilize some variation of rainbow tables) and is often used in conjunction with key stretching.

Hash-based

Many libraries provide functions which perform key stretching as part of their function. PBKDF2 is for generating an encryption key from a password, and not necessarily for password authentication. PBKDF2 can be used for both if the number of output bits is less than or equal to the internal hashing algorithm used in PBKDF2, which is usually SHA-2 (up to 512 bits), or used as an encryption key to encrypt static data.

Strength and Time

These examples assume that a personal computer can do about 65,000 SHA-1 hashes in one second. Thus a program that uses key stretching can use 65,000 rounds of hashes and delay the user for at most one second.

Testing a trial password or passphrase typically requires one hash operation. But if key stretching was used, the attacker must compute a strengthened key for each key they test, meaning there are 65,000 hashes to compute per test. This increases the attacker's workload by a factor of 65,000, approximately 2^{16}, which means the enhanced key is worth about 16 additional bits in key strength.

Moore's law asserts that computer speed doubles roughly every 1.5 years. Under this assumption, every 1.5 years one more bit of key strength is plausibly brute-forcible. This implies that 16 extra bits of strength is worth about 16×1.5 = 24 years later cracking, but it also means that the number of key stretching rounds a system uses should be doubled about every 1.5 years to maintain the same level of security (since most keys are more secure than necessary, systems that require consistent deterministic key generation will likely not update the number of iterations used in key stretching. In such a case, the designer should take into consideration how long they wish for the key derivation system to go unaltered and should choose an appropriate number of hashes for the lifespan of the system).

CPU-bound hash functions are still vulnerable to hardware implementations. Such implementations of SHA-1 exist using as few as 5,000 gates, and 400 clock cycles. With multi-million gate FPGAs costing less than $100, an attacker can build a fully unrolled hardware cracker for about $5,000. Such a design, clocked at 100 MHz can test about 300,000 keys/second. The attacker is free to choose a good price/speed compromise, for example a 150,000 keys/second design for $2,500. The key stretching still slows down the attacker in such a situation; a $5,000 design attacking a straight SHA-1 hash would be able to try $300,000 \div 2^{16} \approx 4.578$ keys/second.

To defend against the hardware approach, memory-bound cryptographic functions have been developed. These access large amounts of memory in an unpredictable fashion such that caches are ineffective. Since large amounts of low latency memory are expensive, a would-be attacker is significantly deterred.

Some Systems that use Key Stretching

- Some but not all disk encryption software.

- Apache. htpasswd "APR1" and OpenSSL "passwd" use 1000 rounds of MD5 key stretching.

- KeePass and KeePassX, open-source password manager utilities.

- Password Safe open-source password manager.

- PGP, GPG encryption software.

- Wi-Fi Protected Access (WPA and WPA2) wireless encryption protocol in personal mode.

PUBLIC KEY CRYPTOGRAPHY

Public-key cryptography or asymmetric cryptography, is an asymmetric form of cryptography in which the transmitter of a message and its recipient use different keys (codes), thereby eliminating the need for the sender to transmit the code and risk its interception.

In 1976, in one of the most inspired insights in the history of cryptology, Sun Microsystems, Inc., computer engineer Whitfield Diffie and Stanford University electrical engineer Martin Hellmanrealized that the key distribution problem could be almost completely solved if a cryptosystem, T (and perhaps an inverse system, T'), could be devised that used two keys and satisfied the following conditions:

- It must be easy for the cryptographer to calculate a matched pair of keys, e (encryption) and d(decryption), for which $T_eT'_d = I$. Although not essential, it is desirable that $T'dTe = I$ and that $T = T'$. Since most of the systems devised to meet points 1–4 satisfy these conditions as well, it will be assumed they hold hereafter—but that is not necessary.

- The encryption and decryption operation, T, should be (computationally) easy to carry out.

- At least one of the keys must be computationally infeasible for the cryptanalyst to recover even when he knows T, the other key, and arbitrarily many matching plaintext and ciphertext pairs.

- It should not be computationally feasible to recover x given y, where $y = T_k(x)$ for almost all keys k and messages x.

Given such a system, Diffie and Hellman proposed that each user keep his decryption key secret and publish his encryption key in a public directory. Secrecy was not required, either in distributing or in storing this directory of "public" keys. Anyone wishing to communicate privately with a user whose key is in the directory only has to look up the recipient's public key to encrypt a message that only the intended receiver can decrypt. The total number of keys involved is just twice the number of users, with each user having a key in the public directory and his own secret key, which he must protect in his own self-interest. Obviously the public directory must be authenticated, otherwise A could be tricked into communicating with Cwhen he thinks he is communicating with B simply by substituting C's key for B's in A's copy of the directory. Since they were focused on the key distribution problem, Diffie and Hellman called their discovery public-key cryptography. This was the first discussion of two-key cryptography in the open literature. However, Admiral Bobby Inman, while director of the U.S. National Security Agency (NSA) from 1977 to 1981, revealed that two-key cryptography had been known to the agency almost a decade earlier, having been discovered by James Ellis, Clifford Cocks, and Malcolm Williamson at the British Government Code Headquarters (GCHQ).

In this system, ciphers created with a secret key can be decrypted by anyone using the corresponding public key—thereby providing a means to identify the originator at the expense of completely giving up secrecy. Ciphers generated using the public key can only be decrypted by users holding the secret key, not by others holding the public key—however, the secret-key holder receives no information concerning the sender. In other words, the system provides secrecy at the expense of completely giving up any capability of authentication. What Diffie and Hellman had done was to separate the secrecy channel from the authentication channel—a striking example of the sum of the parts being greater than the whole. Single-key cryptography is called symmetric for obvious reasons. A cryptosystem satisfying conditions 1–4 above is called asymmetric for equally obvious reasons. There are symmetric cryptosystems in which the encryption and decryption keys are not the same—for example, matrix transforms of the text in which one key is a nonsingular (invertible) matrix and the other its inverse. Even though this is a two-key cryptosystem, since it is easy to calculate the inverse to a non-singular matrix, it does not satisfy condition 3 and is not considered to be asymmetric.

Since in an asymmetric cryptosystem each user has a secrecy channel from every other user to him (using his public key) and an authentication channel from him to all other users (using his secret key), it is possible to achieve both secrecy and authentication using superencryption. Say A wishes to communicate a message in secret to B, but B wants to be sure the message was sent by A. A first encrypts the message with his secret key and then superencrypts the resulting cipher with B's public key. The resulting outer cipher can only be decrypted by B, thus guaranteeing to A that only B can recover the inner cipher. When B opens the inner cipher using A's public key he is certain the message came from someone knowing A's key, presumably A. Simple as it is, this protocol is a paradigm for many contemporary applications.

Cryptographers have constructed several cryptographic schemes of this sort by starting with a "hard" mathematical problem—such as factoring a number that is the product of two very large primes—and attempting to make the cryptanalysis of the scheme be equivalent to solving the hard problem. If this can be done, the cryptosecurity of the scheme will be at least as good as the underlying mathematical problem is hard to solve. This has not been proven for any of the candidate schemes thus far, although it is believed to hold in each instance.

However, a simple and secure proof of identity is possible based on such computational asymmetry. A user first secretly selects two large primes and then openly publishes their product. Although it is easy to compute a modular square root (a number whose square leaves a designated remainder when divided by the product) if the prime factors are known, it is just as hard as factoring (in fact equivalent to factoring) the product if the primes are unknown. A user can therefore prove his identity, i.e., that he knows the original primes, by demonstrating that he can extract modular square roots. The user can be confident that no one can impersonate him since to do so they would have to be able to factor his product. There are some subtleties to the protocol that must be observed, but this illustrates how modern computational cryptography depends on hard problems.

References

- Cryptographic-algorithm, computer-science: sciencedirect.com, Retrieved 19 July, 2019

- Delfs, Hans & Knebl, Helmut (2007). "Symmetric-key encryption". Introduction to cryptography: principles and applications. Springer. ISBN 9783540492436

- One-time-password-otp-algorithm-in-cryptography: geeksforgeeks.org, Retrieved 19 August, 2019

- Mullen, Gary & Mummert, Carl (2007). Finite fields and applications. American Mathematical Society. P. 112. ISBN 9780821844182

- Algorithm-for-dynamic-time-out-timer-calculation: geeksforgeeks.org, Retrieved 10 May, 2019

- Menezes, Alfred J.; Oorschot, Paul C. Van; Vanstone, Scott A. (2001). Handbook of Applied Cryptography (Fifth ed.). P. 251. ISBN 978-0849385230

- Rsa-algorithm-cryptography: geeksforgeeks.org, Retrieved 14 February, 2019

- Van Tilborg, Henk C. A.; Jajodia, Sushil, eds. (2011). Encyclopedia of Cryptography and Security. Springer. ISBN 978-1-4419-5905-8., p. 455

- Custom-building-cryptography-algorithms-hybrid-cryptography: geeksforgeeks.org, Retrieved 25 May, 2019

- Junod, Pascal & Canteaut, Anne (2011). Advanced Linear Cryptanalysis of Block and Stream Ciphers. IOS Press. P. 2. ISBN 9781607508441

- Cryptographic-key, definition: techopedia.com, Retrieved 30 June, 2019

- Jacqui Cheng (2007-05-23). "Researchers: 307-digit key crack endangers 1024-bit RSA". Ars Technica. Retrieved 2016-09-24

- Public-key-cryptography, topic: britannica.com, Retrieved 29 April, 2019

Classical Ciphers

6

Classical cipher is a type of cipher that was used historically, but is no longer used. The main types of classical ciphers are substitution ciphers that include Caesar cipher and playfair cipher, and transportation ciphers such as Hill cipher and polyalphabetic cipher. All the diverse principles related to these types of classical ciphers have been carefully analyzed in this chapter.

The classical ciphers are the absolute simplest forms of encryption; they have been around for thousands of years. There are essentially only two principles that drive all of the classical ciphers: substitution and transposition. Substitution ciphers are simply those that replace symbols in plaintext with another symbol of the same alphabet. To reverse the process, each ciphertext symbol is simply replaced with the corresponding original plaintext symbol. A transposition cipher simply rearranges the symbols in plaintext to produce ciphertext.

Classical ciphers are cryptographic algorithms that have been used in the past (pre WWII). Some of them have only ever been used by amateurs (e.g. Bifid), while some of them have been used by armies to secure their top level communications (e.g. ADFGVX).

None of these algorithms are very secure as far as protecting information goes (with todays computers to break them), so if real data security is needed you should probably look at modern algorithms.

- Atbash Cipher:

  Atbash cipher the Atbash cipher is a substitution cipher with a specific key where the letters of the alphabet are reversed. i.e. all As are replaced with Zs, all Bs are replaced with Ys, and so on.

- ROT13 Cipher:

  Rot13 cipher the ROT13 cipher is not really a cipher, more just a way to obscure information temporarily. It is often used to hide e.g. movie spoilers.

- Caesar Cipher:

  Caesar cipher the caesar cipher (a.k.a the shift cipher, Caesar's Code or Caesar Shift) is one of the earliest known and simplest ciphers.

- Affine Cipher:

  Affine cipher a type of simple substitution cipher, very easy to crack.

- Rail-fence Cipher:

  Rail-fence cipher a simple transposition cipher.

- Baconian Cipher:

Baconian cipher the Baconian cipher is a 'biliteral' cipher, i.e. it employs only 2 characters. It is a substitution cipher.

- Polybius Square Cipher:

Polybius Square cipher the Polybius Square is essentially identical to the simple substitution cipher, except that each plaintext character is enciphered as 2 ciphertext characters.

- Simple Substitution Cipher:

Simple substitution cipher a simple cipher used by governments for hundreds of years. Code is provided for encryption, decryption and cryptanalysis.

- Codes and Nomenclators Cipher:

Codes and nomenclator cipher nomenclators are a mix between substitution ciphers and Codes, used extensively during the middle ages. Codes in various forms were used up until fairly recently.

- Columnar Transposition Cipher:

Columnar transposition cipher another simple transposition cipher in which letters are arranged in rows and the columns are transposed according to a key.

- Autokey Cipher:

Autokey cipher the Autokey cipher is closely related to the Vigenere cipher, it differs in how the key material is generated. The Autokey cipher uses a key word in addition to the plaintext as its key material, this makes it more secure than Vigenere.

- Beaufort Cipher:

Beaufort cipher very similar to the Vigenere cipher, but slightly different algorithm.

- Porta Cipher:

Porta cipher the Porta cipher is a polyalphabetic substitution cipher that uses a keyword to choose which alphabet to encipher letters.

- Running Key Cipher:

Running Key cipher the Running Key cipher is similar to the Vigenere cipher, but the key is usually a long piece of non-repeating text. This makes it harder to break in general than the Vigenere or Autokey ciphers.

- Vigenère and Gronsfeld Cipher:

Vigenere and gronsfeld cipher a more complex polyalphabetic substitution cipher. Code is provided for encryption, decryption and cryptanalysis.

- Homophonic Substitution Cipher:

Homophonic Substitution cipher the Homophonic Substitution cipher is a substitution cipher in which single plaintext letters can be replaced by any of several different ciphertext letters. They are generally much more difficult to break than standard substitution ciphers.

- Four-Square Cipher:

Four-square cipher an algorithm invented by Felix Delastelle, published in 1902.

- Hill Cipher:

Hill cipher an algorithm based on matrix theory. Very good at diffusion.

- Playfair Cipher:

Playfair cipher the technique encrypts pairs of letters (digraphs), instead of single letters as in the simple substitution cipher. The Playfair cipher is thus significantly harder to break since the frequency analysis used for simple substitution ciphers does not work with it.

- ADFGVX Cipher:

ADFGVX cipher a fractionating transposition cipher. Used by the Germans during the first world war, but cracked by the French. Quite a difficult cipher to break.

- ADFGX Cipher:

ADFGVX cipher a fractionating transposition cipher. Used by the Germans during the first world war, closely related to ADFGVX.

- Bifid Cipher:

Bifid cipher a fractionating transposition cipher. Only ever used by amateur cryptographers. Can be broken fairly easily.

- Straddle Checkerboard Cipher:

Straddle checkerboard cipher a substitution cipher with variable length substitutions.

- Trifid Cipher:

Trifid cipher a fractionating transposition cipher. A variant of Bifid.

- Fractionated Morse Cipher:

Fractionated Morse first converts the plaintext to morse code, then enciphers fixed size blocks of morse code back to letters. This procedure means plaintext letters are mixed into the ciphertext letters i.e. one plaintext letter does not map to one ciphertext letter.

SUBSTITUTION CIPHER

A substitution cipher is a method of cryptography (the science of writing, analyzing, and deciphering codes) which converts standard language or plaintext into coded language or ciphertext, by replacing units of plaintext in accordance with a fixed set of rules. These plaintext units may be individual letters or characters, letter pairs, triplets, or other combinations.

Substitution ciphers may replace only the letters of the standard alphabet with ciphertext, or apply substitutions to spaces and punctuation marks as well.

Simple Substitution Ciphers

Simple or monoalphabetic substitution ciphers rely on mapping individual letters of a plaintext alphabet to a particular letter of the ciphertext alphabet.

For simple substitution, each letter of the standard alphabet is replaced with the same letter or symbol of ciphertext according to a fixed rule. So for example, if in a coded message the letter "a" is to be replaced with the "#" symbol, that same substitution will occur in every message encoded according to that particular substitution rule.

Since each letter of the standard alphabet may, in theory be substituted with any other letter or symbol, there's an infinite number of potential monoalphabetic substitution ciphers. In manual coding operations, it's easiest to create the ciphertext alphabet first, then perform encryptions by comparing this with the plaintext alphabet.

Keyword Generators

A popular method used in creating ciphertext alphabets for simple substitution is to begin with a keyword – preferably a word in which each letter of the standard alphabet only occurs once (like "stock" or "cabin"). This word is placed at the beginning of the table, and the remaining alphabet letters are tagged onto the end, in their usual order (i.e. skipping those letters which occur in the keyword).

The Atbash Cipher

One of the earliest recorded substitution ciphers, the Atbash cipher imposed monoalphabetic substitutions on the Hebrew alphabet. It was a simple system in which every passage of plaintext that was encoded used the same ciphertext alphabet.

The Atbash cipher created its ciphertext alphabet by simply reversing the plaintext alphabet, mapping the first letter of the standard alphabet to the last, the second to the second last, and so on. The system derived its name phonetically from its substitution of the Hebrew "aleph" with its cipher form of "tav" and "beth" with "shin".

Naturally, the method may be applied to any language alphabet, and is a quick and easy tool for cloaking messages of non-critical importance from the eyes of casual observers. An element of additional security may be applied to the technique by tagging a string of numbers, symbols or punctuation marks to the end of the ciphertext alphabet before performing the substitutions.

The Caesar Cipher

Slightly more secure than Atbash was the Shift Cipher used by Julius Caesar in sending encrypted communications to his armies in the field. The Shift or Caesar Cipher works by shifting the alphabet a set number of moves and replacing each letter of plaintext with its shifted ciphertext equivalent. In ancient Rome, Caesar replaced the letter "a" with the letter "d" – a "shift of 3", which in essence created an encryption key for the language.

So having decided on a shift number, creating the ciphertext alphabet is a relatively simple matter of shifting the standard alphabet letters by the agreed number of places to the left. This gives "d" as the first letter of the Caesar Cipher alphabet, followed by "efgh" etc., with the letters "abc" tacked on after "z". Encryption of the original message occurs by simple letter substitution with the corresponding ciphertext.

Decryption of the ciphertext may be accomplished by referring to the shifted alphabet table created for encrypting the message, or by creating a fresh table that shifts the standard alphabet letters by the same number of positions in the opposite direction.

The Pigpen Cipher (Freemasons Cipher)

This substitution cipher replaces each letter of the plaintext alphabet with a corresponding symbol. Though its historical origins are unclear, the Pigpen Cipher was used by several groups throughout the years, most notably including Union soldiers imprisoned by the Confederacy during the American Civil War, and by the semi-secret society of Freemasons from the 18th century.

Freemasons used the Pigpen Cipher in many aspects of their daily lives, and even in death: Cryptographic messages have been discovered on the gravestone inscriptions of presumed members of the society.

A grid of symbols is set up to create the ciphertext "alphabet", and each letter of a coded message is simply matched and replaced by its designated symbol.

Digraph Substitution Ciphers

In contrast to monoalphabetic substitution ciphers, digraph substitution ciphers replace pairs of letters from the standard alphabet with a pair of ciphertext letters.

The plaintext message is first split up into pairs of letters, or digraphs. Substitution pairs may be determined using a combination of monoalphabetic techniques, such as two Caesar Shifts. The first shift would be applied to the first letter of each pair, with a second shift dictating the second letter.

Breaking The Code

Despite their success in historical applications, simple, monoalphabetic, and digraph substitution ciphers are quite easy to break – given time and the proper techniques.

Brute force (trial and error) may be sufficient to crack a Caesar Shift cipher, as there are only 26 possible ciphertext alphabets which use all the standard letters.

In other cases, application of a high-sounding process called Frequency Analysis may crack the code. This relatively simple technique involves looking at a piece of encrypted text with letter substitutions in terms of the known rules governing the use of standard language: Most frequently occurring letters ("e" in English), common words ("the", "and") and similar conditions may give a fair initial indication of message content. Some educated guesswork may be used to fill in the remaining gaps.

Polyalphabetic Substitution Ciphers

Because of these inherent weaknesses, attempts were made to develop stronger substitution codes. In about 1467 Leon Battista Alberti created the first known polyalphabetic substitution cipher. The Alberti Cipher used a mixed alphabet for encryption, which would switch to a different ciphertext alphabet at random points in the text. These points were marked in the code by an uppercase letter. Alberti encoded keys to this system on sets of cipher discs.

Building on Alberti's work, a diverse group including the German monk Johannes Trithemius, Italian scientist Giovanni Porta, and most notably the 16th century French diplomat Blaise de Vigenère distilled polyalphabetic substitution into the Vigenère Cipher, which made full use of up to 26 different ciphertext alphabets and remained until 1854 as 'Le Chiffre Undechiffrable', or 'The Unbreakable Cipher'.

Modern Applications

Of course, even the strongest substitution code wouldn't stand up to five minutes of intense hacking using today's technology. But though these techniques are in no way secure enough for modern applications, they did pave the way for the development of contemporary methods of encryption and cryptographic analysis.

Affine Cipher

The affine cipher is a type of monoalphabetic substitution cipher, wherein each letter in an alphabet is mapped to its numeric equivalent, encrypted using a simple mathematical function, and converted back to a letter. The formula used means that each letter encrypts to one other letter, and back again, meaning the cipher is essentially a standard substitution cipher with a rule governing which letter goes to which. As such, it has the weaknesses of all substitution ciphers. Each letter is enciphered with the function $(ax + b)$ mod 26, where b is the magnitude of the shift.

In the affine cipher the letters of an alphabet of size m are first mapped to the integers in the range 0 $m - 1$. It then uses modular arithmetic to transform the integer that each plaintext letter corresponds to into another integer that correspond to a ciphertext letter. The encryption function for a single letter is:

$$E(x) = (ax + b) \bmod m,$$

where modulus m is the size of the alphabet and a and b are the keys of the cipher. The value a must be chosen such that a and m are coprime. The decryption function is:

$$D(x) = a^{-1}(x - b) \bmod m,$$

where a^{-1} is the modular multiplicative inverse of a modulo m. i.e., it satisfies the equation:

$$1 = aa^{-1} \bmod m.$$

The multiplicative inverse of a only exists if a and m are coprime. Hence without the restriction on a, decryption might not be possible. It can be shown as follows that decryption function is the inverse of the encryption function,

$$D(E(x)) = a^{-1}(E(x)-b) \bmod m$$
$$= a^{-1}(((ax+b) \bmod m)-b) \bmod m$$
$$= a^{-1}(ax+b-b) \bmod m$$
$$= a^{-1}ax \bmod m$$
$$= x \bmod m.$$

Weaknesses

Since the affine cipher is still a monoalphabetic substitution cipher, it inherits the weaknesses of that class of ciphers. The Caesar cipher is an Affine cipher with $a = 1$ since the encrypting function simply reduces to a linear shift.

Considering the specific case of encrypting messages in English (i.e. $m = 26$), there are a total of 286 non-trivial affine ciphers, not counting the 26 trivial Caesar ciphers. This number comes from the fact there are 12 numbers that are coprime with 26 that are less than 26 (these are the possible values of a). Each value of a can have 26 different addition shifts (the b value); therefore, there are 12×26 or 312 possible keys. This lack of variety renders the system as highly insecure when considered in light of Kerckhoffs' Principle.

The cipher's primary weakness comes from the fact that if the cryptanalyst can discover (by means of frequency analysis, brute force, guessing or otherwise) the plaintext of two ciphertext characters then the key can be obtained by solving a simultaneous equation. Since we know a and m are relatively prime this can be used to rapidly discard many "false" keys in an automated system.

The same type of transformation used in affine ciphers is used in linear congruential generators, a type of pseudorandom number generator. This generator is not a cryptographically secure pseudorandom number generator for the same reason that the affine cipher is not secure.

Examples:

In these two examples, one encrypting and one decrypting, the alphabet is going to be the letters A through Z, and will have the corresponding values found in the following table.

A	B	C	D	E	F	G	H	I	J	K	L	M	N	O	P	Q	R	S	T	U	V	W	X	Y	Z
0	1	2	3	4	5	6	7	8	9	10	11	12	13	14	15	16	17	18	19	20	21	22	23	24	25

Encrypting

In this encrypting example, the plaintext to be encrypted is "AFFINE CIPHER" using the table mentioned above for the numeric values of each letter, taking a to be 5, b to be 8, and m to be 26 since there are 26 characters in the alphabet being used. Only the value of a has a restriction since it has to be coprime with 26. The possible values that a could be are 1, 3, 5, 7, 9, 11, 15, 17, 19, 21, 23, and 25. The value for b can be arbitrary as long as a does not equal 1 since this is the shift of the cipher. Thus, the encryption function for this example will be $y = E(x) = (5x + 8) \bmod 26$. The first step in encrypting the message is to write the numeric values of each letter.

plaintext	A	F	F	I	N	E	C	I	P	H	E	R
x	0	5	5	8	13	4	2	8	15	7	4	17

Now, take each value of x, and solve the first part of the equation, $(5x + 8)$. After finding the value of $(5x + 8)$ for each character, take the remainder when dividing the result of $(5x + 8)$ by 26. The following table shows the first four steps of the encrypting process.

plaintext	A	F	F	I	N	E	C	I	P	H	E	R
x	0	5	5	8	13	4	2	8	15	7	4	17
$(5x + 8)$	8	33	33	48	73	28	18	48	83	43	28	93
$(5x + 8) \bmod 26$	8	7	7	22	21	2	18	22	5	17	2	15

The final step in encrypting the message is to look up each numeric value in the table for the corresponding letters. In this example, the encrypted text would be IHHWVCSWFRCP. The table below shows the completed table for encrypting a message in the Affine cipher.

plaintext	A	F	F	I	N	E	C	I	P	H	E	R
x	0	5	5	8	13	4	2	8	15	7	4	17
$(5x + 8)$	8	33	33	48	73	28	18	48	83	43	28	93
$(5x + 8) \bmod 26$	8	7	7	22	21	2	18	22	5	17	2	15
ciphertext	I	H	H	W	V	C	S	W	F	R	C	P

Decrypting

In this decryption example, the ciphertext that will be decrypted is the ciphertext from the encryption example. The corresponding decryption function is $D(y) = 21(y - 8) \bmod 26$, where a^{-1} is calculated to be 21, and b is 8. To begin, write the numeric equivalents to each letter in the ciphertext, as shown in the table below.

ciphertext	I	H	H	W	V	C	S	W	F	R	C	P
y	8	7	7	22	21	2	18	22	5	17	2	15

Now, the next step is to compute $21(y - 8)$, and then take the remainder when that result is divided by 26. The following table shows the results of both computations.

ciphertext	I	H	H	W	V	C	S	W	F	R	C	P
y	8	7	7	22	21	2	18	22	5	17	2	15
21(y − 8)	0	−21	−21	294	273	−126	210	294	−63	189	−126	147
21(y − 8) mod 26	0	5	5	8	13	4	2	8	15	7	4	17

The final step in decrypting the ciphertext is to use the table to convert numeric values back into letters. The plaintext in this decryption is AFFINECIPHER. Below is the table with the final step completed.

ciphertext	I	H	H	W	V	C	S	W	F	R	C	P
y	8	7	7	22	21	2	18	22	5	17	2	15
21(y − 8)	0	−21	−21	294	273	−126	210	294	−63	189	−126	147
21(y − 8) mod 26	0	5	5	8	13	4	2	8	15	7	4	17
plaintext	A	F	F	I	N	E	C	I	P	H	E	R

Entire Alphabet Encoded

To make encrypting and decrypting quicker, the entire alphabet can be encrypted to create a one-to-one map between the letters of the cleartext and the ciphertext. In this example, the one-to-one map would be the following:

letter in the cleartext	A	B	C	D	E	F	G	H	I	J	K	L	M	N	O	P	Q	R	S	T	U	V	W	X	Y	Z
number in the cleartext	0	1	2	3	4	5	6	7	8	9	10	11	12	13	14	15	16	17	18	19	20	21	22	23	24	25
(5x + 8) mod 26	8	13	18	23	2	7	12	17	22	1	6	11	16	21	0	5	10	15	20	25	4	9	14	19	24	3
ciphertext letter	I	N	S	X	C	H	M	R	W	B	G	L	Q	V	A	F	K	P	U	Z	E	J	O	T	Y	D

Programming Examples

Using the Python programming language, the following code can be used to create an encrypted alphabet using the Roman letters A through Z.

```
#Prints a transposition table for an affine cipher.

#a must be coprime to m=26.

def affine(a, b):

  for i in range(26):

    print(chr(i+ord('A')) + ": " + chr(((a*i+b)%26)+ord('A')))

#An example call


affine(5, 8)
```

Or in Java:

```
public void Affine(int a, int b){

        for (int num = 0; num < 26; num++)

          System.out.println(((char)('A'+num)) + ":" + ((char)('A'+(a*num + b)% 26)) );

    }

Affine(5,8)
```

Or in Pascal:

```
Procedure Affine(a,b : Integer);
 begin
  for num := 0 to 25 do
   WriteLn(Chr(num+65) , ': ' , Chr(((a*num + b) mod 26) + 65);
 end;


begin
 Affine(5,8)
end.
```

In PHP:

```
function affineCipher($a, $b) {
  for($i = 0; $i < 26; $i++) {
    echo chr($i + 65) . ' ' . chr(65 + ($a * $i + $b) % 26) . '<br>';
  }
}


affineCipher(5, 8);
```

CAESAR CIPHER

In cryptography, a Caesar cipher, also known as Caesar's cipher, the shift cipher, Caesar's code or Caesar shift, is one of the simplest and most widely known encryption techniques. It is a type of substitution cipher in which each letter in the plaintext is replaced by a letter some fixed number of positions down the alphabet. For example, with a left shift of 3, D would be replaced by A, E would become B, and so on. The method is named after Julius Caesar, who used it in his private correspondence.

The encryption step performed by a Caesar cipher is often incorporated as part of more complex schemes, such as the Vigenère cipher, and still has modern application in the ROT13 system. As with all single-alphabet substitution ciphers, the Caesar cipher is easily broken and in modern practice offers essentially no communications security.

Example:

The transformation can be represented by aligning two alphabets; the cipher alphabet is the plain alphabet rotated left or right by some number of positions. For instance, here is a Caesar cipher using a left rotation of three places, equivalent to a right shift of 23 (the shift parameter is used as the key):

```
Plain:    ABCDEFGHIJKLMNOPQRSTUVWXYZ

Cipher:   XYZABCDEFGHIJKLMNOPQRSTUVW
```

When encrypting, a person looks up each letter of the message in the "plain" line and writes down the corresponding letter in the "cipher" line.

```
Plaintext:  THE QUICK BROWN FOX JUMPS OVER THE LAZY DOG

Ciphertext: QEB NRFZH YOLTK CLU GRJMP LSBO QEB IXWV ALD
```

Deciphering is done in reverse, with a right shift of 3.

The encryption can also be represented using modular arithmetic by first transforming the letters into numbers, according to the scheme, A → 0, B → 1,..., Z → 25. Encryption of a letter x by a shift n can be described mathematically as,

$$E_n(x) = (x+n) \bmod 26.$$

Decryption is performed similarly,

$$D_n(x) = (x-n) \bmod 26.$$

(There are different definitions for the modulo operation. In the above, the result is in the range 0 to 25; i.e., if $x + n$ or $x - n$ are not in the range 0 to 25, we have to subtract or add 26.)

The replacement remains the same throughout the message, so the cipher is classed as a type of *monoalphabetic substitution*, as opposed to polyalphabetic substitution.

Breaking the Cipher

Decryption shift	Candidate plaintext
0	exxegoexsrgi
1	dwwdfndwrqfh
2	cvvcemcvqpeg
3	buubdlbupodf
4	attackatonce
5	zsszbjzsnmbd

6	yrryaiyrmlac
	...
23	haahjrhavujl
24	gzzgiqgzutik
25	fyyfhpfytshj

The Caesar cipher can be easily broken even in a ciphertext-only scenario. Two situations can be considered:

1. An attacker knows (or guesses) that some sort of simple substitution cipher has been used, but not specifically that it is a Caesar scheme;

2. An attacker knows that a Caesar cipher is in use, but does not know the shift value.

In the first case, the cipher can be broken using the same techniques as for a general simple substitution cipher, such as frequency analysis or pattern words. While solving, it is likely that an attacker will quickly notice the regularity in the solution and deduce that a Caesar cipher is the specific algorithm employed.

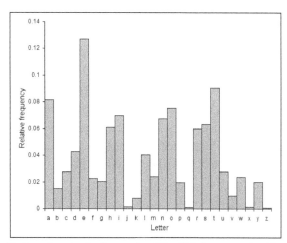

The distribution of letters in a typical sample of English language text has a distinctive and predictable shape. A Caesar shift "rotates" this distribution, and it is possible to determine the shift by examining the resultant frequency graph.

In the second instance, breaking the scheme is even more straightforward. Since there are only a limited number of possible shifts (26 in English), they can each be tested in turn in a brute force attack. One way to do this is to write out a snippet of the ciphertext in a table of all possible shifts – a technique sometimes known as "completing the plain component". The example given is for the ciphertext "EXXEGOEXSRGI"; the plaintext is instantly recognisable by eye at a shift of four. Another way of viewing this method is that, under each letter of the ciphertext, the entire alphabet is written out in reverse starting at that letter. This attack can be accelerated using a set of strips prepared with the alphabet written down in reverse order. The strips are then aligned to form the ciphertext along one row, and the plaintext should appear in one of the other rows.

Another brute force approach is to match up the frequency distribution of the letters. By graphing the frequencies of letters in the ciphertext, and by knowing the expected distribution of those letters in the original language of the plaintext, a human can easily spot the value of the shift by looking at the displacement of particular features of the graph. This is known as frequency analysis. For example, in the English language the plaintext frequencies of the letters E, T, (usually most frequent), and Q, Z (typically least frequent) are particularly distinctive. Computers can also do this by measuring how well the actual frequency distribution matches up with the expected distribution; for example, the chi-squared statistic can be used.

For natural language plaintext, there will typically be only one plausible decryption, although for extremely short plaintexts, multiple candidates are possible. For example, the ciphertext MPQY could, plausibly, decrypt to either "aden" or "know" (assuming the plaintext is in English); similarly, "ALIIP" to "dolls" or "wheel"; and "AFCCP" to "jolly" or "cheer".

With the Caesar cipher, encrypting a text multiple times provides no additional security. This is because two encryptions of, say, shift A and shift B, will be equivalent to a single encryption with shift $A + B$. In mathematical terms, the set of encryption operations under each possible key forms a group under composition.

PLAYFAIR CIPHER

The Playfair cipher was the first practical digraph substitution cipher. The scheme was invented in 1854 by Charles Wheatstone, but was named after Lord Playfair who promoted the use of the cipher. The technique encrypts pairs of letters (digraphs), instead of single letters as in the simple substitution cipher. The Playfair is significantly harder to break since the frequency analysis used for simple substitution ciphers does not work with it. Frequency analysis can still be undertaken, but on the 25*25=625 possible digraphs rather than the 25 possible monographs. Frequency analysis thus requires much more ciphertext in order to work. For a tutorial on breaking Playfair with a simulated annealing algorithm.

It was used for tactical purposes by British forces in the Second Boer War and in World War I and for the same purpose by the Australians during World War II. This was because Playfair is reasonably fast to use and requires no special equipment. A typical scenario for Playfair use would be to protect important but non-critical secrets during actual combat. By the time the enemy cryptanalysts could break the message the information was useless to them .

From Kahn's 'The CodeBreakers':

> Perhaps the most famous cipher of 1943 involved the future president of the U.S., J. F. Kennedy, Jr. On 2 August 1943, Australian Coastwatcher Lieutenant Arthur Reginald Evans of the Royal Australian Naval Volunteer Reserve saw a pinpoint of flame on the dark waters of Blackett Strait from his jungle ridge on Kolombangara Island, one of the Solomons. He did not know that the Japanese destroyer Amagiri had rammed and sliced in half an American patrol boat PT-109, under the command of Lieutenant John F. Kennedy, United States Naval Reserve. Evans received the following message at 0930 on the morning of the 2 of August 1943:
>
> ```
> KXJEY  UREBE  ZWEHE  WRYTU  HEYFS
>
> KREHE  GOYFI  WTTTU  OLKSY  CAJPO
> ```

```
BOTEI   ZONTX   BYBWT   GONEY   CUZWR

GDSON   SXBOU   YWRHE   BAAHY   USEDQ
```

The translation:

```
PT BOAT ONE OWE NINE LOST IN ACTION IN BLACKETT

STRAIT TWO MILES SW MERESU COVE X CREW OF TWELVE

X REQUEST ANY INFORMATION.
```

The coastwatchers regularly used the Playfair system. Evans deciphered it with the key ROYAL NEW ZEALAND NAVY [this is key square ROYALNEWZDVBCFGHIKMPQSTUX] and learned of Kennedy's fate. About ten hours later, at 10:00 p.m. Kennedy and his crew was rescued.

The Algorithm

The 'key' for a playfair cipher is generally a word, for the sake of example we will choose 'monarchy'. This is then used to generate a 'key square', e.g.

```
m o n a r

c h y b d

e f g i k

l p q s t

u v w x z
```

Any sequence of 25 letters can be used as a key, so long as all letters are in it and there are no repeats. Note that there is no 'j', it is combined with 'i'. We now apply the encryption rules to encrypt the plaintext.

1. Remove any punctuation or characters that are not present in the key square (this may mean spelling out numbers, punctuation etc.).

2. Identify any double letters in the plaintext and replace the second occurence with an 'x' e.g. 'hammer' -> 'ha mx er'.

3. If the plaintext has an odd number of characters, append an 'x' to the end to make it even.

4. Break the plaintext into pairs of letters, e.g. 'hamxer' -> 'ha mx er'

5. The algorithm now works on each of the letter pairs.

6. Locate the letters in the key square, (the examples given are using the key square above)

   a. If the letters are in different rows and columns, replace the pair with the letters on the same row respectively but at the other pair of corners of the rectangle defined by the original pair. The order is important – the first encrypted letter of the pair is the one that lies on the same row as the first plaintext letter. 'ha' -> 'bo', 'es' -> 'il'

   b. If the letters appear on the same row of the table, replace them with the letters to their immediate right respectively (wrapping around to the left side of the row if a letter in the original pair was on the right side of the row). 'ma' -> 'or', 'lp' -> 'pq'

c. If the letters appear on the same column of the table, replace them with the letters immediately below respectively (wrapping around to the top side of the column if a letter in the original pair was on the bottom side of the column). 'rk' -> 'dt', 'pv' -> 'vo'

Clarification with pictures - Assume one wants to encrypt the digraph OR. There are three general cases:

```
m  *  *  a  *

*  *  *  *  *

*  *  *  *  *

l  *  *  s  *

*  *  *  *  *
```

Hence, al -> ms

```
*  *  *  *  *

*  h  y  b  d

*  *  *  *  *

*  *  *  *  *

*  *  *  *  *
```

Hence, hb -> yd

```
*  *  n  *  *

*  *  y  *  *

*  *  *  *  *

*  *  q  *  *

*  *  w  *  *
```

Hence, nq -> yw

An example encryption, "we are discovered, save yourself" using the key square shown at the beginning of this section:

```
plaintext:   wearediscoveredsaveyourselfx

ciphertext:  ugrmkcsxhmufmkbtoxgcmvatluiv
```

Two-square Cipher

The Two-square cipher, also called double Playfair, is a manual symmetric encryption technique. It was developed to ease the cumbersome nature of the large encryption/decryption matrix used in the four-square cipher while still being slightly stronger than the single-square Playfair cipher.

The technique encrypts pairs of letters (*digraphs*), and thus falls into a category of ciphers known as polygraphic substitution ciphers. This adds significant strength to the encryption when compared with monographic substitution ciphers, which operate on single characters. The use of digraphs makes the two-square technique less susceptible to frequency analysis attacks, as the analysis must be done on 676 possible digraphs rather than just 26 for monographic substitution. The frequency analysis of digraphs is possible, but considerably more difficult, and it generally requires a much larger ciphertext in order to be useful.

Using Two-square

The two-square cipher comes in two varieties: horizontal and vertical. The vertical two-square uses two 5x5 matrices, one above the other. The horizontal two-square has the two 5x5 matrices side by side. Each of the 5x5 matrices contains the letters of the alphabet (usually omitting "Q" or putting both "I" and "J" in the same location to reduce the alphabet to fit). The alphabets in both squares are generally mixed alphabets, each based on some keyword or phrase.

To generate the 5x5 matrices, one would first fill in the spaces in the matrix with the letters of a keyword or phrase (dropping any duplicate letters), then fill the remaining spaces with the rest of the letters of the alphabet in order (again omitting "Q" to reduce the alphabet to fit). The key can be written in the top rows of the table, from left to right, or in some other pattern, such as a spiral beginning in the upper-left-hand corner and ending in the center. The keyword together with the conventions for filling in the 5x5 table constitute the cipher key. The two-square algorithm allows for two separate keys, one for each matrix.

As an example, here are the vertical two-square matrices for the keywords "example" and "keyword:"

```
E X A M P

L B C D F

G H I J K

N O R S T

U V W Y Z


K E Y W O

R D A B C

F G H I J

L M N P S

T U V X Z
```

Algorithm

Encryption using two-square is basically the same as the system used in four-square, except that the plaintext and ciphertext digraphs use the same matrixes.

To encrypt a message, one would follow these steps:

- Split the payload message into digraphs. (*help me obi wan kenobi* becomes *he lp me ob iw an ke no bi*)

- For a vertical two-square, the first character of both plaintext and ciphertext digraphs uses the top matrix, while the second character uses the bottom.

- For a horizontal two-square, the first character of both digraphs uses the left matrix, while the second character uses the right.

- Find the first letter in the digraph in the upper/left text matrix.

```
E  X  A  M  P

L  B  C  D  F

G  H  I  J  K

N  O  R  S  T

U  V  W  Y  Z


K  E  Y  W  O

R  D  A  B  C

F  G  H  I  J

L  M  N  P  S

T  U  V  X  Z
```

- Find the second letter in the digraph in the lower/right plaintext matrix.

```
E  X  A  M  P

L  B  C  D  F

G  H  I  J  K

N  O  R  S  T

U  V  W  Y  Z


K  E  Y  W  O

R  D  A  B  C

F  G  H  I  J

L  M  N  P  S

T  U  V  X  Z
```

A rectangle is defined by the two plaintext characters and the opposite corners define the ciphertext digraph.

```
E  X  A  M  P

L  B  C  D  F

G  H  I  J  K

N  O  R  S  T

U  V  W  Y  Z


K  E  Y  W  O

R  D  A  B  C

F  G  H  I  J

L  M  N  P  S

T  U  V  X  Z
```

Using the vertical two-square example given above, we can encrypt the following plaintext:

```
Plaintext:  he lp me ob iw an ke no bi

Ciphertext: XG DL XW SD JY AN HO TK DG
```

Here is the same two-square written out again but blanking all of the values that aren't used for encrypting the digraph "LP" into "DL":

```
-  -  -  -  -

L  -  -  D  -

-  -  -  -  -

-  -  -  -  -

-  -  -  -  -


-  -  -  -  -

-  -  -  -  -

-  -  -  -  -

L  -  -  P  -

-  -  -  -  -
```

The rectangle rule used to encrypt and decrypt can be seen clearly in this diagram. The method for decrypting is identical to the method for encryption.

Just like Playfair (and unlike four-square), there are special circumstances when the two letters in a digraph are in the same column for vertical two-square or in the same row for horizontal two-square. For vertical two-square, a plaintext digraph that ends up with both characters in the same column gives the same digraph in the ciphertext. For horizontal two-square, a plaintext digraph with both characters in the same row gives (by convention) that digraph with the characters reversed in the ciphertext. In cryptography this is referred to as a transparency. (The horizontal version is sometimes called a reverse transparency.) Notice in the above example how the digraphs "HE" and "AN" mapped to themselves. A weakness of two-square is that about 20% of digraphs will be transparencies.

```
E X A M P

L B C D F

G H I J K

N O R S T

U V W Y Z


K E Y W O

R D A B C

F G H I J

L M N P S

T U V X Z
```

Two-square Cryptanalysis

Like most pre-modern era ciphers, the two-square cipher can be easily cracked if there is enough text. Obtaining the key is relatively straightforward if both plaintext and ciphertext are known. When only the ciphertext is known, brute force cryptanalysis of the cipher involves searching through the key space for matches between the frequency of occurrence of digraphs (pairs of letters) and the known frequency of occurrence of digraphs in the assumed language of the original message.

Cryptanalysis of two-square almost always revolves around the transparency weakness. Depending on whether vertical or horizontal two-square was used, either the ciphertext or the reverse of the ciphertext should show a significant number of plaintext fragments. In a large enough ciphertext sample, there are likely to be several transparent digraphs in a row, revealing possible word fragments. From these word fragments the analyst can generate candidate plaintext strings and work backwards to the keyword.

TRANSPOSITION CIPHER

In cryptography, a transposition cipher is a method of encryption by which the positions held by units of plaintext (which are commonly characters or groups of characters) are shifted according to a regular system, so that the ciphertext constitutes a permutation of the plaintext. That is, the order of the units is changed (the plaintext is reordered). Mathematically a bijective function is used on the characters' positions to encrypt and an inverse function to decrypt.

Rail Fence Cipher

The Rail Fence cipher is a form of transposition cipher that gets its name from the way in which it is encoded. In the rail fence cipher, the plaintext is written downwards on successive "rails" of an imaginary fence, then moving up when we get to the bottom. The message is then read off in rows. For example, using three "rails" and a message of 'WE ARE DISCOVERED. FLEE AT ONCE', the cipherer writes out:

```
W . . . E . . . C . . . R . . . L . . . T . . . E
. E . R . D . S . O . E . E . F . E . A . O . C .
. . A . . . I . . . V . . . D . . . E . . . N . .
```

Then reads off:

```
WECRL TEERD SOEEF EAOCA IVDEN
```

(The cipher has broken this ciphertext up into blocks of five to help avoid errors. This is a common technique used to make the cipher more easily readable. The spacing is not related to spaces in the plaintext and so does not carry any information about the plaintext.)

The rail fence cipher was used by the ancient Greeks in the scytale, a mechanical system of producing a transposition cipher. The system consisted of a cylinder and a ribbon that was wrapped around the cylinder. The message to be encrypted was written on the coiled ribbon. The letters of the original message would be rearranged when the ribbon was uncoiled from the cylinder. However, the message was easily decrypted when the ribbon was recoiled on a cylinder of the same diameter as the encrypting cylinder.

Route Cipher

In a route cipher, the plaintext is first written out in a grid of given dimensions, then read off in a pattern given in the key. For example, using the same plaintext that we used for rail fence:

```
W R I O R F E O E
E E S V E L A N J
A D C E D E T C X
```

The key might specify "spiral inwards, clockwise, starting from the top right". That would give a cipher text of:

```
EJXCTEDEC DAEWRIORF EONALEVSE
```

Route ciphers have many more keys than a rail fence. In fact, for messages of reasonable length, the number of possible keys is potentially too great to be enumerated even by modern machinery. However, not all keys are equally good. Badly chosen routes will leave excessive chunks of plaintext, or text simply reversed, and this will give cryptanalysts a clue as to the routes.

A variation of the route cipher was the Union Route Cipher, used by Union forces during the American Civil War. This worked much like an ordinary route cipher, but transposed whole words instead of individual letters. Because this would leave certain highly sensitive words exposed, such words would first be concealed by code. The cipher clerk may also add entire null words, which were often chosen to make the ciphertext humorous.

Columnar Transposition

In a columnar transposition, the message is written out in rows of a fixed length, and then read out again column by column, and the columns are chosen in some scrambled order. Both the width of the rows and the permutation of the columns are usually defined by a keyword. For example, the keyword ZEBRAS is of length 6 (so the rows are of length 6), and the permutation is defined by the alphabetical order of the letters in the keyword. In this case, the order would be "6 3 2 4 1 5".

In a regular columnar transposition cipher, any spare spaces are filled with nulls; in an irregular columnar transposition cipher, the spaces are left blank. Finally, the message is read off in columns, in the order specified by the keyword. For example, suppose we use the keyword ZEBRAS and the message WE ARE DISCOVERED. FLEE AT ONCE. In a regular columnar transposition, we write this into the grid as follows:

```
6 3 2 4 1 5

W E A R E D

I S C O V E

R E D F L E

E A T O N C

E Q K J E U
```

Providing five nulls (QKJEU), these letters can be randomly selected as they just fill out the incomplete columns and are not part of the message. The ciphertext is then read off as:

```
EVLNE ACDTK ESEAQ ROFOJ DEECU WIREE
```

In the irregular case, the columns are not completed by nulls:

```
6 3 2 4 1 5

W E A R E D

I S C O V E

R E D F L E

E A T O N C

E
```

This results in the following ciphertext:

```
EVLNA CDTES EAROF ODEEC WIREE
```

To decipher it, the recipient has to work out the column lengths by dividing the message length by the key length. Then he can write the message out in columns again, then re-order the columns by reforming the key word.

In a variation, the message is blocked into segments that are the key length long and to each segment the same permutation (given by the key) is applied. This is equivalent to a columnar transposition where the read-out is by rows instead of columns.

Columnar transposition continued to be used for serious purposes as a component of more complex ciphers at least into the 1950s.

Double Transposition

A single columnar transposition could be attacked by guessing possible column lengths, writing the message out in its columns (but in the wrong order, as the key is not yet known), and then looking for possible anagrams. Thus to make it stronger, a double transposition was often used. This is simply a columnar transposition applied twice. The same key can be used for both transpositions, or two different keys can be used.

As an example, we can take the result of the irregular columnar transposition, and perform a second encryption with a different keyword, STRIPE, which gives the permutation "564231":

```
5 6 4 2 3 1

E V L N A C

D T E S E A

R O F O D E

E C W I R E

E
```

As before, this is read off columnwise to give the ciphertext:

```
CAEEN SOIAE DRLEF WEDRE EVTOC
```

If multiple messages of exactly the same length are encrypted using the same keys, they can be anagrammed simultaneously. This can lead to both recovery of the messages, and to recovery of the keys (so that every other message sent with those keys can be read).

During World War I, the German military used a double columnar transposition cipher, changing the keys infrequently. The system was regularly solved by the French, naming it Übchi, who were typically able to quickly find the keys once they'd intercepted a number of messages of the same length, which generally took only a few days. However, the French success became widely known and, after a publication in *Le Matin*, the Germans changed to a new system on 18 November 1914.

During World War II, the double transposition cipher was used by Dutch Resistance groups, the French Maquis and the British Special Operations Executive (SOE), which was in charge of managing underground activities in Europe. It was also used by agents of the American Office of Strategic Services and as an emergency cipher for the German Army and Navy.

Until the invention of the VIC cipher, double transposition was generally regarded as the most complicated cipher that an agent could operate reliably under difficult field conditions.

Cryptanalysis

The double transposition cipher can be treated as a single transposition with a key as long as the product of the lengths of the two keys.

In late 2013, a double transposition challenge, regarded by its author as undecipherable, was solved by George Lasry using a divide-and-conquer approach where each transposition was attacked individually.

Myszkowski Transposition

A variant form of columnar transposition, proposed by Émile Victor Théodore Myszkowski in 1902, requires a keyword with recurrent letters. In usual practice, subsequent occurrences of a keyword letter are treated as if the next letter in alphabetical order, *e.g.*, the keyword TOMATO yields a numeric keystring of "532164."

In Myszkowski transposition, recurrent keyword letters are numbered identically, TOMATO yielding a keystring of "432143."

```
4  3  2  1  4  3

W  E  A  R  E  D

I  S  C  O  V  E

R  E  D  F  L  E

E  A  T  O  N  C

E
```

Plaintext columns with unique numbers are transcribed downward; those with recurring numbers are transcribed left to right:

```
ROFOA CDTED SEEEA CWEIV RLENE
```

Disrupted Transposition

The disrupted transposition cipher is a further complication to the normal transposition technique. Instead of filling the matrix row by row, the rows are all filled in irregular fashion. This results in a very complex transposition of the characters. First, we determine the exact number of rows and columns to fill. Next we fill a row until we reach the first alphabet sequence from the keyword sequence. If the first digit is at the 8th place, we will only fill that row up to that position. We continue the next row until the second position and so on based on the given example. If we have reached the end position of the last line we continue by filling the remaining empty places at each line. In our example the difference between the two areas is visible by the lower and upper case characters.

The plain text:

"We confirm the delivery of the documents later"

We use the key BIRTHDAY

On the matrix1: after filling the first area

On the matrix2: we see the same matrix filled completely:

Matrix1:

```
2   5   6   7   4   3   1   8
B   I   R   T   H   D   A   Y
W   E   C   O   N   F   I
R
M   T   H   E   D   E
L   I   V   E   R
Y   O
F   T   H
E   D   O   C
U   M   E   N   T   S   L   A
```

Matrix2:

```
2   5   6   7   4   3   1   8
B   I   R   T   H   D   A   Y
W   E   C   O   N   F   I   t
R   e   r
M   T   H   E   D   E
L   I   V   E   R
Y   O
F   T   H
E   D   O   C
U   M   E   N   T   S   L   A
```

Once the matrix is filled we read it off by the columns, according to the keyword sequence.

The Cipher Text:

ILWRMLYFEUFESNDRTEETIOTDMCRHVHOEOEECNTA

Grilles

Another form of transposition cipher uses grilles, or physical masks with cut-outs. This can produce a highly irregular transposition over the period specified by the size of the grille, but requires the correspondents to keep a physical key secret. Grilles were first proposed in 1550, and were still in military use for the first few months of World War One.

Scytale

The Scytale cipher was used in ancient Greek times to encrypt messages. The device used to make these ciphers was a rod with a polygon base, which was wrapped in paper. People could write on the paper horizontally. When the paper was removed from the device, it would make a strip of letters that seemed randomized. The only way to read the message would be to have a Scytale machine of one's own.

Detection and Cryptanalysis

Since transposition does not affect the frequency of individual symbols, simple transposition can be easily detected by the cryptanalyst by doing a frequency count. If the ciphertext exhibits a frequency distribution very similar to plaintext, it is most likely a transposition. This can then often be attacked by anagramming—sliding pieces of ciphertext around, then looking for sections that look like anagrams of English words, and solving the anagrams. Once such anagrams have been found, they reveal information about the transposition pattern, and can consequently be extended.

Simpler transpositions also often suffer from the property that keys very close to the correct key will reveal long sections of legible plaintext interspersed by gibberish. Consequently, such ciphers may be vulnerable to optimum seeking algorithms such as genetic algorithms.

Combinations

Transposition is often combined with other techniques such as evaluation methods. For example, a simple substitution cipher combined with a columnar transposition avoids the weakness of both. Replacing high frequency ciphertext symbols with high frequency plaintext letters does not reveal chunks of plaintext because of the transposition. Anagramming the transposition does not work because of the substitution. The technique is particularly powerful if combined with fractionation. A disadvantage is that such ciphers are considerably more laborious and error prone than simpler ciphers.

Fractionation

Transposition is particularly effective when employed with fractionation – that is, a preliminary stage that divides each plaintext symbol into several ciphertext symbols. For example, the plaintext alphabet could be written out in a grid, and every letter in the message replaced by its co-ordinates. Another method of fractionation is to simply convert the message to Morse code, with a symbol for spaces as well as dots and dashes.

When such a fractionated message is transposed, the components of individual letters become widely separated in the message, thus achieving Claude E. Shannon's diffusion. Examples of ciphers that combine fractionation and transposition include the bifid cipher, the trifid cipher, the ADFGVX cipher and the VIC cipher.

Another choice would be to replace each letter with its binary representation, transpose that, and then convert the new binary string into the corresponding ASCII characters. Looping the scrambling process on the binary string multiple times before changing it into ASCII characters would likely make it harder to break. Many modern block ciphers use more complex forms of transposition related to this simple idea.

HILL CIPHER

In classical cryptography, the Hill cipher is a polygraphic substitution cipher based on linear algebra. Invented by Lester S. Hill in 1929, it was the first polygraphic cipher in which it was practical (though barely) to operate on more than three symbols at once.

Operation

Each letter is represented by a number modulo 26. Though this is not an essential feature of the cipher, this simple scheme is often used:

Letter	A	B	C	D	E	F	G	H	I	J	K	L	M	N	O	P	Q	R	S	T	U	V	W	X	Y	Z
Number	0	1	2	3	4	5	6	7	8	9	10	11	12	13	14	15	16	17	18	19	20	21	22	23	24	25

To encrypt a message, each block of n letters (considered as an n-component vector) is multiplied by an invertible $n \times n$ matrix, against modulus 26. To decrypt the message, each block is multiplied by the inverse of the matrix used for encryption.

The matrix used for encryption is the cipher key, and it should be chosen randomly from the set of invertible $n \times n$ matrices (modulo 26). The cipher can, of course, be adapted to an alphabet with any number of letters; all arithmetic just needs to be done modulo the number of letters instead of modulo 26.

Consider the message 'ACT', and the key below (or GYB/NQK/URP in letters):

$$\begin{pmatrix} 6 & 24 & 1 \\ 13 & 16 & 10 \\ 20 & 17 & 15 \end{pmatrix}$$

Since 'A' is 0, 'C' is 2 and 'T' is 19, the message is the vector:

$$\begin{pmatrix} 0 \\ 2 \\ 19 \end{pmatrix}$$

Thus the enciphered vector is given by:

$$\begin{pmatrix} 6 & 24 & 1 \\ 13 & 16 & 10 \\ 20 & 17 & 15 \end{pmatrix} \begin{pmatrix} 0 \\ 2 \\ 19 \end{pmatrix} = \begin{pmatrix} 67 \\ 222 \\ 319 \end{pmatrix} \equiv \begin{pmatrix} 15 \\ 14 \\ 7 \end{pmatrix} (\mod 26)$$

It corresponds to a ciphertext of 'POH'. Now, suppose that our message is instead 'CAT', or:

$$\begin{pmatrix} 2 \\ 0 \\ 19 \end{pmatrix}$$

This time, the enciphered vector is given by:

$$\begin{pmatrix} 6 & 24 & 1 \\ 13 & 16 & 10 \\ 20 & 17 & 15 \end{pmatrix} \begin{pmatrix} 2 \\ 0 \\ 19 \end{pmatrix} \equiv \begin{pmatrix} 31 \\ 216 \\ 325 \end{pmatrix} \equiv \begin{pmatrix} 5 \\ 8 \\ 13 \end{pmatrix} (\bmod\, 26)$$

It corresponds to a ciphertext of 'FIN'. Every letter has changed. The Hill cipher has achieved Shannon's diffusion, and an n-dimensional Hill cipher can diffuse fully across n symbols at once.

Decryption

In order to decrypt, we turn the ciphertext back into a vector, then simply multiply by the inverse matrix of the key matrix (IFK/VIV/VMI in letters). We find that, modulo 26, the inverse of the matrix used in the previous example is:

$$\begin{pmatrix} 6 & 24 & 1 \\ 13 & 16 & 10 \\ 20 & 17 & 15 \end{pmatrix}^{-1} \equiv \begin{pmatrix} 8 & 5 & 10 \\ 21 & 8 & 21 \\ 21 & 12 & 8 \end{pmatrix} (\bmod\, 26)$$

Taking the previous example ciphertext of 'POH', we get:

$$\begin{pmatrix} 8 & 5 & 10 \\ 21 & 8 & 21 \\ 21 & 12 & 8 \end{pmatrix} \begin{pmatrix} 15 \\ 14 \\ 7 \end{pmatrix} \equiv \begin{pmatrix} 260 \\ 574 \\ 539 \end{pmatrix} \equiv \begin{pmatrix} 0 \\ 2 \\ 19 \end{pmatrix} (\bmod\, 26)$$

which gets us back to 'ACT', as expected.

Two complications exist in picking the encrypting matrix:

1. Not all matrices have an inverse. The matrix will have an inverse if and only if its determinant is not zero.

2. The determinant of the encrypting matrix must not have any common factors with the modular base.

Thus, if we work modulo 26 as above, the determinant must be nonzero, and must not be divisible by 2 or 13. If the determinant is 0, or has common factors with the modular base, then the matrix cannot be used in the Hill cipher, and another matrix must be chosen (otherwise it will not be possible to decrypt). Fortunately, matrices which satisfy the conditions to be used in the Hill cipher are fairly common.

For our example key matrix:

$$\begin{vmatrix} 6 & 24 & 1 \\ 13 & 16 & 10 \\ 20 & 17 & 15 \end{vmatrix} \equiv 6(16 \cdot 15 - 10 \cdot 17) - 24(13 \cdot 15 - 10 \cdot 20) + 1(13 \cdot 17 - 16 \cdot 20) \equiv 441 \equiv 25 \,(\bmod\, 26)$$

So, modulo 26, the determinant is 25. Since this has no common factors with 26, this matrix can be used for the Hill cipher.

The risk of the determinant having common factors with the modulus can be eliminated by making the modulus prime. Consequently, a useful variant of the Hill cipher adds 3 extra symbols (such as a space, a period and a question mark) to increase the modulus to 29.

Example:

Let $K = \begin{pmatrix} 3 & 3 \\ 2 & 5 \end{pmatrix}$ be the key and suppose the plaintext message is HELP.

Then this plaintext is represented by two pairs.

$$HELP \rightarrow \begin{pmatrix} H \\ E \end{pmatrix}, \begin{pmatrix} L \\ P \end{pmatrix} \rightarrow \begin{pmatrix} 7 \\ 4 \end{pmatrix}, \begin{pmatrix} 11 \\ 15 \end{pmatrix}$$

Then we compute:

$$\begin{pmatrix} 3 & 3 \\ 2 & 5 \end{pmatrix}\begin{pmatrix} 7 \\ 4 \end{pmatrix} \equiv \begin{pmatrix} 7 \\ 8 \end{pmatrix}(\mathrm{mod}\,26), \text{ and}$$

$$\begin{pmatrix} 3 & 3 \\ 2 & 5 \end{pmatrix}\begin{pmatrix} 11 \\ 15 \end{pmatrix} \equiv \begin{pmatrix} 0 \\ 19 \end{pmatrix}(\mathrm{mod}\,26)$$

and continue encryption as follows:

$$\begin{pmatrix} 7 \\ 8 \end{pmatrix}, \begin{pmatrix} 0 \\ 19 \end{pmatrix} \rightarrow \begin{pmatrix} H \\ I \end{pmatrix}, \begin{pmatrix} A \\ T \end{pmatrix}$$

The matrix K is invertible, hence K^{-1} exists such that $KK^{-1} = K^{-1}K = I$. The inverse of K can be computed by using the formula $\begin{pmatrix} a & b \\ c & d \end{pmatrix}^{-1} = (ad-bc)^{-1}\begin{pmatrix} d & -b \\ -c & a \end{pmatrix}$

This formula still holds after a modular reduction if a modular multiplicative inverse is used to compute $(ad-bc)^{-1}$. Hence in this case, we compute

$$K^{-1} \equiv 9^{-1}\begin{pmatrix} 5 & 23 \\ 24 & 3 \end{pmatrix} \equiv 3\begin{pmatrix} 5 & 23 \\ 24 & 3 \end{pmatrix} \equiv \begin{pmatrix} 15 & 17 \\ 20 & 9 \end{pmatrix}(\mathrm{mod}\,26)$$

$$HIAT \rightarrow \begin{pmatrix} H \\ I \end{pmatrix}, \begin{pmatrix} A \\ T \end{pmatrix} \rightarrow \begin{pmatrix} 7 \\ 8 \end{pmatrix}, \begin{pmatrix} 0 \\ 19 \end{pmatrix}$$

Then we compute:

$$\begin{pmatrix} 15 & 17 \\ 20 & 9 \end{pmatrix}\begin{pmatrix} 7 \\ 8 \end{pmatrix} \equiv \begin{pmatrix} 7 \\ 4 \end{pmatrix}(\mathrm{mod}\,26), \text{ and}$$

$$\begin{pmatrix} 15 & 17 \\ 20 & 9 \end{pmatrix}\begin{pmatrix} 0 \\ 19 \end{pmatrix} \equiv \begin{pmatrix} 11 \\ 15 \end{pmatrix}(\mathrm{mod}\,26)$$

Therefore,

$$\begin{pmatrix} 7 \\ 4 \end{pmatrix}, \begin{pmatrix} 11 \\ 15 \end{pmatrix} \rightarrow \begin{pmatrix} H \\ E \end{pmatrix}, \begin{pmatrix} L \\ P \end{pmatrix} \rightarrow HELP\,.$$

Security

The basic Hill cipher is vulnerable to a known-plaintext attack because it is completely linear. An opponent who intercepts n plaintext/ciphertext character pairs can set up a linear system which can (usually) be easily solved; if it happens that this system is indeterminate, it is only necessary to add a few more plaintext/ciphertext pairs. Calculating this solution by standard linear algebra algorithms then takes very little time.

While matrix multiplication alone does not result in a secure cipher it is still a useful step when combined with other non-linear operations, because matrix multiplication can provide diffusion. For example, an appropriately chosen matrix can guarantee that small differences before the matrix multiplication will result in large differences after the matrix multiplication. Indeed, some modern ciphers use a matrix multiplication step to provide diffusion. For example, the MixColumns step in AES is a matrix multiplication. The function g in Twofish is a combination of non-linear S-boxes with a carefully chosen matrix multiplication (MDS).

Key size

The key size is the binary logarithm of the number of possible keys. There are 26^{n^2} matrices of dimension n × n. Thus $\log_2(26^{n^2})$ or about $4.7n^2$ is an upper bound on the key size of the Hill cipher using n × n matrices. This is only an upper bound because not every matrix is invertible and thus usable as a key. The number of invertible matrices can be computed via the Chinese Remainder Theorem. i.e., a matrix is invertible modulo 26 if and only if it is invertible both modulo 2 and modulo 13. The number of invertible n × n matrices modulo 2 is equal to the order of the general linear group GL(n, Z_2). It is:

$$2^{n^2}(1-1/2)(1-1/2^2)\cdots(1-1/2^n).$$

Equally, the number of invertible matrices modulo 13 (i.e. the order of GL(n,Z_{13})) is:

$$13^{n^2}(1-1/13)(1-1/13^2)\cdots(1-1/13^n).$$

The number of invertible matrices modulo 26 is the product of those two numbers. Hence it is:

$$26^{n^2}(1-1/2)(1-1/2^2)\cdots(1-1/2^n)(1-1/13)(1-1/13^2)\cdots(1-1/13^n).$$

Additionally it seems to be prudent to avoid too many zeroes in the key matrix, since they reduce diffusion. The net effect is that the effective keyspace of a basic Hill cipher is about $4.64n^2$-17. For a 5×5 Hill cipher, that is about 114 bits. Of course, key search is not the most efficient known attack.

Mechanical Implementation

When operating on 2 symbols at once, a Hill cipher offers no particular advantage over Playfair or the bifid cipher, and in fact is weaker than either, and slightly more laborious to operate by pencil-and-paper. As the dimension increases, the cipher rapidly becomes infeasible for a human to operate by hand.

A Hill cipher of dimension 6 was implemented mechanically. Hill and a partner were awarded a patent (U.S. Patent 1,845,947) for this device, which performed a 6×6 matrix multiplication modulo 26 using a system of gears and chains.

Unfortunately the gearing arrangements (and thus the key) were fixed for any given machine, so triple encryption was recommended for security: a secret nonlinear step, followed by the wide diffusive step from the machine, followed by a third secret nonlinear step. (The much later Even-Mansour cipher also uses an unkeyed diffusive middle step). Such a combination was actually very powerful for 1929, and indicates that Hill apparently understood the concepts of a meet-in-the-middle attack as well as confusion and diffusion. Unfortunately, his machine did not sell.

POLYALPHABETIC CIPHER

A polyalphabetic cipher is any cipher based on substitution, using multiple substitution alphabets. The Vigenère cipher is probably the best-known example of a polyalphabetic cipher, though it is a simplified special case. The Enigma machine is more complex but is still fundamentally a polyalphabetic substitution cipher.

The work of Al-Qalqashandi, based on the earlier work of Ibn al-Durayhim, contained the first published discussion of the substitution and transposition of ciphers, as well as the first description of a polyalphabetic cipher, in which each plaintext letter is assigned more than one substitute. However, it has been claimed that polyalphabetic ciphers may have been developed by the Arab cryptologist Al Kindi centuries earlier.

The Alberti cipher by Leon Battista Alberti around 1467 was an early polyalphabetic cipher. Alberti used a mixed alphabet to encrypt a message, but whenever he wanted to, he would switch to a different alphabet, indicating that he had done so by including an uppercase letter or a number in the cryptogram. For this encipherment Alberti used a decoder device, his *cipher disk*, which implemented a polyalphabetic substitution with mixed alphabets.

Johannes Trithemius invented a *progressive key* polyalphabetic cipher called the Trithemius cipher. Unlike Alberti's cipher, which switched alphabets at random intervals, Trithemius switched alphabets for each letter of the message. He started with a tabula recta, a square with 26 letters in it (although Trithemius, writing in Latin, used 24 letters). Each alphabet was shifted one letter to the left from the one above it, and started again with A after reaching Z.

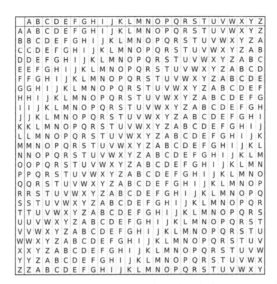

Trithemius's idea was to encipher the first letter of the message using the first shifted alphabet, so A became B, B became C, etc. The second letter of the message was enciphered using the second shifted alphabet, etc. Alberti's cipher disk implemented the same scheme. It had two alphabets, one on a fixed outer ring, and the other on the rotating disk. A letter is enciphered by looking for that letter on the outer ring, and encoding it as the letter underneath it on the disk. The disk started with A underneath B, and the user rotated the disk by one letter after encrypting each letter.

The cipher was trivial to break, and Alberti's machine implementation not much more difficult. *Key progression* in both cases was poorly concealed from attackers. Even Alberti's implementation of his polyalphabetic cipher was rather easy to break (the capitalized letter is a major clue to the cryptanalyst). For most of the next several hundred years, the significance of using multiple substitution alphabets was missed by almost everyone. Polyalphabetic substitution cipher designers seem to have concentrated on obscuring the choice of a few such alphabets (repeating as needed), not on the increased security possible by using many and never repeating any.

The principle (particularly Alberti's unlimited additional substitution alphabets) was a major advance—the most significant in the several hundred years since frequency analysis had been developed. A reasonable implementation would have been (and, when finally achieved, was) vastly harder to break. It was not until the mid-19th century (in Babbage's secret work during the Crimean War and Friedrich Kasiski's generally equivalent public disclosure some years later), that cryptanalysis of well-implemented polyalphabetic ciphers got anywhere at all.

Vigenère Cipher

Vigenere Cipher is a method of encrypting alphabetic text. It uses a simple form of polyalphabetic substitution. A polyalphabetic cipher is any cipher based on substitution, using multiple substitution alphabets. The encryption of the original text is done using the *Vigenère square or Vigenère table.*

- The table consists of the alphabets written out 26 times in different rows, each alphabet shifted cyclically to the left compared to the previous alphabet, corresponding to the 26 possible Caesar Ciphers.

- At different points in the encryption process, the cipher uses a different alphabet from one of the rows.

- The alphabet used at each point depends on a repeating keyword.

Example:

```
Input : Plaintext :   GEEKSFORGEEKS

            Keyword :  AYUSH

Output : Ciphertext :  GCYCZFMLYLEIM

For generating key, the given keyword is repeated

in a circular manner until it matches the length of

the plain text.

The keyword "AYUSH" generates the key "AYUSHAYUSHAYU"

The plain text is then encrypted using the process

explained below.
```

Encryption

The first letter of the plaintext, G is paired with A, the first letter of the key. So use row G and column A of the Vigenère square, namely G. Similarly, for the second letter of the plaintext, the second letter of the key is used, the letter at row E and column Y is C. The rest of the plaintext is enciphered in a similar fashion.

Table to encrypt – Geeks

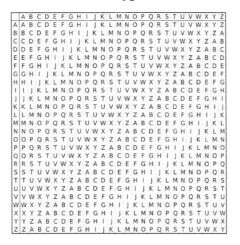

Decryption

Decryption is performed by going to the row in the table corresponding to the key, finding the position of the ciphertext letter in this row, and then using the column's label as the plaintext. For example, in row A (from AYUSH), the ciphertext G appears in column G, which is the first plaintext letter. Next we go to row Y (from AYUSH), locate the ciphertext C which is found in column E, thus E is the second plaintext letter.

A more easy implementation could be to visualize Vigenère algebraically by converting [A-Z] into numbers [0–25].

Encryption

The the plaintext(P) and key(K) are added modulo 26.

Ei = (Pi + Ki) mod 26

Decryption

Di = (Ei - Ki + 26) mod 26

Note: D_i denotes the offset of the i-th character of the plaintext. Like offset of A is 0 and of B is 1 and so on.

Below is the implementation of the idea.

C++

```cpp
// C++ code to implement Vigenere Cipher

#include<bits/stdc++.h>

using namespace std;


// This function generates the key in
// a cyclic manner until it's length isi'nt
// equal to the length of original text
string generateKey(string str, string key)
{
    int x = str.size();


    for (int i = 0; ; i++)
    {
        if (x == i)
            i = 0;
        if (key.size() == str.size())
            break;
        key.push_back(key[i]);
    }

    return key;
```

```cpp
}


// This function returns the encrypted text
// generated with the help of the key
string cipherText(string str, string key)
{
    string cipher_text;

    for (int i = 0; i < str.size(); i++)
    {
        // converting in range 0-25
        int x = (str[i] + key[i]) %26;

        // convert into alphabets(ASCII)
        x += 'A';

        cipher_text.push_back(x);
    }
    return cipher_text;
}


// This function decrypts the encrypted text
// and returns the original text
string originalText(string cipher_text, string key)
{
    string orig_text;

    for (int i = 0 ; i < cipher_text.size(); i++)
    {
        // converting in range 0-25
        int x = (cipher_text[i] - key[i] + 26) %26;
```

```
        // convert into alphabets(ASCII)

        x += 'A';

        orig_text.push_back(x);

    }

    return orig_text;

}


// Driver program to test the above function

int main()

{

    string str = "GEEKSFORGEEKS";

    string keyword = "AYUSH";


    string key = generateKey(str, keyword);

    string cipher_text = cipherText(str, key);


    cout << "Ciphertext : "

        << cipher_text << "\n";


    cout << "Original/Decrypted Text : "

        << originalText(cipher_text, key);

    return 0;

}
```

Java

```
// Java code to implement Vigenere Cipher


class GFG

{


// This function generates the key in

// a cyclic manner until it's length isi'nt
```

```
// equal to the length of original text
static String generateKey(String str, String key)
{
    int x = str.length();


    for (int i = 0; ; i++)
    {
        if (x == i)
            i = 0;
        if (key.length() == str.length())
            break;
        key+=(key.charAt(i));
    }
    return key;
}


// This function returns the encrypted text
// generated with the help of the key
static String cipherText(String str, String key)
{
    String cipher_text="";


    for (int i = 0; i < str.length(); i++)
    {
        // converting in range 0-25
        int x = (str.charAt(i) + key.charAt(i)) %26;


        // convert into alphabets(ASCII)
        x += 'A';


        cipher_text+=(char)(x);
    }
```

```java
        return cipher_text;
}


// This function decrypts the encrypted text
// and returns the original text
static String originalText(String cipher_text, String key)
{
    String orig_text="";

    for (int i = 0 ; i < cipher_text.length() &&
                        i < key.length(); i++)
    {
        // converting in range 0-25
        int x = (cipher_text.charAt(i) -
                key.charAt(i) + 26) %26;

        // convert into alphabets(ASCII)
        x += 'A';
        orig_text+=(char)(x);
    }
    return orig_text;
}


// Driver code
public static void main(String[] args)
{
    String str = "GEEKSFORGEEKS";
    String keyword = "AYUSH";

    String key = generateKey(str, keyword);
    String cipher_text = cipherText(str, key);
```

```
        System.out.println("Ciphertext : "

            + cipher_text + "\n");


        System.out.println("Original/Decrypted Text : "

            + originalText(cipher_text, key));

    }

}


// This code has been contributed by 29AjayKumar
```

Python3

```python
# Python code to implement

# Vigenere Cipher


# This function generates the

# key in a cyclic manner until

# it's length isn't equal to

# the length of original text
def generateKey(string, key):

    key = list(key)

    if len(string) == len(key):

        return(key)

    else:

        for i in range(len(string) -

                        len(key)):

            key.append(key[i % len(key)])

    return("" . join(key))


# This function returns the

# encrypted text generated

# with the help of the key
def cipherText(string, key):

    cipher_text = []
```

```
    for i in range(len(string)):
        x = (ord(string[i]) +
            ord(key[i])) % 26
        x += ord('A')
        cipher_text.append(chr(x))
    return("" . join(cipher_text))


# This function decrypts the
# encrypted text and returns
# the original text
def originalText(cipher_text, key):
    orig_text = []
    for i in range(len(cipher_text)):
        x = (ord(cipher_text[i]) -
            ord(key[i]) + 26) % 26
        x += ord('A')
        orig_text.append(chr(x))
    return("" . join(orig_text))


# Driver code
if __name__ == "__main__":
    string = "GEEKSFORGEEKS"
    keyword = "AYUSH"
    key = generateKey(string, keyword)
    cipher_text = cipherText(string,key)
    print("Ciphertext :", cipher_text)
    print("Original/Decrypted Text :",
        originalText(cipher_text, key))


# This code is contributed
# by Pratik Somwanshi
```

C#

```
// C# code to implement Vigenere Cipher
using System;

class GFG
{

// This function generates the key in
// a cyclic manner until it's length isi'nt
// equal to the length of original text
static String generateKey(String str, String key)
{
    int x = str.Length;

    for (int i = 0; ; i++)
    {
        if (x == i)
            i = 0;
        if (key.Length == str.Length)
            break;
        key+=(key[i]);
    }
    return key;
}

// This function returns the encrypted text
// generated with the help of the key
static String cipherText(String str, String key)
{
    String cipher_text="";

    for (int i = 0; i < str.Length; i++)
```

```
    {
        // converting in range 0-25
        int x = (str[i] + key[i]) %26;


        // convert into alphabets(ASCII)
        x += 'A';


        cipher_text+=(char)(x);
    }
    return cipher_text;
}


// This function decrypts the encrypted text
// and returns the original text
static String originalText(String cipher_text, String key)
{
    String orig_text="";


    for (int i = 0 ; i < cipher_text.Length &&
                     i < key.Length; i++)
    {
        // converting in range 0-25
        int x = (cipher_text[i] -
                 key[i] + 26) %26;


        // convert into alphabets(ASCII)
        x += 'A';
        orig_text+=(char)(x);
    }
    return orig_text;
}
```

```
// Driver code

public static void Main(String[] args)

{

    String str = "GEEKSFORGEEKS";

    String keyword = "AYUSH";


    String key = generateKey(str, keyword);

    String cipher_text = cipherText(str, key);


    Console.WriteLine("Ciphertext : "

        + cipher_text + "\n");


    Console.WriteLine("Original/Decrypted Text : "

        + originalText(cipher_text, key));

    }

}


/* This code contributed by PrinciRaj1992 */
```

Output

```
Ciphertext : GCYCZFMLYLEIM

Original/Decrypted Text : GEEKSFORGEEKS
```

References

- Classical-era, ciphers: practicalcryptography.com, Retrieved 19 August, 2019

- Substitution-ciphers-a-look-at-the-origins-and-applications-of-cryptography: finjan.com, Retrieved 30 June, 2019

- Pieprzyk, Josef; Thomas Hardjono; Jennifer Seberry (2003). Fundamentals of Computer Security. Springer. P. 6. ISBN 3-540-43101-2

- Playfair-cipher, ciphers: practicalcryptography.com, Retrieved 10 May, 2019

- "TICOM I-20 Interrogation of sonderfuehrer Dr Fricke of OKW/CHI". Sites.google.com. NSA. 28 June 1945. P. 2. Retrieved 29 August 2016

- Vigenere-cipher: geeksforgeeks.org, Retrieved 14 February, 2019

- Churchhouse, Robert (2002), Codes and Ciphers: Julius Caesar, the Enigma and the Internet, Cambridge: Cambridge University Press, ISBN 978-0-521-00890-7

PERMISSIONS

All chapters in this book are published with permission under the Creative Commons Attribution Share Alike License or equivalent. Every chapter published in this book has been scrutinized by our experts. Their significance has been extensively debated. The topics covered herein carry significant information for a comprehensive understanding. They may even be implemented as practical applications or may be referred to as a beginning point for further studies.

We would like to thank the editorial team for lending their expertise to make the book truly unique. They have played a crucial role in the development of this book. Without their invaluable contributions this book wouldn't have been possible. They have made vital efforts to compile up to date information on the varied aspects of this subject to make this book a valuable addition to the collection of many professionals and students.

This book was conceptualized with the vision of imparting up-to-date and integrated information in this field. To ensure the same, a matchless editorial board was set up. Every individual on the board went through rigorous rounds of assessment to prove their worth. After which they invested a large part of their time researching and compiling the most relevant data for our readers.

The editorial board has been involved in producing this book since its inception. They have spent rigorous hours researching and exploring the diverse topics which have resulted in the successful publishing of this book. They have passed on their knowledge of decades through this book. To expedite this challenging task, the publisher supported the team at every step. A small team of assistant editors was also appointed to further simplify the editing procedure and attain best results for the readers.

Apart from the editorial board, the designing team has also invested a significant amount of their time in understanding the subject and creating the most relevant covers. They scrutinized every image to scout for the most suitable representation of the subject and create an appropriate cover for the book.

The publishing team has been an ardent support to the editorial, designing and production team. Their endless efforts to recruit the best for this project, has resulted in the accomplishment of this book. They are a veteran in the field of academics and their pool of knowledge is as vast as their experience in printing. Their expertise and guidance has proved useful at every step. Their uncompromising quality standards have made this book an exceptional effort. Their encouragement from time to time has been an inspiration for everyone.

The publisher and the editorial board hope that this book will prove to be a valuable piece of knowledge for students, practitioners and scholars across the globe.

INDEX